Currency Risk and Business Management

Currency Risk and Business Management

ALFRED KENYON

Basil Blackwell

First published 1990
First published in USA 1991

Basil Blackwell Ltd
108 Cowley Road, Oxford, OX4 1JF, UK

Basil Blackwell, Inc.
3 Cambridge Center
Cambridge, Massachusetts 02142, USA

British Library Cataloguing in Publication Data

A CIP catalogue record for this book is available from the British Library.

Library of Congress Cataloging in Publication Data

Kenyon, Alfred.
Currency risk and business management/Alfred Kenyon.
p. cm.
Includes bibliographical references (p. 247).
ISBN 0-631-17749-3
1. Foreign exchange. 2. Risk management. 3. Foreign exchange futures.
I.Title.
HG3851.K368 1991
658.15'5-dc20 90-283 CIP

Typeset in 10 on 12pt Times
by Hope Services (Abingdon) Ltd
Printed in Great Britain by
T. J. Press Ltd,
Padstow,
Cornwall

Contents

Acknowledgements

With pleasure and gratitude I acknowledge the immense help I have had from many friends and colleagues.

In the City University Business School, Shelagh Heffernan has helped me throughout the task. Others who have been most helpful include Shiv Mathur, Roy Batchelor, Gordon Gemmill, Sudi Sudarsanam, Gerald Dickinson and Alec Chrystal.

I am especially indebted to the unnamed finance directors and treasurers who generously supplied the information summarized in the appendix to chapter 9.

Very special thanks are due to Paul Richardson, who worked painstakingly through a complete draft, preserved me from major errors and suggested a number of great improvements, and to Dr Stephen Taylor of Lancaster University, whose advice has been salutary and most helpful. Norma Whitcombe worked miracles as typescript editor.

On technical issues I have had invaluable help from John Heywood and Philip Bryan of Hambros Bank, Geoffrey Dicks of London Business School, and Bill Robinson of the Institute of Fiscal Studies. I am grateful to London Business School for generously permitting me to use their real exchange rate graphs.

Finally I must thank all my students from whom I have learned so much. Among them I must single out Simon Wilson. With so much help from so many, I must own that all the remaining errors are entirely mine.

AK

Acknowledgements

1

Building Bridges

1.1 Message of the book

The main message of this book is to all those in business who either face or manage currency risk: currencies are a *business* challenge. Few currency risks are just something for the financial specialist. Some are purely financial, but many more are problems or opportunities of the whole business. Famous companies like Laker Airways and J. Lyons have ascribed their demise to currency losses. Many companies' annual reports highlight currencies as major factors in their performance. If currencies have such major effects, then they are surely of concern to general management, not just to the financial specialist.

Currencies are traded in financial markets. Currency risks therefore *originate* in those financial markets, and the technical instruments by which they are traded and hedged are financial. Yet many of the *impacts* of exchange rate movements affect how the business wins orders from customers, how it keeps costs competitive, or whether an overseas subsidiary stays solvent. Few of these issues can be managed by the mere use of currency market instruments.

1.2 Different business functions

Currency risk therefore presents managers with problems which cut across functional responsibilities. Many of the problems are neither just financial nor just commercial: they are *business* problems. There are also some purely commercial problems which are widely mistaken for financial ones because they are caused by events in financial markets. It takes multi-disciplinary teams to respond to these challenges. Other problems again are purely financial in the sense that they affect how the business is financed, yet they compel further choices, for example between short- and long-term financial objectives.

If much of the emphasis in this book is on the relationship between currency issues and commercial management, management motivation is not forgotten, and surfaces especially in chapter 17, where decentralization is discussed.

1.3 Multidisciplinary management: the key role of pricing decisions

The same theme pervades our understanding of business problems and opportunities. An understanding of the currency markets is a financial discipline. However, as so many major impacts of currency risk are on the commercial management of the business, those who manage currency risk need an intimate grasp of its commercial markets and its objectives in those markets. Why has this side of currency risk management received relatively little attention? A possible clue is that currency issues depend far less on commercial objectives in a very important set of industries; industries which need to make few or no pricing decisions. They serve commodity or near-commodity markets, in which there are mainly price takers, and few, if any, price setters. Where what is sold is homogeneous and the suppliers many and small, pricing decisions are relatively unimportant or even non-existent.

Industries with relatively few pricing decisions include large parts of the chemical, petrochemical, petroleum and mining industries. The largest units in these industries need to be very large to realize economies of scale, and in many of their products they have few pricing decisions to make: they are price takers, not price setters. Most of them are multinational, and need relatively strong head offices.

Some of them have developed highly professional expert treasury management teams, using the most advanced techniques. They are deservedly influential in the world of currency risk management practice. They are naturally prominent among those practitioners who become writers and speakers on currency risk. Yet these industries by their nature have relatively little need to integrate currency with commercial management. This coincidence may have helped to steer the business literature on currency management away from the need for multidisciplinary teams to manage currency risk.

This book seeks to redress the balance. This main theme runs through the whole book, but the central arguments are in part II, chapters 6–9.

1.4 Accounting v. economic framework

In the United States the trauma of SFAS 8, the accounting standard in force during the 1970s, focused attention on the accounting effect of exchange rate movements to a point where those effects dominated all discussion of currency management. With its replacement by SFAS 52 much heat has been taken out of the controversy. However, whereas in the 1970s, the danger was that economic views of business objectives might be overlooked altogether, the pendulum has now swung to a point where the need to watch accounting implications is in danger of being ignored altogether. Yet accounting implications can have legal and financial consequences of their own.

1.5 Practitioners and theorists

If the main message is about the need to integrate currency management in business management, a second message aims to build bridges across the gulf between managers and business academics.

The present writer, after years as a corporate treasurer, became a business school academic. After some years in a business school he has not yet overcome his sense of wonder at how little the two worlds understand each other. Yet the effort to bridge this gulf is worth while; for there is little doubt that each side has much to give to the other. Wide-eyed disbelief is not enough.

A caricature might show each of the two sides of the gulf obsessed with its own pet techniques. A caricature of the practitioner might show him (throughout this book masculine pronouns refer to persons of either sex: excellence among treasurers and economists is self-evidently not the preserve of either gender!) facing a video screen, with many different and attractive instruments on offer. Forwards, futures, swaps, options, and an ever-growing crop of derivatives and combinations of these instruments. The figure in our caricature takes it as axiomatic that he must use this array of shiny tools.

The academic in the caricature uses his statistical tools and models, but his models do not always fit the real world of the manager. He is tempted to impose unreal patterns both on the currency markets and on the relationship between risk management and the hierarchy of objectives of the business.

Financial theorists have of course made many valuable discoveries about the way markets work or do not work, but the questions they ask may differ from the questions that practitioners have to answer. The problems of managers are sometimes identified by a priori reasoning, not by sitting with managers to see what they are busy with. One result is that some writers at least make quite inadequate distinctions between the functions of owners and investors on the one hand and the manager on the other.

These are of course caricatures, and thus distorted and unrepresentative. There are many thoughtful practitioners who concentrate hard on fundamentals, and many painstaking academics who take infinite care to study the real world of business management and to check their models of the world for realism.

1.6 Different perceptions of how the currency markets work

At a more detailed level the two sides do not communicate too well about the nature of the foreign exchange markets. The practitioner is conscious of levels of exchange rate volatility which vary greatly between time-spans. He has experienced major changes in the way the currency markets behave whenever governments change their methods of economic management, or when external shocks like the oil shocks of the 1970s change the environment. He is very much alive to the differences between the courses of freely floating and managed currencies. The practitioner is bemused when asked to look at data that span these major divides. He also notes with some surprise that a few textbooks still use concepts which belonged to the pastiche world of Bretton Woods, when major currencies were 'devalued'.

Again, some economists regard currency risk as a dispersion of outcomes which 'in the long run' must average out the gains and losses. So why bother to manage currency risk at all? One element in this view is that it attaches less importance to results in a fairly short term. A year for example falls well short of the 'long term' in which currency outcomes might average out. Company managers do not live in such a far-sighted world!

The academic, on the other hand, is taken aback when he sees business managers paying relatively large fees for professional exchange rate forecasts. Academics know that these forecasts do not systematically succeed in doing appreciably better than the highly unreliable forward rate of exchange, which can be read from the video screen or obtained free of charge by telephone from the dealing room of any bank.

Bridges are evidently being built in a number of places. Several companies examined in the appendix to chapter 9 show considerable awareness of modern portfolio theory in framing their objectives for managing currency or currency-related risks.

This book places special emphasis on the critical importance of different time-spans. Exchange rates behave rather differently over a few hours, a few months or a few years.

1.7 Layout of the book

Part I, chapters 2–5, describes the currency markets and the problems of forecasting exchange rates. The dramatic differences between different time-frames are stressed in chapters 4 and 5. Part II, chapters 6–9, looks at the management problems of the company and how currency risk management can best be integrated into the general tasks and objectives of managing a business. Chapter 7 attempts an outline of how business objectives fit into some kind of hierarchy. This serves to show some priorities, but also some interdisciplinary links without which a business cannot expect to be successful. Chapter 8, as part of this discussion, classifies currency risks as either competitiveness, trading or position risks. Chapter 9 enquires into some companies' corporate objectives in the field of currency risk management, with some interesting results. It also finds some practical and legal reasons why managers cannot completely ignore the accounting effects of currency movements. However, it is suggested that the cash view of currency risk should ultimately prevail.

Parts III and IV, together with chapter 2, are the main practical parts of the book. Part III, chapters 10–16, examines each of the three risks and the techniques for managing them. Part IV, chapter 17, deals with the consequent lessons for organizing, controlling and measuring currency risk management. Chapter 18 is an executive summary.

Some business readers may wish to skip the more reflective parts of the book. They may prefer to concentrate on the practical advice in parts III and IV (chapters 10–17) and on the executive summary in chapter 18. However, part II is concerned with the principles of business management and the place of currency risk in it. It is very much addressed to the business reader.

1.8 We have a lot to learn from each other

This book is designed for practitioners, academics and students. The author has learned a great deal from all of them, has a great deal more to learn from all of them but feels that perhaps they may also have something to learn from each other.

Part I

The Markets

2

Spot, Forward, Interbank Swap and Futures Deals

2.1 Introduction

This chapter gives a general introduction to the basic exchange deals and to the fundamental mechanics of the foreign exchange and currency futures markets. These basic building bricks are essential to an understanding of business currency risk. More advanced techniques like currency options and long-term currency swaps are introduced in part III, chapters 12 and 15.

2.2 The spot exchange deal

A **spot exchange deal** is a binding contract to exchange agreed amounts of two currencies at an agreed rate of exchange on the conventional date for implementing spot deals between the two currencies.

Its detailed characteristics are as follows:

- Like all other contracts in the foreign exchange markets, a spot deal is strictly binding on both parties.
- At least one of the two parties must be a bank.
- No cash passes at the time the deal is struck.
- The rate of exchange is determined by the state of the market at the time when the deal is agreed.
- The conventional date for implementing spot deals between major currencies is the second dealing day after date of contract; it is later for spot deals in less heavily traded currencies.
- Saturdays, Sundays and bank holidays in either of the countries are not dealing days: so if a $/£ spot deal was entered into on a Thursday, and if the following Monday was a bank holiday in either New York

or London, the exchange of currencies would take place on the Tuesday following the date of the deal.

- Electronic banking may speed these processes up.
- In wholesale dealing, there are no commissions or charges payable, except the banks' normal turnover charges; the banks are remunerated exclusively by the dealing spreads discussed below.

2.3 Illustration from *The Financial Times* quotations

The Financial Times of Saturday 9 July 1988, in the table 'Pound spot–forward against the pound', reported the closing rates at close of business on Friday 8 July for US$/£ and DM/£ as follows:

	Close
US	1.7015–1.7025
W Germany	3.12½–3.13

This means that at the close of business an average wholesale bank would have offered to another interbank party these rates:

Quoting bank will

sell dollars for sterling at $1.7015 = £1
buy dollars for sterling at $1.7025 = £1
sell DM for sterling at DM3.125 = £1
buy DM for sterling at DM3.13 = £1

The differences of 0.1 US cent and 0.5 pfennig between the bank's buy and sell rates represent its dealing margins, called 'bid–offer spreads'. From these margins the bank has to cover its transaction costs, risks, overheads and return on capital. The risks are discussed in chapter 3.

Beginners should be warned that each one of the rates could have been expressed as its reciprocal, with the non-sterling currency taken as the unit. For example the quoting bank's rate for buying dollars for sterling could have been expressed as 1/1.7015, i.e. as £0.5877 = $1. Similarly its selling rate for dollars against sterling could be stated as £0.5874 = $1. The same quotation in the *Wall Street Journal* might therefore well have been £0.5874–0.5877. This time the selling rate for dollars against sterling would have appeared as the left-hand quotation instead of the buying rate. The only safe rule is to remember that the bid–offer spread is always to the quoting bank's advantage.

2.4 The forward exchange deal

A **forward exchange deal** is a binding contract to exchange agreed amounts of two currencies on an agreed future date at a rate of exchange agreed now.

The definition of the forward contract is identical with that of the spot exchange contract except for the implementation date. In the case of deals between two major currencies like dollar/sterling, if the deal is for the second dealing day, then it is a spot deal. If on the other hand it is for the third or any later date, then it is a forward deal.

Like spot deals therefore, forward deals are strictly binding, require at least one bank party, involve no cash transaction when entered into, are implemented on the agreed date or the next dealing day common to both centres (New York and London for dollar/sterling), but at market rates ruling at the earlier time when the deal was made. Forward contracts occur in the wholesale markets, and carry no charges except those covered by the spread.

2.4.1 *Illustration from* The Financial Times

The Financial Times quotes forward rates for one month and for three months forward. On 9 July 1988 it reported 8 July closing rates \$/£ and DM/£ for one month as shown in table 2.1. The % p.a. column expresses the forward premium or discount as an *annualized* (multiplying by, for example, 365/30) percentage of the spot rate.

Table 2.1

	Close	One month	% p.a.
US	1.7015–1.7025	0.32–0.29 cpm	2.15
W Germany	3.12½–3.13	1½–1⅜ pfpm	5.52
Italy	2315½–2316½	par–2 lire dis	−0.52

The key to the symbols is:

pm = premium c = cents (\$¹⁄₁₀₀)
dis = discount pf = pfennig (DM ¹⁄₁₀₀)

A forward **premium** quotation means that the currency in which the rates are quoted (in this case the dollar or D-Mark), buys more units of the other currency (in this case sterling) forward than spot. The market evidently expects the quoted currencies (dollar, D-Mark) to rise against sterling during the one-month period. **Discount** means the reverse, i.e.

the lira buys less sterling forward than spot, and is therefore expected by the market to fall against sterling.

The forward premium or discount is not necessarily quoted in the same unit as the spot rate. For both the dollar and the D-Mark the forward premium is quoted at 1/100 of the main currency unit.

We can now derive the forward rates from the FT quoted closing rates for 8 July 1988. These are shown in table 2.2.

Table 2.2

	Quoting bank offers to	
	Buy £	Sell £
$ spot	1.7015	1.7025
deduct 1 month premium	0.0032	0.0029
1 month forward	1.6983	1.6996
DM spot	3.1250	3.1300
deduct 1 month premium	0.0150	0.0138
1 month forward	3.1100	3.1162
Lire spot	2315.5	2316.5
add 1 month discount	0000.0	0002.0
1 month forward	2315.5	2318.5

There are some instructive points to note here:

1 Buy £ = sell the other, the non-sterling currency, and sell £ = buy the other, the non-sterling currency.

2 The dollar and the D-Mark are at a forward premium to sterling, so £1 buys *less* D-Marks or dollars forward than spot, and the premium has to be deducted. The lira is (just) at a forward discount to sterling, so £1 buys *more* lire forward than spot, and the discount has to be added. It is equally correct of course to say that sterling is at a forward discount to the D-Mark and at a forward premium to the lira.

3 In all three cases the spread for the spot rate plus the spread for the forward premium/discount equals the spread for the forward rate. The forward spread is always the sum of the other two spreads, irrespective of whether the *rates* are added or subtracted.

4 The lira was at a one-month par with sterling for buying or selling lire, and at a very small discount at the sell or buy lire rate. The market evidently regarded the two currencies as almost equally strong.

5 We were able to place the left-hand premium under the left-hand (buy sterling) spot rate for both the dollar and the D-Mark because *The Financial Times* follows the usual London convention in quoting the **premium downwards** (0.32–0.29 instead of 0.29–0.32) precisely for this convenience, whereas for the lira the **discount is quoted upwards** (par–2). In London we can thus always tell whether the forward differential is a premium or a discount without the symbols pm or dis: if the higher figure is quoted first, it is a premium; if the lower, then a discount.

2.5 The significance of the forward contract

The forward contract is a foreign exchange deal done at today's rate for a future date or maturity. It locks the parties into today's foreign exchange rate structure. As the deal is binding, they must deal at that rate, irrespective of what the spot rate will turn out to be at the future date. Each party knows that it will not do any better or worse than today's forward rate.

2.6 Forward rates and Eurocurrency interest rates

The table in *The Financial Times* of 9 July contains two more columns, which deal with three-month forward rates. In table 2.3 we substitute the two three-month columns for the two one-month columns in table 2.1. Here we should note particularly that the symbol for the currency unit, in which the pm/dis is quoted, is not repeated by *The Financial Times* in the three-month column: the reader has to look that up in the one-month column.

Table 2.3

	Close	Three months	% p.a.
US	1.7015–1.7025	0.95–0.90 pm	2.17
W Germany	3.12½–3.13	4⅜–4¾ pm	5.52
Italy	2315½–2316½	3–5 dis	−0.69

Lower on the same *Financial Times* page we find another table headed 'Eurocurrency interest rates'.

This shows the average Eurocurrency interest rates quoted interbank in the wholesale Eurocurrency deposit market at the close of business in

London on 8 July, i.e. synchronized with the above foreign exchange rate quotations. Once again each quotation is a two-way quotation. The quoting bank offers a higher rate to borrowers than to depositors, the difference being again called the bid–offer spread. Table 2.4 gives extracts from the three-month column:

Table 2.4

	Quoting bank offers to:	
	Lend 3-months deposits at % p.a.	Accept 3-months deposits at % p.a.
Sterling	10⅜	10¼
Dollar	8⅛	8
D-Mark	4¾	4⅝
Italian lire	11	10½

If we placed the interest rates in a *rising* order, this would be D-Mark, dollar, pound, lira: the same ranking as the descending strength of the forward premiums or discounts. The forward foreign exchange market clearly saw the DM as the strongest and the lira as (just) the weakest of these four currencies.

If we now work out the differences between the three-months Eurointerest rates, and compare them with the % p.a. forward rates from table 2.4, we get the comparison shown in table 2.5 showing a fairly close correspondence and a very high correlation. The correspondence would be still closer if quoted closing rates were actual dealing rates of a single bank instead of averages of five banks' quotations, rounded off and converted to annualized rates by *The Financial Times*.

We shall show in chapter 3 that the premium or discount is in fact derived from the Eurointerest differential, so that the forward rate is

Table 2.5

	Eurointerest differential		Forward % p.a.
	Lend	Borrow	
£–$	2¼	2¼	2.17
£–DM	5⅝	5⅝	5.52
£–lira	–⅝	–¼	–0.69

composed of two elements: (a) the spot rate, and (b) the premium or discount derived from Eurocurrency interest rates. Thus the forward rate between major freely floating currencies is not an autonomously traded rate, but a rate determined by two other markets, the spot foreign exchange market and the market in Eurodeposit interest rates. This deposit market will be described in chapter 3.

2.7 The interbank swap deal

Beside the spot and the forward deal there is also the interbank swap deal. This consists simply of a simultaneous spot and reverse forward deal between the same two parties. Its effect is very similar to that of a forward deal, except that there is also an exchange of deposits at the outset, i.e. on the date for implementing a spot deal, say on the second dealing day.

A three-month DM/$ swap entered into on day 0, a Tuesday, then consists of bank A delivering D-Marks for dollars to bank B on (working) day 2, and receiving a smaller amount of D-Marks for dollars on day 91. The reduction in the amount represents the 'swap rate', which is almost the same rate as the forward premium of the D-Mark against the dollar.

The two important differences between a forward and a swap deal are first that the swap changes both parties' balance sheets during the forward period, and secondly that the swap is cheaper because spreads tend to be thinner for swaps than for outright forwards.

The balance sheet effect comes from the first, the spot leg of the swap. Suppose the swap consists of an exchange of DM18 million for $10 million. Bank A must part with DM18 million, either by running down its existing stock of D-Marks or by borrowing D-Marks, perhaps from bank X. It will also add to its dollar position, either by adding $10 million to its dollar assets or by repaying dollar liabilities. Its balance sheet position in the two currencies will have changed for the period from day 2 to day 91, and so will that of bank B.

The thinner spread is due to the much heavier volume of business in the swap than in the outright forward market. We have seen that bid–offer spreads are a bank's cover for its costs and return on capital in all the markets, spot, forward, Eurointerest and swap markets, and that the costs include its risks. These risks include the counterparty credit risk and the market risk of not finding an offsetting transaction at the same or nearby rate. We shall return to this last risk in chapter 3, but it must evidently be greater in a thin than in a very liquid market. It explains why spreads are wider in thin markets.

Interbank swaps must be distinguished from currency swaps, which are discussed in chapter 15. The differences are that currency swaps are generally for much longer periods, do not need a bank as one of the parties, are usually reversed on maturity at the *same* exchange rate and in that case require periodical mutual payments of interest. The two legs of the interbank swap are at *different* exchange rates (the difference is the swap rate), and the interbank swap involves no mutual interest payments.

2.8 The use of interbank swaps and outright forwards

Beginners are often puzzled why swaps are used at all, as the swap is so similar to the forward deal and the forward deal looks so much simpler. The pattern is that swaps are largely used in interbank dealing, whereas outright forwards are mainly used in deals between banks and non-bank customers. Corporate customers prefer the outright forward because it causes no balance sheet effect: it cannot increase the debt equity gearing ratio of the corporate hedger during the forward period. In any case, the corporate user achieves the exact equivalent of a swap only by combining it with a spot deal to counteract the spot leg of the swap.

The swap on the other hand is preferred by banks for dealing with each other. The volume of reciprocal interbank dealing results in a multitude of interbank positions between the same parties, which affect their balance sheets only at the level of the net position with each party. Above all, swaps are cheaper than outrights. The key to all this is that the volume of interbank transactions is many times as large as that of forward transactions with corporate customers: the cost saving will therefore be substantial.

2.9 Currency futures

Currency futures have virtually the same effect as forward contracts, but the market and its mechanics are very different. In a currency futures contract, A buys from B the obligation to deliver a standard amount of a non-dollar currency such as British pound sterling at a fixed dollar price on a fixed delivery date. Futures markets are formal 'open outcry' markets in which instruments are traded in standard form, not unlike exchange-traded currency options. Futures markets are designed to make trading free from credit risk. The exchange has a clearing house which guarantees the transaction. Each party must make a security deposit ('margin') of around 1 per cent. This is maintained at or near its original value by daily cash adjustments representing daily gains and losses from fluctuations in spot rates in the cash market each day. The effect is that, if a trader fails before closing out its contract, the clearing house can, without loss, close it out in the trader's place. The clearing house can do this without risk of loss, because any shortfall between current and contractual prices is covered by the margin held by the clearing house. Futures contracts are tradable in the secondary market until delivery date. This feature and the low dealing costs are an attraction, but the restrictions caused by standardization, and the administrative effort of frequent margin transactions explain why the larger non-financial businesses prefer the forward to the futures market for their currency hedging. The futures market is, however, useful to the business which is too small to obtain adequate forward dealing limits from banks. Futures deals are also available for smaller amounts than forward contracts.

2.10 Summary

This chapter has introduced the basic features of spot, forward, interbank swap and futures contracts and the interrelation between the forward premium or discount and Eurocurrency interest rates. Fuller descriptions of these markets are found in Heywood (1984a, b), Walmsley (1983), Bell and Kettell (1983) and other texts.

3 Interrelations of Markets

3.1 Why relations between markets matter

The behaviour of exchange rates is intimately related with the economic environment. As exchange rates are the cause of currency risk, we must look at that background, without pretending that this is an economic textbook.

The business manager is operating in a number of markets and environments. He is above all competing in his commercial markets. He also has to finance his business in the financial markets, which include the equity, debt and currency markets. Moreover, these commercial and financial markets are part of the national and world economic systems, and powerfully affected by them. As we set out to understand the issues of currency risk and its management, we have to obtain some appreciation not only of the economic logic of some of these markets and systems, but also how they affect one another. If this sounds abstract and remote from the corporate treasurer's Reuter screen, an illustration may help.

Example 3.1

General Industries plc (GI), a public company with headquarters in the UK, contemplates a \$200 million manufacturing investment in the United States. GI's markets are global: its customers can buy from competitors whose head offices or supply sources are in other countries. The purpose of GI's project is to expand its world capacity so as to improve its share of the world market. The goods to be produced are light, compact and cheap to transport between different parts of the world.

Is the United States the best place to locate the plant? The dollar is rising strongly despite the external and internal deficits of the US. It is possible that over the next few years the dollar will be uncompetitive or overvalued. In that case US manufacturing costs might be uncompetitive over that period compared with costs in other developed countries such as West Germany. We are now comparing relative costs of factors of production in different countries or currency areas. To evaluate this, GI has to look at the macroeconomic logic of the world and US economies, which involves exchange rates, relative price levels, and therefore the general aggregate levels of demand and supply in different countries. GI must in any case look at that outlook for demand and supply, because it will affect the demand for the products of its proposed new US plant. If the demand were to be weak, then volume and prices would be under pressure, the returns from the project might be less than GI's cost of capital, and its stock market rating might drop. The question now links up with the logic of the equity market.

In any case GI has to finance the project, perhaps initally with debt. In what currency should GI borrow? Will the cost vary from currency to currency? Will the choice of currency raise GI's exposure to currency risk? Would such exposure affect the risk rating of GI's shares in the stock market, and thus its cost of capital yet again?

We are now concerned with the way the international debt and currency markets are linked, and how a company's currency risk affects its rating in its equity market.

3.2 Separating external from managerial issues

Can we put some order into this apparently chaotic set of issues? The first step is to distinguish external from managerial issues. External issues are those over which GI has no influence: it must take them as given. On managerial issues, on the other hand, GI's own actions affect its destiny. Most managers believe that their dominant problems and tasks are in their commercial markets.

In this chapter we set out the main relationships between the foreign exchange and other markets. These are clearly external to the company.

3.3 The Eurocurrency deposit market

The most important market to look at is the Eurocurrency deposit market. It is the most important, because it is fully integrated with the foreign exchange market. It is practically the same market. A single network of dealers operates in currencies and Eurodeposits, in the same way and over the same telephone and telex lines. A Eurodeposit is simply a bank deposit outside the country which issues the currency of the deposit.

Strictly, since the introduction in 1981 of 'international banking facilities' (IBFs) in the United States, we should not say 'outside the country', but 'outside the *banking regulations* of the country' that issues the currency. Banking regulations here include

- any foreign exchange regulations,
- reserve requirements (the obligation to make interest-free deposits with the central bank) which represent a significant cost to the banks,
- restrictive regulations like the famous Regulation Q in the US which used to impose ceilings on the deposit rates that US commercial banks could offer,
- 'prudential' regulations (like capital adequacy requirements) to protect depositors against the failure of a bank.

A sterling deposit in Paris, or a dollar or D-Mark deposit in London, is not subject to any such regulations and is thus a Eurodeposit. So, however, is a dollar deposit in an IBF located in the United States. Provided IBFs conduct no domestic US business, they can accept dollar deposits free from US banking regulations. In other words dollar deposits in an IBF are Eurodollar deposits, even though they are not held outside the United States.

The Eurodeposit market was born in 1958. When the Bank of England in that year deregulated the non-sterling markets in London, it suddenly became cheaper to borrow, and more profitable to lend, US dollars in London than in New York. The new market grew explosively, reaching total deposits of $1000 billion by 1981. The growth of this market caused many structural changes; one of the most visible ones was the arrival of some 400 foreign banks in London in the 1960s.

The Eurodeposit market is a wholesale market, about 70 per cent of it is in US dollars, 70 per cent is interbank, only about 15 per cent of balances are with private non-bank entities such as corporate customers. It operates by telex, telephone and computer links, not on a public trading floor. Dealers sit in bank dealing-rooms. The market trades round the world, and therefore virtually round the clock from London via New York, San Francisco, Tokyo, Singapore and Hong Kong, Bahrain and back to London, It is at least relatively 'efficient', both in the sense of low transaction costs and in the sense that all information is promptly and equally known to all participants and absorbed in interest rates. Arbitrage is what integrates the market so well. It unifies the money markets in the major currencies.

It may now be apparent why the international deposit and currency markets are so closely interwoven that they are no longer separate markets. Eurodeposits can be freely and cheaply traded. However, every time a trader wishes to switch from a D-Mark to a sterling deposit, he has to sell D-Marks for sterling, i.e. do an exchange deal.

3.4 Market efficiency and arbitrage

The concept of the efficient market was developed by Fama (1970). It describes a market in which all relevant information is instantly absorbed in market prices, so that abnormal profits cannot be made by operators. In an efficient market the present structure of rates (including forward rates) is the best available forecast. A thorough discussion of whether the forward exchange market is efficient is found in MacDonald and Taylor (1989).

Arbitrage, or rather **covered arbitrage**, is strictly defind as making a riskless profit by simultaneously dealing in two related, but temporarily misaligned markets. The process is sometimes called a 'free lunch'.

Example 3.2

I could right now buy £1 sterling for $1.70. However, I could instead obtain £1 for $1.6990 by buying DM3.177 with $1.70 at DM1.87 = $1, and then buying £1 for DM3.177, doing both deals with the same bank which is quoting me DM1.87 for selling dollars and DM3.177 for buying pounds. Those quotations are misaligned with the quotation of $1.70 for buying pounds for dollars. My saving of 0.1 cents is riskless. At the wholesale level of £1 million, my 'free lunch' would have been $1,000.

We can now extend this concept to deals other than spot deals.

Example 3.3

A trader can deposit DM2 million for three months at 4.75 per cent p.a. If, instead of doing this, he could simultaneously

1 sell the D-Mark spot for dollars,
2 deposit the dollars for three months, and
3 sell the dollars and the dollar interest forward three months for D-Marks,

and obtain a higher total of principal and interest at the end of the three months without taking any risk, then he would effectively have obtained a rate of D-Mark interest of more than 4.75 per cent by means of covered arbitrage, and earned himself a free lunch!

Now suppose the bank that made the free lunch was Lloyds Bank in London, and that it achieved its coup by doing all three deals with

Deutsche Bank. Deutsche Bank must have misaligned its quotations to the point where it gave Lloyds Bank the arbitrage opportunity. Lloyds Bank would have made money out of Deutsche Bank. Clearly Deutsche Bank's dealers are strongly motivated not to give other banks such opportunities. Every bank has every incentive to align its quotations of spot, forward, swap and Eurodeposit rates in such a way as to preclude that kind of arbitrage at its own expense.

From chapter 2 we know that all these rates are quoted as dual prices, with a bid–offer spread between them. Arbitrage is therefore profitable only if it overcomes the combination of all three spreads in the example: on the DM/£ spot, Eurosterling deposit and three-months forward quotations offered by Deutsche Bank. To the extent of these spreads the dice are therefore loaded against arbitrage.

3.5 Brendan Brown's currency triangles

The full mechanics and implications of this linkage between the deposit and currency markets are very clearly set out in Brendan Brown's excellent study *The Forward Market in Foreign Exchange* (1983). Brown points out the triangular shape of each potential arbitrage link; with all the triangles also interlinked with one another.

The simplest link is that between three spot rates in example 3.2. The DM/\$, \$/£ and DM/£ spot rates form a triangle. The DM/\$ spot rate is of course also in the triangle linking the DM/\$ spot, forward and swap rates with one another, as in example 3.3. And of course the DM/\$ swap rate is also in a triangle with the D-Mark and dollar Eurointerest rates. To avoid arbitrage against itself, a bank must align its quotations within each triangle and between the triangles, so that the entire market becomes an integrated network of well-aligned, virtually arbitrage-proof rates.

Brown (1983) adds the useful perception that, in any one triangle, the three corners attract spreads of varying width. The spread is always narrowest in the corner which carries the largest stream of transactions, called the most 'liquid' corner. For example, in the \$/DM/£ spot triangle the most liquid corner is DM/\$, and the least liquid DM/£. Similarly, the spot rate is the most liquid corner in the spot, swap and outright forward triangle, with the outright the least liquid. In each case the width of the spread is in inverse order to the liquidity of the corners. The logic of this is that the less liquid the market is, the greater is the bank's risk of not finding a matching deal to balance its position; a risk which it seeks to protect by the wider spread. We saw in chapter 2 that the function of the spread is to remunerate the bank for its costs and risks. This market risk is not the least of these risks.

Brown goes on to call the least liquid the 'dominant' corner. It is here that arbitrage opportunities are most likely to occur.

3.6 How banks balance out their mismatches

In 1989, the foreign exchange market trades currencies worth $500 billion or more each day. Each of the major dealing banks has a huge daily turnover, many times the size of its own capital. If any one bank simply went on trading without worrying, for example, whether it was a couple of billion dollars either short or long in, say, Swiss francs, then any unexpected movement in Swiss francs could quite quickly jeopardize its solvency. Ordinary prudence therefore compels banks to control their positions in each currency at short intervals, perhaps several times each hour, and to contain imbalances within predetermined limits by successive offsetting deals (often swaps) in the interbank market. So if our bank is getting long in Swiss francs, it will sell them interbank for a currency in which it is short.

A bank's own prudence would dictate that kind of control, but regulators make doubly sure that banks do not put their depositors' funds at risk by imposing some specific disciplines. Thus the Bank of England expects the banks under its control to carry overnight no currency mismatch in excess of 10 per cent of the bank's capital.

Each bank therefore tends to match its deals with its customers with offsetting deals in the interbank market; not deal by deal, but whenever its total currency balance gets near its internal position limits or (near the end of the day) the regulator's mismatch limits.

This pattern explains a number of the facts already described. One is that market risks in a narrow or relatively illiquid market cause spreads to widen. This risk is more acute in a thin market. Banks' need to offset mismatched positions also helps to explain why some 70 per cent of Eurodeposit market balances tend to be interbank.

3.7 Spot, forward, interest and inflation rates

Financial economics recognizes Brown's triangular arbitrage relationships as part of a wider set, which include not only *actual* Eurodeposit interest rates and forward exchange rates, but also *expected* future spot and inflation rates.

These relationships are usually shown in a diagram like figure 3.1.

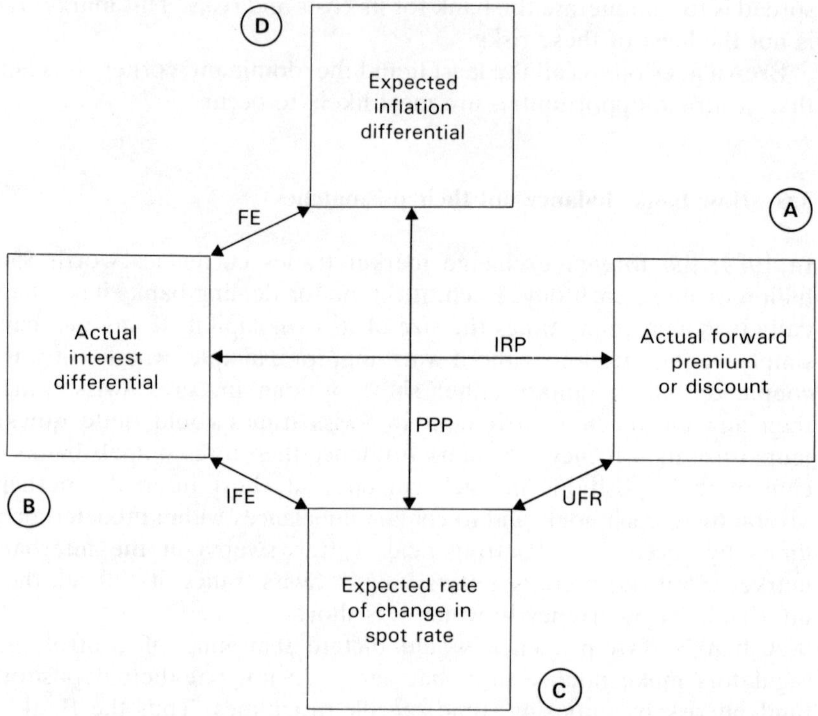

Figure 3.1 Arbitrage relationships: IRP, interest parity; IFE, international Fisher effect; UFR, unbiased forward rate; FE, Fisher effect; PPP, purchasing power parity

The diagram links the following relevant four market rates for a single forward period, say three months, for a pair of currencies, such as the US dollar and the pound sterling:

- A the forward premium or discount,
- B the difference between their Eurointerest rates,
- C the market's *expectation* of the change in the spot rate over the period,
- D the market's *expectation* of the difference between their inflation rates over the period.

The relationships in figure 3.1 are given in the following sections.

3.7.1 A and B: interest parity (IRP) (also known as covered interest parity)

A and B are linked by the interest parity theorem. This merely states that the forward premium or discount tends to be equal to the difference between the Eurointerest rates of the two currencies for the period, both expressed as per cent per annum. In other words covered interest arbitrage opportunities are likely to be very rare. Brendan Brown would see it as an expression of the fact that the swap rate links the spot, forward and swap triangle with the triangle linking the swap rate and the two Eurointerest rates, Eurosterling and Eurodollar.

As A and B are the only **actual** – as distinct from **expected** – rates in figure 3.1, this relationship is the closest and best documented of the relationships.

3.7.2 B and C: international Fisher effect (IFE) (also known as uncovered interest parity)

B and C are linked by the international Fisher effect. The IFE holds that B, the Eurointerest differential, is an unbiased predictor of the prospective rate of change in C, the future spot rate. This is really a double proposition. It suggests

1 that the interest differential represents the market's collective opinion of the speed at which the spot rate will move during the period, and *therefore* (as the market knows the current spot rate) of its value at the end of the period, and
2 that this prediction is unbiased, i.e. that over a period the sum of the errors in this prediction will tend to be equal on both sides. Bias is more fully discussed in chapter 5.

Of these two propositions, the first causes much less difficulty than the second. In the absence of market imperfections, arbitrage (see below) will ensure that a typical portfolio investor might be indifferent between holding his asset in a Eurodollar deposit earning 8.125 per cent p.a. or a Eurosterling deposit earning 10.375 per cent p.a. for the next three months. The market must have a mean collective expectation that the dollar will rise against sterling by 1.10375/1.08125 p.a. over the next three months, so that at the end of three months the amount of the deposit plus the different amounts of interest which he will have earned in each currency will give him the same value at the *then* ruling *spot* rate.

This appeals to common sense. If the market believed that the spot rate would remain unchanged at the end of the three months, then everybody in that market would invest in sterling and borrow dollars.

The massive outflow of funds from New York to London would make money scarce in New York and plentiful in London. This would pull interest rates up in New York and down in London, and the spot rate towards a higher value of sterling against the dollar, until the three rates would find a new equilibrium at a point where the interest differential would once again express the market's expectation of changes in the spot rate over the period.

In the last two paragraphs we have used the word 'arbitrage' in the sense of **uncovered** arbitrage. In section 3.4 we defined **covered** arbitrage. Uncovered arbitrage includes expectations and risk perceptions as well as known actual market prices: in the absence of market imperfections, risk-adjusted expected returns on financial assets in different markets should be equal (Shapiro, 1989).

This framework does, however, presuppose that capital rather than trading transactions predominate in the foreign exchange market. If the main weight of the market were in trading transactions, in settling payments for exports and imports, then the described arbitrage process would not be effective. In fact, ever since the early 1970s, the overwhelming weight of the market has been in capital or financial rather than trade-related transactions. World trade is dwarfed by the $500 billion a day, which was the estimated size of the foreign exchange market in 1989!

Proposition 1 thus merely affirms that present rates in this market must reflect its current expectations. Proposition 2 goes much further: it suggests that the market has some actual capacity to forecast, that its expectations are at least on average borne out by subsequent exchange rate movements.

3.7.3 A and C: forward rate as unbiased predictor (UFR)

A and C are linked by the theory that the forward rate is an unbiased predictor of the future spot rate. As interest parity (which links A with B) holds so strongly, this A–C link is simply a corollary of the IFE, the B–C link.

Once again we can analyse this into (1) a collective expectation and (2) an unbiased forecast. The forward rate must obviously represent the market's present mean expectation of the future spot rate. It consists of (a) the present spot rate and (b) the present premium or discount. This last is derived from the interest differential. This in turn through the IFE is the market's view of the change in the spot rate over the period.

Is the forward rate in fact an unbiased forecast of the future spot rate? This has been empirically researched by many, and the results are inconclusive. Excellent reviews of the literature on this are found in

MacDonald and Taylor (1989) and Heffernan and Sinclair (1990). The balance of evidence is beginning to tilt decisively towards the presence of bias. Some researchers have also found that the evidence varies between different maturities.

Most practical market operators would be surprised to hear that the issue was ever regarded as finely balanced; that the forward rate could even be thought to have a capacity to predict! There is of course a misunderstanding here. Market operators are aware that an *individual* bank quoting a forward rate is not attempting to predict the future spot rate. The researchers are finding that the market *collectively* has some (probably biased) view of the future spot rate, a view which influences the Eurointerest differential.

3.7.4 D and B: Fisher effect (FE)

D and B are linked by the (closed) Fisher effect (FE). This states that the interest differential will tend to be equal to the expected difference between the inflation rates in the two countries which issue the two currencies. In our example, this would mean that the market expects the inflation rate in the UK to be 2.25 per cent p.a. above that in the US. This proposition really suggests that expected *real* interest rates (i.e. actual interest rates less expected rates of inflation) tend to be equal in all currencies.

Another way of putting this is to say that differences between Eurointerest rates in different currencies are accounted for by differences between inflation expectations for those currencies. The relationship may well hold for expectations, but actual real interest rates diverge considerably. Inflation measures changes in purchasing power. It affects prices in the goods markets, not in the financial markets. Prices in goods markets do not adjust as quickly or as easily as prices in financial markets. Consequently arbitrage between actual goods and financial markets is slow and uncertain.

On the other hand, the FE has a lot of credibility if applied to a pair of currencies like the dollar and the Brazilian cruzeiro, in which inflation is usually running at several hundred per cent p.a. and highly volatile. Against this very high and volatile inflation rate, real interest rates in Brazil are relatively stable. They may swing within a 30 per cent band while both inflation and nominal interest rates may swing within a 100 per cent band over the same period. Consequently, both expected and actual interest differentials between these two currencies are *relatively* close to the rapidly changing differences between their inflation rates.

The clue from this hyperinflation example is that the applicability of the FE to actual price levels seems to depend on the degree of volatility of inflation rates. In hyperinflation countries like Brazil they are very volatile, more volatile than real interest rates. Between stable developed countries with relatively low inflation, inflation differentials are very slow to change, and much less volatile than interest differentials. This is the core of the logic. Where interest differentials are seen to be much more volatile than inflation differentials, the FE is unlikely to hold for actual levels of prices. Investors are unlikely to pay much attention to purchasing power when investing for short periods like three months. They are much more likely to be concerned about the competitive attractions of other financial instruments in terms of their expected financial returns. The investor who invests for the long term, say for five years, may well take a different view. Over that longer period the outlook for inflation differentials may cause greater concern than the outlook for interest rate differentials. Deviant inflation rates take that much longer to return to equilibrium.

We conclude that in actual terms (as opposed to expectations) the FE is more likely to hold either in the very long term or for hyperinflation currencies than for major currencies in the short term.

3.7.5 D and C: purchasing power parity (PPP)

D and C link two *expectations:* that of future changes in the spot rate, and that of the inflation differential over the period. This is the theory of purchasing power parity. PPP is held in two forms, absolute and relative. Absolute PPP is 'the law of one price'. It suggests that the same item, like a can of Coca Cola, cannot have a different price in different currencies or countries, because consumers would arbitrage and buy wherever it is cheapest, until PPP was restored.

The relative form of PPP is more influential. It merely suggests that the spot rate between two currencies will change at an annual rate equal to their inflation differential. Once again this presupposes arbitrage occurring between the goods and financial markets, and once again the theory seems to have more validity in the long term and in hyperinflation countries. Certainly very few people find it plausible for, say, the dollar/sterling spot rate for three months.

This topic is discussed in greater detail in chapter 4, Sections 4.8–10.

3.8 Expected and actual rates

The wider relationships in figure 3.1 are between four rates, all concerned with one pair of currencies (like DM/$) for one maturity period (say three months), all of which interact with present market sentiment.

Two of these rates (the Eurointerest differential and the forward premium or discount) are actual and verifiable, and two of them (prospective inflation differential and prospective change in spot rate) are market expectations.

Of the two rates which constitute expections, the expected change in the spot rate is within the financial markets. The market by its nature forms a collective view of the future spot rate (by forecasting its rate of change, and applying it to the known current spot rate) so that it can be arbitraged in arriving particularly at the Eurointerest differential. This extended meaning of 'arbitrage' (uncovered arbitrage) was explained in section 3.7.2.

On the other hand the fourth item, expected relative rates of inflation, is neither a present known fact nor internal to the financial markets. The process of arbitrage concerns expected price levels in the commercial market in traded goods and services, and arbitrage in the goods markets is notoriously slow. If it were fast, there would be no structural unemployment.

Table 3.1

	Characteristics of linkage	
1 IRP	Actual F	with actual F
2 IFE and UFR	Actual F	with expected F
3 FE	Actual F	with expected G
4 PPP	Expected F	with expected G

F = financial markets, G = goods markets

The order in which the relationships tell us something about the real world is shown in table 3.1. Figure 3.1 thus contains some concealed asymmetries which explain why some of the relationships are so much closer than others. Deviations from the FE and from PPP are normal and long-lived. The Eurointerest differential and the forward premium or discount may be unbiased predictors of the future spot rate, but they are far from accurate predictors.

3.9 Summary

The chapter has reviewed how the process of arbitrage keeps the Eurocurrency deposit and foreign exchange markets in alignment and how the combination of investors' expectations and arbitrage ensures that the Eurointerest differential and the forward premium/discount (or swap rate) express the market view of future movement in the spot rate. The balance of the evidence suggests that the market's expectations are *not* an unbiased forecast of the future spot rate.

Different individual markets like those between different spot rates or spot, swap and outright forward markets for the same pair of currencies carry different trading volumes, known as 'liquidities', and the lower the liquidity, the wider will be the spread and the greater the chance of arbitrage opportunities.

Relative inflation rates also have some links with relative interest rates, and in the long term there may be a weak tendency for real interest rates to be similar in different countries. Relative inflation rates also have some links with long-term movements in exchange rates, but again these links appear to be weak and irregular.

4

Time Spans and Volatilities in the Currency Markets

4.1 Introduction

This chapter reviews how patterns in nominal and real exchange rates and their relations with interest rates are characterized by different volatilities for different time-frames.

4.2 Nominal spot exchange rates

Figure 4.1 is a plot of the monthly average closing rate for spot US dollars against £1 sterling, from 1973 to early 1990. We call this the **nominal** spot rate to distinguish it from the real exchange rate. The **real** exchange rate is the subject of section 4.8. It measures variations in the relative purchasing power of currencies, by adjusting changes in the nominal rate for differences in the countries' inflation rates.

By averaging fluctuations within each month, figure 4.1 understates the actual volatility of this rate. It nevertheless appears to show large jagged movements, with some major trends, some of them persisting for several years before they are reversed. The graph appears to show a long-term declining trend of the pound against the dollar, but there are upward trends persisting for example for four years in 1977–81 and again in 1985–8.

4.3 Long-term volatility of spot rates

The plot of a spot rate between two currencies, as in figure 4.1, does not of course show which of the two currencies, dollar or sterling, or both, is moving. It would take weighted indices of each currency against a

Figure 4.1 US dollars to £1 sterling – spot exchange rates from 1/1/73 to 9/3/90 monthly
Source: Datastream

basket of its main competitor currencies to show the separate course of each currency.

Figure 4.1 does, however, show how sharply the nominal rate can move. Sterling fell against the dollar by 32 per cent in 19 months from March 1975 to October 1976, and even more spectacularly by 24 per cent in 7 months from January to August 1981. That particular trend continued to February 1985, achieving a total fall of 55 per cent over 49 months, to less than half the peak value of January 1981. If we were using daily instead of monthly average rates, peaks and troughs would diverge even more.

4.4 Shorter-term volatility of spot rates

Heywood (1984b) has calculated that the percentage variation high v. low during calendar years from 1973 to 1981 for a number of cross exchange rates could reach 39 per cent (for DM/$) at the peak, that the minimum swing was between 5 per cent and 9 per cent, and that the average over the 9 years was in the range 16–18 per cent. Chart 13 of the 1985 Annual Report of the IMF (IMF, 1985) suggests that daily swings in the case of $/£ in 1985 reached a peak of around 5 per cent and anecdotal experience suggests possible swings of up to 10 per cent in a month and 20 per cent in 6 months. Volatility of this order has important implications for currency risk management.

Other studies, particularly Wolff and Reyes (1989) show that volatility is itself variable over time. These fluctuations in volatility have important effects, for example on the pricing of currency options, as we shall see in chapter 12.

De Grauwe (1988), in an interesting paper, draws attention to a number of puzzling phenomena. One is that nominal exchange rates are relatively less volatile than equity prices, and less volatile in the short term than commodity prices. To de Grauwe this suggests that the exchange market behaves with more limited rationality because the fundamentals driving the exchange markets are 'highly uncertain, and much more uncertain' than those driving the commodity and equity markets. It follows, says de Grauwe, that the exchange market operates with bounded rationality, in which the market only moves if newly available data are outside the bounds of the original range of agnosticism.

De Grauwe's view is in harmony with the general intuitive observation that the market tends to move sideways most of the time, and sharply in one direction or the other for the rest of the time.

De Grauwe has not, however, looked at very short periods. His shortest statistic is weekly data for the yen/dollar rate. A real difficulty is that data for very short periods are very hard to obtain and analyse. To some observers, including technical forecasters (see chapter 5, section 5.13.2), exchange rates appear to form a pattern of big waves, smaller waves and finally ripples, which would affect statistical interperiod comparisons.

Meanwhile our concern here is not whether other markets like commodity and equity markets are still more volatile. What concerns us is that exchange markets can be very volatile, and that volatility itself varies over different time-spans and over calendar time. These perceptions have important lessons for risk management.

4.5 Relative volatility of forward exchange rates

In chapters 2 and 3 we found that the forward exchange rate has two independently determined elements, the spot rate and the premium/discount. We also found that the premium/discount is derived from the Eurointerest differential. Chart 14 of the 1985 Annual Report of the IMF and similar charts in Levich (1982) and MacDonald and Taylor

(1989) show that for most pairs of currencies the spot rate was perhaps at least twice as volatile as the interest differential, over the period 1981–4. The exception to this and other rules is that the Canadian/US dollar relationship is more stable than other relationships.

There is anecdotal experience to suggest that the disparity between the volatility of spot rates and that of interest differentials is much greater still over very short periods, such as one day or less. Interest rates tend to be less jumpy than spot rates.

If these observations are accepted, they have some very important implications for how valuable the IFE and the UFR, discussed in chapter 3, section 3.7, are to the currency manager. To the extent that there is a strong disparity between the volatility of the spot rate and that of the interest differential, the usefulness of the forward rate as an accurate (rather than unbiased) predictor of the future spot rate is impaired.

4.6 Beating the market over very short periods

All this confirms empirical evidence that the market is a poor predictor, irrespective of whether it is biased or not. Much more startling are the implications of the suggested view that, for very short periods, spot rates are several times more volatile than interest differentials. If interest differentials approach stability in the very short term, so that only spot rates move, then the currency manager can in that very short term concentrate on spot rates and ignore all other variables. He can do this profitably if over a time-span of hours rather than days he can deploy superior techniques for forecasting spot rate movements.

This conclusion again is consistent with anecdotal evidence that some banks and some large companies make consistent gains in managing their short-term positions. Banks have to comply with supervisory limits for overnight mismatches: the bulk of their speculative positions must therefore be open for less than a day.

In any event, the IFE and UFR can hardly be expected to 'hold', i.e. to have predictive power, over periods in which there is no scope for arbitrage. Banks not only need not, but cannot, use interest-bearing deposits or borrowings to hedge spot deals which are reversed or closed out within the same dealing day, if a spot deal takes two days to implement!

4.7 Currencies and inflation: sea change in the early 1970s

We saw in chapter 3 how the expected difference between two countries' inflation rates is believed

1 through PPP to influence the financial markets' expectation of the rate of change in the future spot rate, and
2 through the FE to be equal to the differential between nominal interest rates in the two currencies.

In their strict forms these propositions cannot be tested because *expectations* of future inflation rates are not easy to measure empirically. Valuable studies of survey data to measure expectations of exchange rates and other variables, like that by Frankel and Froot (1987), deal with the expectations of relatively few, though influential, experts.

In this chapter we are more concerned with the actual behaviour of foreign exchange markets. It may well be that goods market price levels take much longer to adjust to equilibrium than financial markets, but the dominant fact in the real world is the sea change which has come over the foreign exchange markets since the breakdown in 1971–3 of the Bretton Woods system of fixed but adjustable exchange rates.

This sea change – like a coin – has two sides. First, overwhelmingly the main weight of transactions across the exchanges shifted from trading to capital transactions. Secondly, portfolio investors have taken over from central banks as the largest international asset holders, with the predominant collective power to move exchange rates. Indeed one technical reason for the breakdown of Bretton Woods was that the central banks had lost much of their market power to control exchange rates in accordance with the Bretton Woods rules. Their immediate successors as the largest asset holders were OPEC countries; they in their turn were replaced by wider circles and especially Japanese institutions.

If only a small proportion of the demand and supply of currencies serves the purpose of settling trade payments, then trade competitiveness will have only a minor influence on the foreign exchange market. Any such influence of trade factors must work via the trade balance of the country.

Example 4.1

Suppose we start from equilibrium (defined in section 4.10), with an exchange rate which represents equal price levels in Germany and USA for internationally traded goods. Now suppose that inflation in USA is 4 per cent p.a., inflation in Germany is 2 per cent p.a., but that the DM/$

exchange rate remains stable. The dollar price level of traded goods will rise against the D-Mark price level of traded goods at the rate of 1.04/1.02 p.a., reaching 8.08 per cent at the end of four years. At that time the dollar will be uncompetitive against the D-Mark by 8.08 per cent. An uncompetitive exchange rate will make German goods more attractive to US importers, and US goods less attractive to German importers. The US trade balance will go into deficit, Germany's into surplus. The demand for US dollars declines, the demand for D-Marks rises. *Other things being equal,* the D-Mark will rise against the US dollar until competitive equilibrium is restored between the two currencies.

In practice we know that other things are not equal. Currencies are now bought and sold mainly as investments. The dollar may well be more attractive, perhaps because US interest levels are higher or because investors place a high risk discount on the D-Mark, perhaps for political reasons. A risk adjustment seems to have occurred when Solidarity first rose to fame in Poland, uncomfortably near, at that time, to West Germany's Eastern border.

In the very long run the trade balance cannot of course go on being financed by capital inflows into the US from Germany, notwithstanding the interest differential in the dollar's favour. This is for several reasons. A direct effect is that the rise in US external debt generates a growing interest deficit, which will itself aggravate the current account deficit of the US. Indirectly both the growing external debt and continuing trade uncompetitiveness of the US would gradually make the market progressively more nervous of the US dollar. At first a risk premium on the currency would cause dollar interest rates to rise, and finally the market would fall back to and beyond its PPP. In the long run PPP would thus become effective.

4.8 The real exchange rate

The analytical tool for measuring the competitiveness of a currency is its weighted average *real* exchange rate. Shapiro (1989) defines the real exchange rate as 'the nominal, or actual, exchange rate adjusted for changes in the relative purchasing power of each currency since some base period'.

The **real exchange rate** can be defined as a measure of the relative purchasing powers

1 of a given *pair* of currencies, like US dollar/D-Mark, or
2 of a single currency against a basket of other relevant currencies, usually its main trading partner currencies.

Item 2 can be expressed as

(a) $\dfrac{\text{price of tradable goods}}{\text{price of non-tradable goods}}$

in the country which issues the currency (Edwards 1988), or

(b) an index of the currency's weighted average competitiveness, or relative purchasing power against the basket of other currencies.

In section 4.3 we came across the concept of the weighted index of a currency against its main competitor currencies. The weighting is usually by relative amounts of trade with countries issuing other currencies. The index is therefore 'trade weighted'. We can multiply that index A by a further index B, with the same weights, but this time of the relative inflation rates of the other currencies. Movements in the resulting index C represent movements in the relative purchasing power of the currency against its competitor currencies. In other words, index C measures movements in the **competiveness** of the currency. It is usually described as an index of changes in its weighted average **real** exchange rate. Index A, by contrast, was an index of movements in its **nominal** exchange rate.

Strictly, therefore, the real exchange rate,

1 is an index number, not an exchange rate,
2 measures *changes* in relative purchasing power.

Changes in purchasing power are, of course, the reciprocal of changes in the rate of inflation, so that the real exchange rate can also be described as a measure of how far movements in the exchange rate deviate from the difference between the two countries' inflation rates since the base period. In other words real exchange rates measure the ups and downs of the competitiveness of a currency.

4.9 Purchasing power parity

PPP was discussed in chapter 3, section 3.7.5, It takes two forms: absolute and relative, its view of the future spot rate can be regarded as an *ex ante* expectation or as having some predictive power, perhaps in terms of lack of bias.

To the extent that forward exchange rates are believed to be driven by market expectations, it seems plausible to infer that one element in those expectations is the market's view of countries' relative prospective inflation rates.

4.10 Real exchange rates: the track record

In the real world there are more than two currencies, and exchange rates are at any given point the result of demand and supply for a large number of currencies. The best way therefore to track the course of the real exchange rate of a currency is to construct an index, like index C in section 4.8, which compares exchange rates and price levels between that currency and a weighted average of its main competitor currencies. Figures 4.2 and 4.3 show two such representations. Figures 4.2 and 4.3 are so drawn that a rise in the real exchange rate shows a worsening, and a fall shows an improvement in the competitiveness of the currency concerned.

The weighted average exchange rates are compared with a calculated PPP line. Figures 4.2 and 4.3 derive PPP data from studies by the United Nations. Figure 4.2 shows calculated 'actual' PPP values, whereas figure 4.3 shows them as a straight horizontal line. Both are from a model devised by London Business School.

Edwards (1988) defines the equilibrium real exchange rate as

> That relative price of tradeables that, for given long-run equilibrium (or sustainable) values of other relevant variables such as trade taxes, international prices, capital and aid flows, and technology, results in the simultaneous attainment of external and internal equilibrium. In this context internal equilibrium means that the non-tradeable goods market clears in the current period and is expected to be in equilibrium in the future.

Figures 4.2 and 4.3 must not be interpreted as precision measurements. Measuring price parities is fraught with statistical difficulties. For example Japan and USA have very different consumption 'baskets'. The four diagrams give the impression that the four depicted currency areas collectively tend to have predominantly undervalued currencies, with only the US dollar predominantly overvalued. However, the rest of the world has correspondingly overvalued currencies in relation to PPP. The measurements should be accurate enough to indicate when a currency is moving towards a more or a less competitive real parity with its main trading partners.

4.11 Patterns of real exchange rate movements

There are a number of interesting and practical, if intuitive lessons in the two diagrams. The real exchange rate periodically, but infrequently, changes its vertical direction. In a majority of cases it appears to be

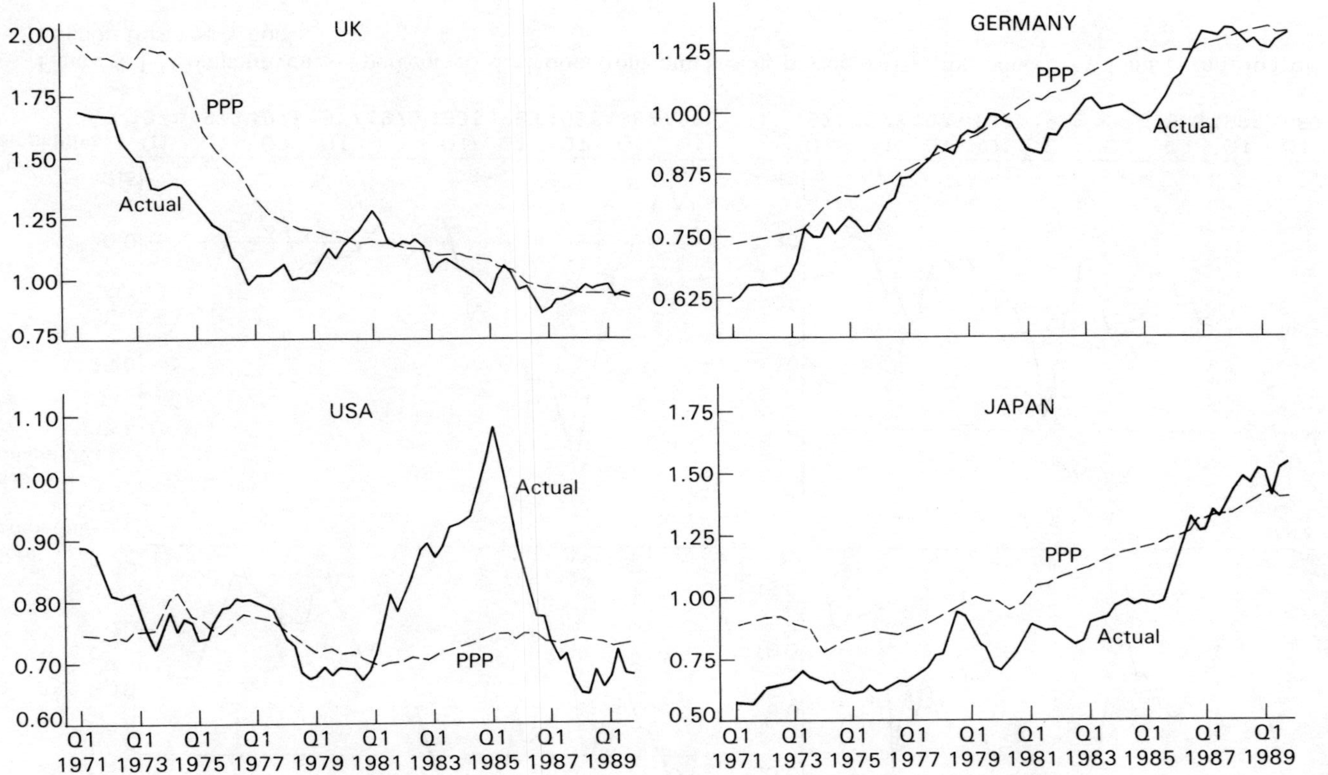

Figure 4.2 Trade weighted exchange rates, plotted against purchasing power parity, 1985 = 1 (reproduced by kind permission of London Business School)

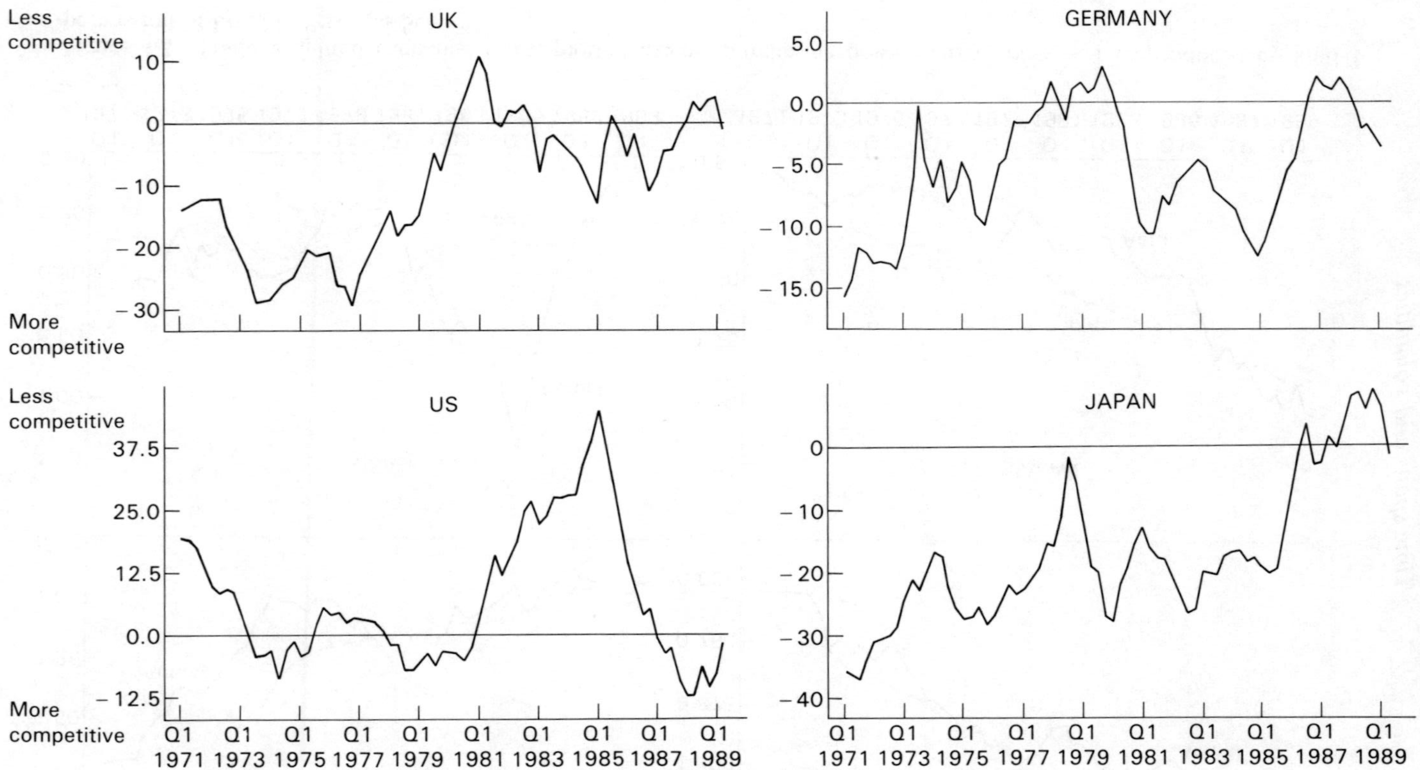

Figure 4.3 Competitiveness, percentage deviation from purchasing power parity (reproduced by kind permission of London Business School)

relatively competitive or uncompetitive for fairly long periods, typically several years. The real exchange rate is less volatile than the nominal exchange rate. Nevertheless over- and undervaluations can be of significant sizes. A level of deviation of 20 per cent in either direction from the currency's average (not its PPP) value is not unusual. In practice, what matters is that competitiveness rises and falls relatively slowly, and that trends are usually reversed, but after some time.

We have already seen, in chapter 3, section 3.8, and in section 4.7, that the economic logic behind the slow adjustment of exchange rates to relative purchasing power changes is the relative inflexibility of certain prices in non-financial markets (the 'real economy'), particularly the price of labour. Those prices will eventually adjust to market factors, but the process is slow and its momentum not easily halted. This elephantine quality of prices in goods markets contrasts with the much greater sensitivity of the purely financial markets in which the nominal exchange rate is traded.

De Grauwe (1988) points out that his near-rational model predicts that real exchange rates 'move in a particular direction for many years without a clear tendency . . . to return to equilibrium value'. Only when the movements away from equilibrium travel outside the 'range of agnosticism' of bounded rationality, will there be fundamental forces to drive them back to where they came from.

If this intuitive pattern were reliable, then competitiveness would be open to at least a modest degree of prediction. For example, at the point where competitiveness has just shown an improving trend, there is a fair chance that the currency will remain relatively competitive for some months or even years, before becoming less competitive again. That conclusion would of course be speculative, but would have some positive probability. This could have important implications for managing what later chapters will call competitiveness risk.

One technical point needs to be made. PPP is not constant, but rises for some and falls for other currencies. A full theoretical explanation is beyond the scope of this book. In broad terms the explanation is that PPP might be constant if *all* goods and services in every economy were *internationally traded.* In that case arbitrage in the goods market would affect the general price level. In fact, however, by no means all goods and services are traded, i.e. exported and imported. Quite large proportions of economic activity, especially services, do not enter into trade and do not therefore affect exchange rate equilibrium. Moreover, productivity improvements are unlikely to be equal in the traded and non-traded sectors. The upshot is that PPP rises in countries with the highest rate of increase in productivity and falls in those with the lowest rate of increase.

4.12 Interrelation between nominal and real exchange rate movements

Chapter 8 will argue that nominal and real exchange rate movements cause different categories of business risk. Nominal movements cause financial risks, i.e. trading and position risk, whereas real exchange rate movements cause competitiveness risk as defined in that chapter. We must therefore examine just how different these two types of exchange rate movement actually are. If they were very highly correlated, the distinction between different risks caused by the two categories (see chapter 8) would lose some of its usefulness.

The pattern here, as elsewhere, shows a sharp contrast between short and long time-spans. Inflation rates do not normally change quickly. In fact the normal order of volatility is spot rates first, interest rates second and inflation rates last. Interest rates too are more volatile than price levels in commercial goods markets. Financial markets are normally nimbler and less impeded by rigidities and information delays than commercial markets in goods and services.

Spot rates, then relative interest rates, then relative inflation rates: that is the normal descending order of volatilities. The important exception to this order, as we saw in chapter 3, is an economy with hyperinflation. In fact the best definition of hyperinflation may be that it is a state in which variability of the rate of inflation is the dominant volatility.

The implication of the normal state is that in the very short term there is little difference between nominal and real exchange rate movements: inflation and therefore inflation differentials are close to zero in that very short run. In the very long run, on the other hand, intuitive evidence suggests that real exchange rate movements have a tendency to approach and cross the long-term trend line, whereas nominal movements tend to widen as long as there is an inflation differential with the same sign, positive or negative.

To sum up, in the very short term, nominal exchange rate fluctuations are virtually identical with real exchange rate fluctuations; as time-spans lengthen, the differences become substantial, and the competitiveness sign is reversed when the real exchange rate crosses the trend line.

4.13 The very short period

If the discussion in this chapter strikes the business reader as a little dry or even dull, then he has missed a very startling lesson in section 4.6, which corporate currency management can exploit with very significant benefits. In the currency markets the very short term, consisting of a few dealing hours, is important, because in it only spot rates are really volatile. Within those short periods, spot rate changes are in practice identical with real exchange rate movements.

There are two reasons for this. First, the disparity between the volatility of spot exchange rates, on the one hand, and interest rates and inflation rates, on the other, is much sharper in the very short period. Secondly, the arbitrage relationship between spot rates and interest rate differentials does not apply in the very short period because regulatory constraints on banks' open position do not apply intraday, and spot deals take at least two working days to settle. These special features of the very short period attract a large interbank trading volume.

In the slightly less short period, interest rates are more volatile than inflation rates, so that during such short periods real interest rates have much greater volatility than in the longer run. The FE operates only in that longer run.

4.14 Summary

The chapter has reviewed the significantly different patterns of nominal and real exchange rates, and attempted to interpret the differences.

The central message of the chapter is the importance of different time-frames and their very different volatilities. In the very short period – a few dealing hours – the volatility of the spot rate dominates the picture. In the very long term – some years – real exchange rates and purchasing power parity may dominate. In the very short term the interest parity relationship cannot hold because interest rates do not move at anything like the speed of spot rates, and in any case arbitrage is not possible; at least until electronic means speed up the implementation of spot exchange contracts.

The very special features of very short periods are in fact the most striking lesson from these perceptions. The relationship between spot, forward, interest and inflation rates is not what it is in longer periods. This is exploited by some of the larger market operators. When we look at longer horizons, say up to 12 months, the IFE and therefore the forward rate are much harder to beat, and in the much longer period of several years PPP may be a stronger predictor than interest rates.

5 Forecasting Exchange Rates

This chapter reviews first the long-standing divergence between the views of practitioners and finance theorists about the possibility of beating the market's forecast incorporated in its forward rate, and then the different types of professional forecasting services.

5.1 Can the market's view be beaten?

An MBA student from a well-known business school, in the course of research on his project dissertation, had interviewed a number of senior treasurers of companies. When asked how he assessed their competence and intelligence, he said he had reservations. 'They all think they can forecast.'

The anecdote brings out the conflict of views between many practitioners and most financial theorists. Theorists tend to have some measure of belief in the efficiency of the market, and therefore in the futility of any attempts to outguess the forward rate. Practitioners believe that they either are or should be able to beat the market, at least sometimes. This argument can hardly be resolved without first defining and refining the positions much more closely.

This book will not attempt to outline the entire theory of currency determination. The various models are very helpfully set out and compared in Heffernan and Sinclair (1990). We shall merely try to refer to the main features of the present floating currency environment, and the main fallacies, and to distinguish what seem to be reasonable from unreasonable conclusions.

5.2 Market efficiency and the forward rate

An efficient market was defined by Fama (1970) as one which 'fully reflects' all relevant information promptly, so that agents in that market should not be able to earn abnormal returns.

In the foreign exchange markets, market efficiency, coupled with rational expectations, implies that however widely actual spot rates differ from the views implied in past forward rates, those differences should over time add to zero, showing the absence of bias. We came across this concept in the '*ex post*' versions of the IFE and the UFR in chapter 3, sections 3.7.2–3 and 3.8.

In the *ex ante* – expectations – sense, the IFE and UFR are simply equilibrium conditions, and are very likely to hold. This is because investors' preferences between Eurocurrency deposits in different freely floating currencies would not be in equilibrium if the interest differential were not equal to the market's collective expectation of the future movement of the spot rate. It is quite another matter whether this collective view will in fact have some verifiable relationship like lack of bias with the **subsequent out-turn**.

The literature on this has been thoroughly reviewed in MacDonald and Taylor (1989). The test of market efficiency in this sense is whether actual out-turns vary randomly or with bias from the forecasts of the market. Deviations should be due to fresh news not available to market agents at the time of their forecasts. The balance of the evidence according to the authors has recently swung fairly decisively towards the existence of bias.

The evidence for bias includes the success of filter rules which made systematic profits (Sweeney, 1986). Explanations put forward in that paper include intervention by central banks under rules (as in the European Monetary System) which compel them to deal at a loss. Speculators can then systematically gain at the central banks' expense. In that case the currency float is imperfect.

Unfortunately proof of bias gives no guidance as to whether bias is due to a risk premium or to a lack of rationality in expectations. However, an attempt can be made to resolve that question by using data from survey enquiries, as was done by Frankel and Froot (1987). The results suggest that bias is not due to risk premia, but to less than perfectly rational expectations. This conclusion is of course congruous with de Grauwe's hypothesis of bounded rationality.

However, what precisely is meant here by the expression 'risk premium'? Certainly nothing like an insurance premium. Researchers use the word 'premium' to denote the degree by which risk aversion causes the interest differential to underestimate the actual subsequent movement in the exchange rate. The expression 'risk premium' implies that bias in the forward rate takes the form of underforecasting subsequent movements in the spot rate. It should not therefore be mistaken for a kind of reward to banks for relieving hedgers of risks by selling them forward contracts. The forward contract does not transfer risk. The banks' reward is contained in the spread. In any case different hedgers deal in opposite directions with the banks in the *same* pair of currencies: for every hedger *selling* D-Marks three months forward for dollars there is one *buying* D-Marks forward for dollars for the same maturity. Banks merely deal at the market rate for the forward date.

If bias is accepted, its degree need not be high. The remarkable feature of the evidence is how little bias the forward rate appears to have. Most market participants have a profound appreciation of the fact that the quoting bank is not normally even thinking of the expected future course of the exchange rate, only the Eurointerest differential. It does not easily occur to them that the forward rate can have any validity as a forecast. Yet all the evidence suggests that it has some predictive power, however unimpressive. This must evidently be ascribed to the market as a whole, not to its individual participants.

5.3 Are the IFE and UFR useful pointers to the future spot rate?

To the practitioner the efficient markets hypothesis and the test of bias are of less interest than whether the forward rate is a reasonably accurate forecast, and whether it does better or worse that other types of forecast. This question has been researched in a series of studies like those of Levich (1982), Brasse (1983) and Blake, Beenstock and Brasse (1986) which have compared the accuracy of the forward rate with the accuracy of professional forecasts. These tests on balance confirm that the reviewed forecasts tend to be both biased and very inaccurate. The forward rate seems to compare well with the track record of professional forecasts, or at any rate to do no worse. The forward rate (and thus the IFE and UFR) may well be the *best available, but still poor* predictor of the future spot rate.

Empirical research therefore on balance suggests a rather sceptical conclusion. It is that forecasting is not really possible, and that in any event the very inaccurate forward rate cannot be beaten. There is no consistently better answer than the collective view of the market in the forward rate.

5.4 The perceptions of practioners

The anecdote in section 5.1 seems to show academics and practitioners on a collision course on this issue. Practitioners believe in the possibility of beating the market. Their predominant intuitive conviction is that spot rates tend to develop wavy movements or bandwagons and to move past equilibrium before going into reverse and repeating the process on the other side. On a much milder scale these tendencies are also present in interest differentials or inflation differentials. Chapter 4 described how much less volatile these are. Some academic models like de Grauwe's are consistent with this view.

5.5 Pointers to a resolution of the conflict

Can we suggest any way to resolve the conflict? The last two chapters have already provided a couple of clues.

5.5.1 The importance of different time-frames

It seems likely that very different rules can apply to different time-frames. In the very short period the market provides no forecast while spot rates can be very volatile. The efficient markets hypothesis is largely irrelevant in that time-frame. In the slightly less short term, investment transactions and therefore the IFE and UFR are dominant. In the very long term, on the other hand, we should expect the real economy, the goods markets and therefore PPP to be more influential. These features were explored in chapter 4, sections 4.7 and 4.12.

5.5.2 Relative volatilities

We have seen that spot rates are more volatile than interest and inflation rates. Once again there is at least intuitive evidence that both absolute and relative volatility vary with time-frames. The peak in each case may well be the very short period again. These matters are well worth some empirical research.

5.5.3 Are the two sides asking the same question?

The above two clues came out in earlier chapters. There is, however, a third point. Like the other two, it involves time-frames. Researchers accept a very rigorous discipline. For example, the three-months forward rate is tested against the three-months outcome: the spot rate three months later. However, the practitioner who believes that sterling is undervalued against the dollar, would almost certainly not claim that the undervaluation will correct itself by any particular time, such as day 91 from now. The practitioner merely believes that if he invests in sterling now, then at some time in the future his total sterling principal and interest will – at the then spot rate – be worth more than the corresponding sum which he could then have if he now invested the same sum in dollars instead of sterling.

Intuitively, that is the kind of judgement which would be reasonable at various points on a chart like figure 4.1. Practitioners believe that there are wavy trends, that the waves run on beyond longer-run equilibrium, are then corrected by reverse movements which will in their turn overcorrect, and so on. They do not, however, claim that these waves follow regular time-spans, regular enough to comply with the researcher's rigorous rules. Moreover, many of the decisions which practitioners need to take, do not require that degree of timing precision. They may well need to be right within finite ranges of time, but not at a single point in time, which is the test adopted by the researcher.

Example 5.1

Suppose a UK-based company has a SFr100 million Eurobond outstanding, and no Swiss franc assets. Its treasurer has instructions to neutralize this imbalance, but is free to choose his time. Moreover, the Swiss franc is at present 15 per cent overvalued against sterling in terms of economic fundamentals. He has little doubt that the fundamental disequilibrium will be corrected within the next 15 months. In that case all he has to do is to set himself a trigger exchange rate at which he will take action to balance the company's Swiss franc position. The trigger rate is best defined in terms of the real (inflation-adjusted) exchange rate, so as to allow for the effect of higher sterling than Swiss franc inflation. Perhaps he would place his trigger rate at a 15 per cent fall in the real SFr/£ rate.

His latitude in timing his action gives him an advantage over those situations where timing is more closely constrained. Example 16.1 in section 16.3 explains the practical problem in greater detail.

To sum this up, if practitioners do not ask the same questions as the researchers, then it is not surprising that they do not come up with the same answer.

5.6 Should practitioners ignore the theoretical models?

It is not, however, suggested that business managers and financial theorists have nothing to learn from one another. Many of the business currency manager's actual decisions are about forward periods which are neither very short nor very long. Over that very wide field the market may not be perfectly efficient, but it is efficient enough to be hard to beat. The currency manager here needs a strong case before he bets against the forward rate. The dice are loaded in his favour only if his view of the future spot rate gets a head start from tax arbitrage: for example if the tax rules penalize an interest gain more than they relieve an equal exchange loss on the principal sum.

On the other hand, at least some theorists have not yet taken enough note of how causal frameworks vary with different time-spans and how they relate to different actual business problems. The skilled currency manager may well be able to beat the market if his time-frame is outside that middle range of time-spans or if he can afford to wait long enough to sit out even a fairly long extra duration of the movement which he believes has already gone some way beyond the longer-term equilibrium. The academics may one day disprove the existence of such trends, but in these time-elastic terms they have not so far tried to do that.

5.7 Relative volatilities and risk premia

If markets were perfectly efficient and the forward rate was therefore an unbiased predictor of the future spot rate, what explains the very large errors in those predictions, observed by all who have investigated the track record?

The average size of the error is so great that it is plausible to look for a causal connection with the great volatility of the spot rate which we have noted several times. It is tempting to suggest that the problem should be examined through the other end of the telescope. Perhaps it would be more rewarding to investigate the volatility of the spot rate than just the shortcomings of the forward rate, or rather of the predictive power of the Eurointerest differential.

Some researchers at present ascribe this forecasting 'error' of the forward rate wholly to the arrival of unexpected news after the date on which the forward rate is quoted. Others, including Hacche and Townend (1981) and the IMF Annual Report 1981, bring in the concept of differential **risk premia** for different currencies. (This is not the same kind of risk premium as was discussed in section 5.2. That premium would prompt forward rates and interest differentials generally to underestimate *all* movements in the spot rates of *all currencies*. We are now discussing how investors see *currency A as riskier than currency B)*.

On this view equilibrium in the investment market for currencies A and B depends on the expected relative return on investing in currency A rather than B. The return on investing in a currency is the net sum of

- the expected (usually the quoted) Eurocurrency rate of interest,
- the expected rate of capital gain or loss due to movements in the spot exchange rate,
- a risk factor which measures the investor's relative uncertainty about the above expectations.

Example 5.2

Let us assume

1 that dollars yield 10 per cent and D-Marks 6½ per cent,
2 that the markets are in equilibrium after discounting a risk premium on the dollar over the D-Mark due, say, to instability in Eastern Europe: but for this, the interest differential would have been wider.

Any sudden resolution of the Eastern European turmoil would upset the existing equilibrium. A new equilibrium would now require *either* a widening of the interest differential *or* a fall by the dollar against the D-Mark or a mixture of both.

Equilibrium spot, forward and Eurointerest rates are those at which the investor is indifferent between the various currencies. Equilibrium levels are determined by a mutual process between the spot and Eurointerest rates, but the forces which determine equilibrium are expectations rather than hard actual data. Moreover those expectations appear to be capable of some degree of nervousness.

We do not appear to know what explains high volatility in the spot rate. The available evidence suggests that these high levels of volatility are discontinuous. Taylor (1989) has even found deviations from interest parity (covered interest arbitrage) at times when major policy changes are expected. Some of his earlier examples concern sterling before the abolition of exchange controls. Figure 4 in Wolff and Reyes (1988) charts daily volatility of the dollar/sterling spot rate from 1975 to 1987 varying between 0.3 and 3 per cent. Intuitively one might find it plausible to believe that nervousness reaches its peaks at times of doubt about the monetary and other policies of central banks or at times of political uncertainty. These explanations would perhaps not be inconsistent with de Grauwe's (1988) supposition that bounded rationality is due to uncertainty about the mechanism by which equilibrium is determined.

5.8 Economic forces and short-term expectations

Traditionally, exchange rate forecasting was regarded as a task for economists and economic commentators. Exchange rates were seen as driven by relative inflation rates, the internal balance in each country (broadly whether savings and taxation exceed investment and public expenditure), price-elasticities of imports and exports, relative growth in money supply and resulting trends in external current accounts. These are the meat and drink of econometric forecasts.

Many of these variables are appropriate more to currency markets in which trade rather than capital flows predominate. However, even when portfolio switching is dominant, it must be assumed that the portfolio managers will be conscious of the ultimate pull of economic fundamentals. We saw in section 4.7 of chapter 4 how a persistent trade deficit must ultimately lead to a reassertion of economic fundamentals.

However, all this is an oversimplification, because some of the monetary factors like interest rates and money supply can have a much more direct and faster-acting effect on the markets. We must therefore note the sharp and complex differences between the time-scales over which each of the influences work on *actual,* and therefore indirectly on *expected* data.

Relative *inflation rates,* as we saw in chapter 4, take a very long time to assert themselves. The process described in section 4.7 can take years. Meanwhile relative inflation rates, and especially expected future inflation rates, are also one of the determinants of relative *interest* rates, which in their turn affect exchange market expectations rather faster than trade imbalances. Other things being equal, a rise in yen interest rates will rapidly attract funds into yen deposits and cause the yen to rise.

Differences between rates of growth of the *money supply* in different countries affect exchange rates after a complex pattern of time-lags:

1 they affect exchange rates *instantly* through their impact on expectations, especially expectations of interest and inflation rates,
2 they *fairly rapidly* influence actual rates of interest and investment demand,
3 they have *delayed* effects on economic activity and thus – via the internal balance – on the trade balance: this in turn affects demand and supply for the currency in the medium term.

Some effects are instant, others take years.

5.9 Economic forces and the long term

Once the forecaster or currency risk manager is concerned with periods of several years, the nature of the forecasting task changes materially. As the period lengthens, the influence of the commercial markets in the arbitrage relationships gains in strength. In practice this means that real exchange rate equilibrium becomes more powerful. As the period approaches 3, 4 or 5 years, the probability of competitive equilibrium being reached and crossed rises. Again, the longer the period, the weaker is the pull of the financial equilibrium relationships like the IFE. Financial market arbitrage becomes less important, but within the financial markets the action shifts from the interbank to the bond and other security markets.

Until recently cross-currency arbitrage in, say, the Eurobond markets was less strong than in the interbank markets. This difference is being eroded as the security and bank markets become more and more integrated through swaps and other new instruments, and through the trend towards securitization (BIS, 1986).

5.10 Summary of the forecasting environment

The argument so far suggests that the business currency manager faces a market for freely floating currencies with the following characteristics:

1 Many of its features are still imperfectly understood.
2 It is closely integrated by arbitrage with the global interest rate structure, particularly through the Eurocurrency deposit market. This integration weakens as time-frames approach very long periods.
3 Its collective view of the future course of the spot rate is contained in its forward exchange rate, which is not perfectly unbiased, but not heavily biased and hard to outspeculate over a wide span of time-frames (maturities).
4 Except over very long maturities, it is dominated by buyers and sellers who trade currencies as investment assets rather than to pay for *traded* goods.
5 The investment value of a currency depends on its expected future rise or fall against other currencies, its relative interest rate and its relative risk rating.
6 Spot rates are very volatile, especially in the short term; more volatile than interest rates and interest rate differentials.
7 Over very long maturities, spot rates are more closely related with expected relative inflation rates, and less closely with interest

differentials. The closed Fisher effect does not seem to hold very strongly.

8 Market participants strongly believe that the market develops wavy movements, bandwagons or other departures from longer term equilibrium paths, especially in those very short and very long time-frames where the integration with Eurointerest rates is not very strong.

The importance of every one of these features, including 1 and 5, varies between different time-frames. The need to discriminate between time-frames is perhaps the strongest message that comes from this picture.

5.11 Is forecasting floating exchange rates worth while?

Everything said in this chapter so far applies to freely floating currencies which can be freely traded spot and forward and in the Eurodeposit markets.

We began with a disagreement between many practitioners on the one hand and many financial theorists on the other as to whether forecasting was a waste of time in efficient markets. We have found that market efficiency cannot be used to support a broad-brush rejection of forecasting. Market efficiency is itself open to some doubt. In any case, as the currency manager's time-frame extends from the short to the longer term, the markets which predominate in determining exchange rate equilibrium shift from the short-term market in currency bank deposits towards the commercial market in goods and services. At the shorter end we have found room for bandwagons which may be entirely dominant in the very short period of a few dealing hours and still retain some degree of influence for periods of several months.

At the same time there are time-frames, typically perhaps the 3- to 12-month period, in which it is very difficult for a forecaster to outperform the forward rate and the IFE with any consistency. For these middle periods the financial markets are by and large the best forecasters we have.

That leaves quite a few tasks for the forecaster. Forecasting will never be easy in volatile markets, but there are some prizes for those who acquire skills to identify the following:

5.11.1 Bandwagons and the extent to which they have not yet run their course

- In the very short period this means being very close to the interbank market; as close perhaps as an ordinary interbank party, and combining this with the cool, objective detachment needed to identify and judge the status of bandwagons.
- In the longer period from, say, two days to several months it needs less closeness to the market and even more discrimination between genuine trends and overshooting.

5.11.2 The effect of economic fundamentals in the longer term

The difficulty here is not so much to find the direction in which economic or commercial market fundamentals pull the exchange rate, but to weigh this against the countermagnetism of the interest differential and risk perceptions in the financial markets, and to judge how long it will take the fundamentals to take charge. Timing problems here, as elsewhere, are the hardest.

None of this – we must repeat – suggests that it is easy or even practicable to beat the markets; only that in principle at least it is not always impossible.

5.12 Relaxing the discipline of timing

As noted in section 5.5.3, practitioners do not always have to work within those timing disciplines which researchers need to accept. Researchers cannot test their models without such disciplines. They need to specify the future date for which a forecast is made. The practitioner's forecasting task is often free from that important constraint.

5.13 The forecasters

Three types of professional forecasters are generally recognized: econometric, technical and kitchen sink.

5.13.1 Econometric forecasters

Econometric forecasters are at once the most respectable and perhaps the least successful group. They build and estimate models of how exchange rates are determined by various macroeconomic factors. These factors include inflation rates, economic growth, current account balances, money supply and interest rates. They then use these models to forecast future exchange rates. Hacche and Townend (1981), in a footnote, speak of the widespread failure of econometric forecasts. This failure is of course consistent with what has been suggested in this chapter. First, expectations cannot be measured and fed into models, only past actual data. Secondly, the models attribute too much influence to the real economy and the commercial markets, especially in the shorter term. In any case discontinuities occur over time in economic management by governments. These changes can invalidate the insights yielded by past correlations. Recognized discontinuities can of course be incorporated as independent variables in the equations used for forecasts. However, during the 1980s many econometric forecasting services have adopted technical forecasts to cover the first three months of each forecast.

5.13.2 Technical forecasters

Technical forecasters are popularly known as chartists. They have a better track record in the short term. They plot daily closing exchange rates, and deduce from the behavioural patterns of those charts what bandwagons are running, and how near or far they are from having run their course. Such success as these forecasts have had is evidence that good technical forecasting can capture at least some of these bandwagons. There is much logic in this. If we believe in bandwagons, then we can only hope to explain and capture them in terms of market psychology, and that is best observed by behavioural analysis. That is what technical analysis sets out to do.

De Grauwe's (1988) model is unusual in finding room for technical forecasting. In this model, operators in the markets allot fluctuating weights to backward-looking and forward-looking data in framing their expectations. When information reaching the market is within the 'range of agnosticism' of bounded rationality, the main weight is given to past behaviour, which technical analysis covers. When the information exceeds the bounds of that range, the centre of gravity shifts towards forward-looking rational expectations again.

Technical forecasts have important limitations. Forecasts are usually expressed in terms of spot rates at various future dates. By their self-imposed professional rules the forecasters must derive their forecasts strictly from the information of each chart: it is unprofessional to take account of any information which is not on that particular chart. Thus a forecaster's code of practice requires him to forecast each of the $/DM,

\$/£ and £/DM exchange rates independently. If the charts tell him to forecast for one month from now that \$1 = DM2.00, £1 = DM3.00 and £1 = \$1.70, then his forecasts are glaringly inconsistent. The first two of those rates are consistent only with £1 = \$1.50. Technical forecasters are no fools. Our forecaster very probably knows about Brown's (1983) triangular arbitrage conditions, but there is nothing he can do about it. He knows he is wrong in at least one of the forecasts, but his code of practice does not permit him to modify his forecast to accommodate this fact.

Technical forecasts are respected by many practitioners for their apparently superior performance. Their strength naturally lies in short period forecasts. The shorter the period, the greater is the influence of market bandwagons, and technical forecasts are the only objective method devised to recognize bandwagons. Nevertheless they are not cheap and their success record is not so startling as to make them an obvious bargain. In any case they are of varying quality.

5.13.3 Kitchen sink forecasters

Kitchen sink forecasters are usually economists who do not restrict themselves to econometric models or any other mechanistic tools. They use all the information they can assemble, including public or private policy statements from official sources, market information, economic statistics and sometimes personal interviews with influential sources of information, and build all these into forecasts which they do not publish, but sell as a consultancy service. The kitchen sink school's distinctive concept is that the nature of the market does not lend itself to any mechanistic forecasting technique. However, as neither the forecasts nor the sources of information on which they rest are available for comparison, no track record can be publicly measured.

5.14 Postcript: non-floating currencies

Perhaps 95 per cent of the world's 400-odd currencies do not float freely. Some are heavily controlled and not freely traded. Others are managed by their central banks much closer to their market values, and traded with varying degrees of freedom. It would be impossible to control their exchange rates, least of all at some distance from market values, if the currencies were heavily traded as portfolio assets. Control is in any case possible only if the issuing central bank is the largest single dealer in the currency.

Many **controlled** currencies are overvalued. In most cases that is the central purpose of control. A currency is 'overvalued' if it would drop if allowed to float. As these currencies are not freely tradable, they are not attractive to investors. Trading transactions therefore predominate in their markets.

The key fact about a controlled currency is the degree of its deviation from its competitive equilibrium. As interest rates too are kept below market levels, interest differentials cannot be unbiased predictors.

Controlled currencies can be subdivided into

- currencies with forward and sometimes offshore deposit markets, usually with **moderate inflation**, and
- those with **hyperinflation** and no forward and offshore deposit markets.

Controlled currencies are effectively in a system similar to the old Bretton Woods system. Hyperinflation currencies keep very broadly in line with PPP by means of frequent ('crawling peg') minidevaluations, not through continuous market adjustment. Major deviations from PPP build up until they are corrected by infrequent maxidevaluations. It is always known in which direction the maxi will be, but not *how much* or *when*.

Currencies with moderate inflation rates, e.g. the Scandinavian currencies, are even harder to forecast. They can survive without an adjustment back to competitive equilibrium for quite long periods, and the governments concerned have a considerable measure of control over them. Trade balance considerations tend to have a decisive influence in most cases.

The currency manager who is concerned with a controlled currency like, say, the Egyptian pound, has a task similar to that which faced all currency managers in the Bretton Woods system. His risk is one way. He cannot be in doubt which way the currency will move if it moves. He should

1. ascertain or calculate against what currency or basket (weighted average) of currencies the Egyptian pound is pegged by its central bank, then
2. assume stability against that peg between adjustments (devaluations), and finally,
3. assess the timing and amount of the next adjustment.

The currency manager can refer to a number of sources, including the IMF's International Financial Statistics, to find out whether a currency is floating, pegged against a particular major currency such as the US dollar, or pegged against a basket of currencies, or in a joint float as are the currencies in the European Monetary System.

The way to arrive at a rational forecast for a controlled currency is to find out as much as possible about the policies and intentions of the government or the central bank or whichever minister, official or body makes the effective decision about the exchange parity of the currency. Politics are the key to their decisions.

Managed currencies, like for example most currencies in the European Monetary System (EMS), are generally managed not for overvaluation, but for stable harmonization with the leading currency or basket to which they are hitched. In the EMS this role is played by the D-Mark. Currencies are kept within floating limits by central bank intervention, but monetary and fiscal policies are adjusted so as to harmonize target parities with market values.

Managed currencies are relatively easy to forecast, as long as their management is successful. In the EMS there have been realignments whenever success was incomplete, and although the direction of any realignment is usually known, it is not easy to forecast whether, when, or by how much a currency will be realigned.

5.15 Summary

Forecasting has an uphill task in beating the forward rate over a very large part of the foreign exchange market: the short- to medium-term period in the major floating currencies in which fund holders invest.

However, the forecaster may have a chance to beat the markets expecially in very short and very long time-frames and in managed or controlled currencies. Time-frames are all-important in this field. Also important are relative volatilities and risk premia between currencies.

The pecking order of the competing forces determining exchange rate movements undergoes changes over various time-frames, with relative inflation rates growing in influence over time, bandwagons declining, and arbitrage with the Eurocurrency markets rising in very short periods and then declining again as time-frames get very long.

Econometric forecasters are handicapped by the difficulty of capturing expectations to feed into models. Technical forecasters have other handicaps, but have better track records for short periods. Kitchen sink forecasters cannot be monitored because they do not publish their forecasts.

Part II

Management Principles and Classification of Risks

6

A General Approach to Business Risks

6.1 The issues

A central, but neglected issue in currency risk management is how that task fits into the general task of managing a business, which covers the wider topic of all business risk. It is useful therefore to review briefly the wider spectrum of business risks. This appears not to have been done elsewhere except in a brief article by Kenyon (1988). The topic needs separate attention. Here it can only be outlined to the extent that it affects the place of currency risk management in the wider context.

The issues are as follows:

- One-way v. two-way risks (section 6.2).
- Is risk in business always to be seen as a variety or spread of possible outcomes of some uncertainty, or are there also risks which should be minimized or avoided? Is risk something which can be either valuable, a 'good thing', or at worst value-neutral, or can risk also be a 'bad thing', something undesirable? The former type could be managed as a portfolio by diversification, the latter only by some kind of counteraction or avoidance (section 6.3).
- How can we distinguish between risks which can be treated as portfolios and those which must be managed by varying degrees of either neutralization or avoidance (section 6.4)?
- Is all risk to be managed by direct and sole reference to the financial value of the company (sections 6.4.2–3)?
- Are there risks in business which are intolerable, to be either neutralized or avoided at almost any cost (section 6.5)?

6.2 One-way and two-way risks

Risks which can end in loss, but not gain, are one-way risks: there are no negative floods. Two-way risks can result in either gains or losses. They can be broadly identified with market risks. Their outcomes typically depend on price movements in financial, commodity or commercial markets. Those prices can move favourably or unfavourably. This category includes risks from future fluctuations in market prices of exchange rates, commodities, equity shares, options or futures. Not all two-way risks are concerned with market prices. Some of them turn on non-market forces such as human competence or the tensility of metals, etc. Investment projects too can have successful or unsuccessful outcomes depending among other things on competitive events in commercial markets.

The one-way class of risk includes most insurable risks like earthquake, fire, burglary, personal accident, or credit risk. The distinction between one-way and two-way risks is brought into sharper focus by the nature of insurance itself. To the insured party, the possible loss of his home is a catastrophic loss which he could not average against other out-turns: to him it is a one-way risk. To the insurer, however, the aggregation of risks borne out of a many times larger capital fund, becomes part of a two-way risk in which his gain or loss depends on whether actual loss experience is above or below his mean expectation of, say, 2 per cent of his total portfolio of real estate risks. Viewed in this light, the same external threat is a one-way risk to the insured party and a two-way risk to the insurer. The burning question for those faced with a one-way risk, say a personal accident or burglary, is 'will it occur: yes or no?'

In the two-way category the variability of outcomes as such is not in doubt. Few people expect the price of coffee or the dollar/sterling spot exchange rate to stop fluctuating. What is in some doubt, is the shape of the distribution curve, and even more the price or rate at any particular future point in time. There is usually an expected mean outcome, but few people would bet on that turning up. The risk is strictly an unexpected outcome, a deviation from the expected mean.

Linguistic confusion is partly bred by the different academic disciplines concerned with risk. The insurance literature deals mainly with one-way risks. Financial economics is largely concerned with two-way risks, and therefore does not discuss risk as a feared event. Finally writers on the psychology of risk, like Slovic et al. (1980), note that some outcomes of risk, such as bankruptcy, are so repugnant to business managers as to be wholly unacceptable.

Unacceptable, intolerable outcomes can, however, result both from one-way and from two-way risks. Intolerable risks are discussed in section 8.5. Bankruptcy for example could result from a disastrous fire, but also from a shock movement in prices or exchange rates. The manager has every incentive to see bankruptcy in terms of 'yes or no' rather than 'how much', regardless of whether the cause was a one-way or two-way risk.

6.3 Financial theory and the concept of the risk portfolio

Financial theory has, since the early 1960s, made great strides in illuminating such concepts as the value of the company and the cost of capital. The concepts are of critical importance because they closely and formally define the ultimate objectives of competitive business enterprise, and indeed the conditions of survival. In general terms, a new or continuing business venture is financeable only if its expected returns are at least equal to the cost of capital for that specific venture. The cost of capital is in each case a risk-adjusted rate of return, adjusted for that risk which the financial markets attribute to the particular business or project. Risk here means variablility of the expected returns. The more risky a business is, the greater is the rate of return required and expected by the market. High-risk securities suit some portfolio investors who want high-risk high-return assets in their portfolios. Managers according to this theory should not therefore seek to diversify the risks of their business, for example by turning their companies into conglomerates, but leave it to shareholders to diversify them in their portfolios.

Adler and Dumas (1984) explicitly apply this concept to currency risk, by treating currency risk as a single regression coefficient measuring the sensitivity of a given business to changes in given exchange rates. The application of this coefficient to the foreign currency cash flows of the company establishes the company's exposure, i.e. the amount it has at risk to currency fluctuations. The company can then hedge or diversify this risk by acquiring forward contracts or foreign currency liabilities equal to this exposure. Currency risk management becomes an identical activity for the owner and the manager. The shareholder can hold the same kind of hedge in his portfolio as the manager might arrange for the company to hold. The company might be justified in doing it on the shareholder's behalf if, for example, it was better placed to obtain tax relief on the hedge.

Financial theory gives managers a greatly sharpened perception of the fundamental requirements which a business venture must meet. It is a measure of the writers' achievement that managers the world over are now aware of these concepts and of their fundamental importance. However, financial theorists are less than pleased with the extent to which business managers apply finance theory in their day-to-day decisions.

There has been much speculation about the causes of the apparent conflicts between the assumptions which govern the actual practice of management and the tenets of finance theory, which seem quite clear and authoritative as criteria for all business management. A favourite explanation is agency conflict, a concept which suggests that investors and managers (their agents) have conflicting objectives (Jensen and Meckling, 1976). A manager seeks continuity of employment, whereas the owner-investor would be better served by a sale of the assets or at least by a change of management, if liquidation or take-over would immediately enhance the value of the shares owned by the investor.

Agency conflict is clearly not a fiction. It would be strange if the interests of shareholders and managers were wholly identical. What is less clear is whether agency conflict explains managers' attitudes to risk. What would have to be demonstrated is that the two parties' interests clash at the point where a decision is taken whether to accept a particular risk. The clearest evidence of conflict on the other hand concerns that later stage at which things have turned out badly, when a risk has turned sour. At that point the investors may well be better served by the removal of the managers. Our own interest is, however, in the decision whether to accept any given risk without insurance or hedging or other neutralizing action.

In sections 6.4 and 6.5 we review some reservations about the applicability of the portfolio concept to all business risks. In chapter 7, section 7.3, we shall review some difficulties which apply specifically to currency risk. Some of those difficulties overlap of course.

6.4 Risks which should not be managed as parts of a portfolio

Finance theory is convincing in its belief that the risks peculiar to different commercial trades are both diversifiable and often better diversified by investors than by managers. There may be exceptional reasons for creating conglomerates, or against remaining in a narrow competitive range in which risks are high and prospects poor, but the general rule should be that portfolio diversification is better handled by the investor than by business managers.

What needs to be questioned is

1 whether or how far the principle of diversifiability extends beyond

the sphere of the risks of the various commercial trades in which businesses are engaged,

2 whether managers should manage all other risks by *sole and direct* reference to the financial concept of the value of the company,

3 whether managers should take their company's risk profile in those other risks as given, or whether they have opportunities and duties to improve that profile, i.e. whether their tasks in this field are active or passive.

Some writers assume that the principle of portfolio diversification extends to currency risk, on the assumption that currency issues play a part in investors' construction of their portfolios. Whether the task of hedging or diversification is best handled by investors or by managers, depends in this model on logistics and transaction costs.

If investors were to attempt the task, they might find it hard to acquire the information. The currency exposures of a company can change dramatically every day in the course of ordinary business conduct, and depend on commercial events and on the way the company deals with its changing exposures day by day (or even hour by hour). Are positions hedged, and if so, how quickly does hedging action respond to successive changes? Even on the balance sheet date, accounting standards do not currently require disclosure of all currency positions. If they did, investors would obtain the information just once a year, after a lag of some months; by that time the facts would have changed many times.

The writers do not, however, stop at risks of the trade and currency risks. A framework which sees all business risks in terms of diversifiable portfolio risk presumably includes in that concept all the insurable risks, credit risks, political risks. This framework may be sound, but not free from practical difficulties. Even if unlimited information were available to the fund manager, he would be constrained by the availability of securities which display a sufficient variety of the desired risk characteristics in the desired proportions. If this condition were met, an elaborate computer program would be needed to construct a fine-tuned portfolio, so as to get the proportions of risk right in each of the required dimensions. However, the greatest of all the problems would be the lack of up-to-date information about the various exposures in the various companies whose equity shares are available for investment. That is a practical set of difficulties. There are, however, also some objections of principle to the assumption that all business risks should be managed like a portfolio, and on a calculation of a risk/return trade-off.

6.4.1 Managers have a dynamic responsibility

The first of these objections is that investors are by definition able to act only in the financial markets, by buying and selling financial assets. Managers, on the other hand, are mainly charged with optimizing commercial performance. Investors must take a company's risk profile as given: managers are paid to improve it. Managers have a dynamic, not a static task to perform. Moreover, risk decisions face them in their dozens each week:

> Should we install sprinklers? Should we sell this large foreign currency receipt forward? Can we rely on the Government of Orientica to pay us a large contractual sum when we have performed our contract in four years' time? What chance is there of a change of regime in Latinica, and in that case would our proposed plant there be nationalized without compensation? Can we move the sourcing of costs from an overvalued to a competitive currency, or redesign our product to a higher standard of safety?

By reducing these risks in his company the manager does not just reshuffle risk between different securities which an investor could hold; he actually improves the risk/return profile of the totality of all market securities. The actions expected of the manager are not zero-sum games between different companies competing for capital. Any theory or framework which allots to the manager a mere proxy function on behalf of the investor is surely at odds with the real world of business. This theme will reappear in chapter 7, section 7.3.

Managers do not always explicitly recognize the distinction between one- and two-way risks, but they do have another reason for approaching even two-way risks with a sense of insecurity. They are afraid of taking two-way risks with less than the degree of care and competence expected of them, of doing an unprofessional job. In the capital asset pricing model's sense, a two-way risk should not be shunned if it is a normal business risk in which a greater degree of uncertainty can expect commensurately higher returns. The manager seldom faces such a decision as a yes/no decision. His worry is that he should and could have improved the risk/return expectation before accepting the risk. He may, for example, have made rough assumptions on a technical issue on which expert advice was available in the company. He may have accepted a risk without awareness of a cheap and advantageous hedging tool. Or he may have decided to market a new drug without adequate field tests to identify side-effects. One dilemma is always the trade-off between the competitive need for speed and the time needed to improve his information. Competitive business can never afford to wait for perfect information, but that dilemma is stressful.

6.4.2. Managers must give priority to their commercial markets

The second objection is discussed in greater detail in chapter 7 in the specific context of currency risk. The assumption that either all or a wide range of management decisions can be taken with a single focus on the financial value of the company is unlikely to hold in all cases. The supremacy of the financial markets in deciding the survival of the company in not in question. However, the way a company meets the criteria of the financial markets is by competing successfully in its commercial markets. Many decisions about risk must be subordinated to the overriding aim of supporting the company's competitive effort in those markets. In other words, the financial markets are supreme, but are mainly served not directly, but indirectly, via success in commercial markets.

6.4.3 Enterprise risk is different in kind

Lastly, there is surely a case for regarding the risk of enterprise, the decision to compete in a particular commercial market, in a different light from all other business risks. First, it is the very *raison d'être* of investing in business equity. Other risks are incidental to that decision. Secondly, it is not a simple risk in the sense that its out-turn depends on price developments in a perfect market (as do financial and commodity price risks). The causality which makes the difference between success and failure of a business venture is multiple. It depends on the psychology of customers and competitors, on events in factor markets like labour, management skills and materials bought, on external factors like weather, war and other political events, disruptions from accidents, fire and earthquakes.

Business managers seldom ask whether an insurance premium saved might be a better bet than acceptance of various insurable risks. Perhaps they should ask that question more often; for some insurance premiums exceed the cost of bearing a reasonably predictable stream of uninsured costs from the source of the risk. The mere fact, however, that many managers fail to ask the question shows their preoccupation with the problems of competitive success, a preoccupation which is at the very least a good fault, and in most cases a virtue.

6.5 Are there intolerable risks?

We have now reached another fundamental issue. The likely worst outcome of any given risk can be estimated at the time of the decision whether or not to accept the risk. Each such risk is then seen to have a certain downside potential which can be measured on a money scale. There is a point on that scale beyond which the likely worst outcome would not be tolerable to the managers. We can call this their threshold of tolerable risk (Kenyon, 1985). The intolerable outcome would be the loss of the company's independent survival, either by bankruptcy or by hostile take-over.

Independent survival of a business depends on its critical financial institution. The stock market has for some decades been the critical financial institution for listed companies in the US, UK and other mainly Anglo-Saxon financial systems. In most other systems the company's main bankers are the company's critical financial institution. This category includes all businesses in, for example, Germany, France and Japan and also of course unlisted companies in Anglo-Saxon countries. What the business needs to avoid is a sharp downrating by its critical financial institution, sharp enough to cause the institution to withdraw support. Such an adverse reaction is likely only to the extent that it is unexpected and undiscounted by that institution.

The financial theorist might at this point argue that this description of intolerable risk describes something which only managers, not investors, find intolerable. Investors might well be better off if bankruptcy or take-over occurred: intolerable risk seems to reinforce, not refute, the agency conflict explanation.

Shareholders may indeed, as we noted in section 6.3, be better served by such a change in the control of the assets *after* a risk has turned sour. On the other hand the risk has to be major to be potentially intolerable. So would the shareholders vote in favour of such a major risk at the much earlier stage when the decision is taken to accept or reject it? Is there likely to be a conflict between investors and managers at that stage?

Financial theory concedes that bankruptcy costs may outweigh the benefits of bankruptcy. An increased threat of take-over would follow the sharp fall in the share price triggered by shock news of a major loss from an unexpected and undiscounted risk. This sharp drop in the market capitalization of the company makes it vulnerable to unwelcome bids from a substantially wider circle of predators than before.

It is at least questionable whether the investor *at the point of decision,* if he knew the potential loss from the worst outcome, would wish the managers to accept the risk. The fact that managers regard some risks as intolerable need not therefore be evidence of agency conflict. In any event there is little doubt that managers act with this concept in mind, and that this helps to explain the gulf between the views of business risk taken by financial theory on the one hand, and by managers on the other.

In insurance language the word for 'intolerable' is 'catastrophic'. When managers confront a decision about such a risk, they often treat it as something to be shunned irrespective of expected returns. We could use a somewhat circular definition of an intolerable risk as one to which the risk/return ratio is not applied, were it not for one important exception. This could be called 'the courage of desperation'. Where a business is so near to failure or ruin that it has no solid substance to lose or protect, its managers will take almost any risk because they have so little to lose. Risk is only intolerable where there is something to lose: where there is a business of substance whose independent survival is both probable and valuable. A person on the edge of bankruptcy is less likely to pay a premium to cover his house against fire than a more solvent person.

Currency risk is always a two-way market risk; yet at the intolerable level it makes very little difference whether the risk is one-way or two-way. Managers will reject it. So where is the threshold of tolerable risk? At what level does a risk cross the line from a tolerable level, where a portfolio approach is appropriate, to an intolerable level? This is a very difficult question, because it has some psychological and possibly irrational elements, but from anecdotal observation many business managers will instinctively see that level as geared to the financial size of the business; for example, to its current level of annual pretax profits. Their threshold might be in the region of 15–20 per cent of that level. For this type of calculation to be relevant, the chance of a loss of that order must be appreciable, not zero but not necessarily more than perhaps 1 per cent, and the company must be a listed one in an Anglo-Saxon stock market-driven financial system. For companies outside that environment (including those in France, Germany and Japan) the threshold is likely to be higher, and geared to the net worth on the balance sheet rather than to the profit level. The concept is not at this stage precisely defined, but its existence and its importance is not really in doubt.

As the essence of intolerable levels of risk is that risk/return trade-offs cease to apply, the concept applies to the management of currency risks even though currency risks are two-way risks.

6.6 Financial and insurance theory

The literature of risk falls broadly into financial and insurance theory, and a striking but not surprising difference is that financial theory treats risk as something interesting, but neutral or good, whereas insurance theory treats it as a bad thing, something to mitigate, hedge, insure or shun.

Financial theory regards risk as good – or at least value-neutral – because risk is correlated with returns: the risk-averse investor is stuck with the unexciting returns available from riskless investments.

Insurance theory has many valuable concepts for us. The principal one is perhaps the principle of concentration and fragmentation. The risk carrier accepts a large number of similar but causally independent risks like house fires, car collisions or shipwrecks. Each individual has a major part of his wealth tied up in his house, car or ship – a total loss would be catastrophic to him. The insurer, however, as noted in section 6.2, has a sufficient portfolio of homogeneous but independent risks to be able to predict within fairly narrow limits the statistically probable annual incidence of loss. This enables the insurer to charge premiums for accepting the risk from the numerous individuals. In total this premium income will enable him to meet the cost of claims and the cost of administering the portfolio. The key word here is '**independent**'. An insurer cannot accept a concentration of causally related risks (as may happen with nuclear installations or jumbo aircraft) which is large in relation to the insurer's capital and income stream. The risks must be fragmented enough for the law of large numbers to operate.

A company with a fleet of 1000 cars may expect say 4 per cent of these to crash each year, subject to minor fluctuations, say between 3.8 per cent and 4.2 per cent. After taking into account the administrative burden, it may well decide that this is cheaper than a premium rate of say 5 per cent. So the company will not insure this (except where required by law) with external insurers. The story would be very different if the company held an annual in-house race between all 1000 cars, with the risk that they might all crash into each other. In that case the risks cease to be independent and fragmented: they are now highly concentrated, and will command a high insurance premium which the company will no doubt be glad to pay.

These principles are not without application to non-insurable fields like currency risk.

6.7 Summary

An integrated account of business risk must distinguish between one-way and two-way risks, between risks which managers should and should not seek to manage, between risks which can be managed with an eye solely on the financial value of the company or as subordinate to other, mainly commercial, objectives, and between risks whose potential worst outcomes are tolerable or intolerable. We have also looked at the principle of fragmentation and concentration of risks: the law of large numbers. We shall find that these concepts are helpful in understanding currency risk.

7

The Place of Currency Risk Management in General and Financial Management

7.1 Three conflicting assumptions

What kind of a business phenomenon is currency risk? There are some startling contrasts between the assumptions made by various writers and practitioners. These assumptions appear to be broadly of three types.

1 *The financial management assumption:* This first assumption treats currency risk as a purely financial phenomenon, which can be handled wholly by action in the foreign exchange market and related financial markets. In fact, however, currency risk is not a single management task because exchange rate fluctuations affect the business in different ways which have to be managed in different ways.
2 *The commercial/financial assumption:* This second assumption treats currency risk as a complex and fragmented phenomenon which affects how the business performs in both its financial and its commercial markets. It cannot be managed purely, perhaps not even primarily, by reference to the financial objectives of the business or by means of financial instruments.
3 *The shareholder's portfolio assumption:* This third assumption treats currency risk as a macroeconomic phenomenon, affecting the totality of the cash flows of the business. Its effect on the business is best assessed as a single or multiple regression coefficient, and managed either by the shareholder as part of his portfolio risk diversification, or by the business managers, if they can diversify risk more cheaply internally than the investor can externally.

It is rare for one of these assumptions to be made single-mindedly by any one company or writer. Assumption 1 is certainly followed by many companies, and is implied by Donaldson (1980, 1987). Assumption 2 is also followed by many companies, and implied by Kenyon (1981). Some mixture of 1 and 2 is also common, and implied by Ankrom (1974). Assumption 3 is made by a number of academic writers, beginning perhaps with Adler and Dumas (1984).

Each of the three assumptions was found to be used by at least some of the 13 companies whose objectives are discussed in the appendix to chapter 9. Oxelheim and Wihlborg (1987) come close to an explicit recognition and comparison of the three assumptions.

7.2 Currency risk, financial theory and wider macroeconomic risk

Assumption 3 is mainly made by writers on financial theory. One of the fundamental issues about currency risk management is the extent to which it lends itself to the portfolio approach. In other words, to what extent can and should currency risk be managed by diversification? Companies like Rio Tinto-Zinc Corporation (RTZ) follow the general principles of this assumption, as is set out in chapter 9 and its appendix. Chapter 8 takes the view that the risk managed by companies like RTZ is a wider macroeconomic risk rather than just currency risk.

7.3 Can shareholders diversify currency risk?

7.3.1 In how many dimensions can shareholders diversify risk?

Shareholders can diversify business risks as long as

1 the number of different types of risk is manageable,
2 the categories have a reasonably stable relationship to a company's cash flows.

A fairly small list of factors in fact seems to go into the stock market's beta coefficients for different companies. The dominant factor is the economic profile (e.g. cyclical or non-cyclical) of the company's activities. Portfolio managers probably also try to diversify currency risks – as the dollar/yen rate fluctuates, they may prefer to hold both US and Japanese securities. They may also diversify other dimensions of risk, such as commodity prices where companies are sensitive to their changes. Every time a further risk dimension is added, the diversification problem requires more cross-classification by the classes of risk. The further this process is taken, the more complex the task becomes. The other limiting factor, however, is that there may not be enough securities available with the necessary cross-classifications by the risk factors. There may not be a Japanese equity with a particular degree of exposure to fluctuations in cocoa prices.

Financial theorists tend to discuss the currency risk diversification task as though currency was the only risk dimension which affects portfolio selection. No doubt this simplification is useful for the purpose of exposition. Yet the practical task of cross-classifying by different classes or dimensions of risk is a major one.

7.3.2. Shareholders' information problem in diversifying all business risks

Most of the risks on which managers decide day by day could not possibly come to the shareholders' attention even if companies published daily bulletins at a saturation level of disclosure. Companies make decisions about risks, including currency risks, several times daily. Disclosure requirements may be inadequate in this field, but if they were adequate, they would only show the risks carried on the annual reporting date, and this information would be published some weeks after that date. It is unrealistic to expect investors to be adequately informed in this field at any time.

7.3.3 Diversification is not the only solution: managers have dynamic tasks

We here pick up a theme which in its general form arose in chapter 6. Most writers see portfolio diversification of risk as something to be achieved by the use of financial instruments. Whether it is the shareholder or the manager who is diversifying, he is seen as doing it by acquiring a portfolio of currency assets or liabilities.

The classic 'economic' currency risk is where a country's real exchange rate appreciates against that of a company's competitors. It rises in the exchange markets by more than the relative inflation rates. The company's costs become less competitive by comparison with the costs of competitors. In chapter 8 we shall call this currency risk 'competitiveness' risk. The manager may well be able to switch manufacturing or buying costs to a more competitive currency. Hertzell and Caspar (1988) suggest something on these lines. In short, the manager does not sit in the shareholder's chair. He has wider opportunities, and therefore wider duties in risk management.

The point here is that only the *manager* has that opportunity, *not the investor.* The portfolio model of currency risk assumes that the risk profile of the company is stable, and has to be taken as given. The facts of business are that managers are paid to improve that profile. Their task is dynamic. The risk profile must not be treated as given.

7.4 Currency risk as a single lump

There is another issue embedded in the suggestion that currency risk can be managed as a regression coefficient. The suggestion was made by Adler and Dumas (1984) and has been followed by many writers since. It implies that currency risk is or can be managed as a single phenomenon.

Chapter 8 will define currency risk in different categories, which differ mainly in whether the risk is from nominal or real exchange rate movements. One reservation about the single lump assumption is the contention in this chapter that some currency risks are managed with an eye on commercial rather than purely financial objectives. Currency risks differ also, however, in the time-frame over which they affect the business. The treatment of all currency risk as a single lump, manageable by a single financial hedge, disregards all these distinctions. The categorization in chapter 8 differs from most of its predecessors, but not on this point. Many writers have distinguished between risks which affect the outcome of short-term transactions already in the pipeline, and other risks which determine the company's ability to compete successfully in the future.

One major difficulty with this assumption of the single lump concerns whether the inherent extrapolation is valid. Will the future be like the past? The attraction of regression analysis is that it quantifies the past sensitivity of a business to a given external factor, like movements in the yen/dollar exchange rate. The varying periods over which such movements affect different aspects of the business do not appear to matter, as long as the overall pattern is static enough to be a reliable guide to the future. This may not, however, be the case.

Example 7.1

If the *real* (inflation-adjusted) exchange rate makes the dollar less competitive against the yen, then our factory in California will lose sales to Japanese competitors after some time, that is after the increase in costs has begun to bite and squeeze margins. On the other hand, if the dollar falls against the yen in nominal terms, then our yen payable at the end of this month will cost less and benefit our cash flows now.

All this might be consistent with the single lump assumption, as long as the entire pattern does not change in the future. The pattern in example

7.1 will hold in the future if the following features continue unchanged into the future:

- an unchanged product portfolio,
- Japanese competitors – not German or British,
- Japanese suppliers – not US, French or Swiss,
- stability in the product and its cost structure: it must be exactly the same product with at least a similar cost breakdown, the same degree of vertical integration (value added percentage), and the same production cycle time: if, for example, the production process only takes half the time, then the time pattern in the regresssion equation has also changed.

These matters are seldom static in modern business. To assume that they are static is to assume that the microeconomy stands still while the macroeconomy changes. Commercial markets may have exhibited such continuity in some past golden age, perhaps after some major wars, but that has not been the norm and is not the pattern of markets around 1990.

The time factor is all-important. What we must pay next week is differently affected by exchange rate movements from what we plan to sell in year 2 from now.

In section 7.13, we look at Oxelheim and Wihlborg's framework. These writers very fairly call their book *Macroeconomic Uncertainty* (1987) and go one better than Adler and Dumas by treating currency risk as just one aspect of macroeconomic uncertainty, and considering this wider concept as a single-lump management task.

In chapter 9 and its appendix we shall look at the corporate objectives of some UK companies, and shall find that one of them (RTZ) adopts such a wider approach to this management task. However, this is justified by the fact that this company depends heavily for its performance on producing a commodity, the price of which depends entirely on economic factors. Its trading pattern forces it to be preoccupied with macroeconomic variables rather than manage just currency risk. Only a minority of companies is in that position. To a much greater number, currency risk as such is important; not just in terms of the demand and supply of its end product, but more specifically in terms of particular transactions and asset positions.

7.5 Is currency risk a task just for financial management?

So far we have only examined assumption 3 (the shareholder's portfolio assumption) of those set out in section 7.1. We now examine the other two. We shall find that the contrast between assumptions 1 and 2 sheds further light on assumption 3.

Porter (1980) in his famous five-forces diagram sees competition within an industry as driven by five forces: bargaining power of suppliers and buyers, threats from new entrants or substitutes and rivalry within the industry. We adapt the concept by suggesting that the individual company competes in a number of markets, which above all include the financial markets in which it competes for capital, and the commercial and commodity markets in which it competes for customers and supplies. Other markets are the labour market in which it competes for workers, and the executive market in which it competes for executive talent.

These various financial, commercial, commodity and labour markets are ultimately interrelated, but in the short term at least the interrelations can be tenuous. For our present purposes it is enough to concentrate on two types of market, the commercial markets in which a company meets its customers, competitors and suppliers, and the financial markets in which it competes for capital and on which its independent survival depends. The way companies compete in commercial markets is well described in Mathur (1988).

7.6 Commercialists v. financialists

There is ample common sense and anecdotal evidence to show that most companies give ultimate priority to the financial markets, but that they see their primary route towards satisfying those financial markets through performance in their commercial markets. Nor is that system of priorities irrational. We have already noted earlier in this chapter that financial theory itself, in explaining the beta coefficient in the capital asset pricing model, allots a central role to the commercial profile of the business, and much stock market analysis focuses on a company's competitive position in its commercial markets.

We shall seek to demonstrate in subsequent chapters that various forms of currency risk have a powerful and direct impact on a company's competitive success. It follows that companies should logically manage those currency risks with an eye on their commercial effects. There is evidence that this is indeed how a great many companies approach the matter, and this is overwhelmingly borne out by the case studies examined in the appendix to chapter 9. Companies do not invariably see currency risk as a problem to be managed exclusively in the financial markets, merely because it is caused there. The impact of many currency risks is in the commercial markets; they should be managed by action in either type of market, but with the immediate aim of commercial and competitive success. Survival in the financial market and maximizing the value of the company retain their overriding priorities, but are pursued *indirectly*, via the commercial markets. This indirect pursuit of the survival requirement is illustrated in figure 7.1. It shows some currency risk management directed straight to the overriding financial objective, and the remainder towards commercial objectives, and thus indirectly to the ultimate financial target. Companies with this management approach make commercial/financial assumption 2 rather than our other two assumptions. This goes a long way to explain why so few managers conform to models like that of Adler and Dumas.

Yet many other businesses do not make assumption 2. They see currency risk as a problem or opportunity contained predominantly within the finance function. In their view currency risks should be managed exclusively by financial means and particularly with instruments bought or traded in the financial markets, and by financial managers. Commercial managers may affect the way some of the problems arise, e.g. by choosing currencies of invoice. If so, they need to be educated and informed by financial managers about the way to manage those decisions. This second group of companies believes in assumption 1.

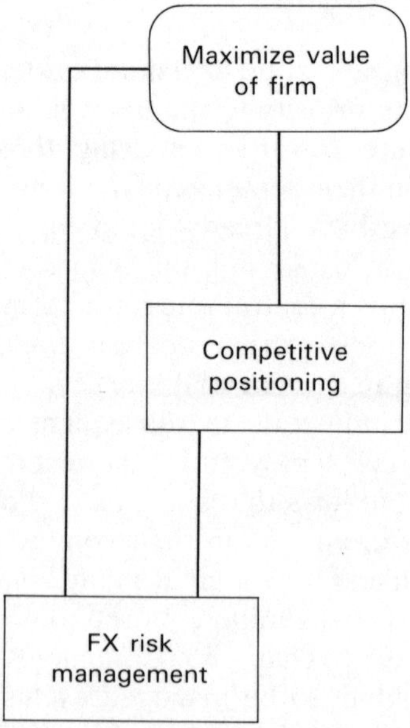

Figure 7.1 Hierarchy of business objectives

We might, by way of shorthand, call those who use the commercial/financial assumption 2 'commercialists' and those who prefer the financial management assumption 1 'financialists'. Before we explore the contrast between them we should pause to remind ourselves of two significant points on which both groups are agreed. First, neither group excludes the use of financial instruments. Secondly, neither of these two groups sees currency risk as something to be reduced to a single regression coefficient in an equation designed to calculate the value of the company or its cost of capital. Neither commercialists nor financialists believe in the shareholder's portfolio assumption 3.

7.7 Why do approaches to business risk vary?

Many divergent practices in business are in fact attributable to the different operating profiles of each business, and particularly to the relative importance of pricing decisions. A process business producing standard commodities, like company K in the appendix to chapter 9, has so large a proportion of total unit costs in fixed or sunk costs that it has to sell at almost any price rather than leave capacity idle. It has very little choice in fixing its selling prices, and very little option but to sell its capacity almost irrespective of price. Price is an important management area only where variable costs are a high proportion of total unit costs. This profile is frequently found in engineering and construction, where single contracts are one-off with high value added. However, it is also found in many service activities.

Wherever pricing decisions are important, their outcomes need to be measured; the business must isolate the effect of exchange rate movements and monitor those effects as a separate, commercially significant issue. This is one important reason why such businesses have to take a commercialist approach to those currency risks that we shall in chapter 8 call trading risks.

In the same way, if a business has important variable costs, if each additional sale incurs fresh costs which constitute a substantial part of the final price, and if those costs are not easily switched from one currency area to another, then risks from the uncompetitiveness of a currency are important to the company. They need to be managed as a commercial problem. In chapter 8 we call this risk 'competitiveness' risk.

Financialist companies tend to have little trading or economic risk. If an overwhelming part of unit costs is fixed or sunk, then opportunity costs are not greatly dependent on any particular exchange rates.

Financialist companies are therefore quite rational in restricting their management of currency risks to the sphere of financial management.

7.8 The role of financial hedging instruments

Some financial theory assumes that currency risk should be exclusively managed by means of financial instruments. In the classical case of 'economic' currency risk, an uncompetitive currency causes a rise in costs against the company's market selling prices. It will suffer either a loss of sales or a shrinkage of margins or both. The writers suggest that the company should hedge its exposure with currency assets or liabilities equal to the size of its exposure, after applying the coefficient of covariance between its cash flows and changes in certain exchange rates. The gain on its financial hedge will then balance the losses caused by its uncompetitive costs.

The commercialist's difficulty with this concept is that a mere cash receipt cannot compensate for the setback to the company's commercial market position: as he sees it, the hedge is in the wrong dimension. In any case, a loss of market share may well have indefinite, not just finite financial consequences. Competitors tend to exploit a gain in competitiveness to make progressively further gains. The coefficient of covariance is unlikely to remain unchanged.

7.9 Models of the business

We have suggested that product profiles will dispose companies to take a commercialist or financialist approach. Yet differences in the approach to currency risk management are not wholly explained by differences between different products and services. They also owe something to the model of the company which is in the mind of the individual or group of people who effectively direct the company. For example, some of those who direct commercial banks see their business as a financial model, mainly perhaps as a balance sheet, to be judged in terms of capital adequacy, return on assets and return on expenses. Others see their bank as a marketing business seeking out profitable customer segments to serve, such as high net worth individuals. Others again see the bank mainly as a lender of deposits to borrowers, and therefore as a manager and processor of credit risks. In some countries, bankers see their business as part of a regulatory nanny system. The model in the mind of the chief executive or inner cabinet has a very great influence on how the business is organized to take its decisions.

In the currency risk field this generates priority judgements of which the following are extreme examples:

- we are here to make *widgets*, not to speculate in the money markets,
- we are here to make *money*, so let us make money out of currencies or cocoa prices or oil futures, as long as it boosts the bottom line.

7.10 The accounting model

One of the cultural divisions among managers and between managers and academics concerns the role of the accounting model in management. Economists, especially in the United States, are more and more frustrated by the persistence of many managers in looking at their tasks in terms of how the accounting results of the business will be affected. This issue is very close to many of the judgements that have to be made about currency risk, and therefore deserves some attention.

Every textbook on financial theory and related topics devotes some space to the inappropriateness of the accounting framework, to the conflict between investors' interests and the goal of maximizing accounting returns, and to the apparent absurdity of that goal: for it fails to minimize the cost of capital, which most managers regard as their fundamental objective. Maximum accounting returns do not hit that target because the financial market has been shown to see through accounting conventions, and straight to the economic value of the business, i.e. the present value of its expected future cash flows. The accounting model also, through its unrealistic asset valuations, misdirects those who want to maximize cash flows.

Most of these criticisms are valid. The weakness of the accounting ethos stems from its search for a *verifiable* account of business results. The backbone of accounting is the auditing process. The accounting profession is well aware that the recording and summarizing of business transactions must always involve a great deal of judgement, but its ethos is to minimize the area of judgement and to maximize that of historical fact. This inevitably builds in a strong reluctance to undertake assessments of the future. The auditor who stakes his professional reputation (and indemnity cover) on what he says in his audit report, cannot be comfortable in pitting his judgement of the future against that of the managers. However, it is the managers whose record is being portrayed and who have prepared the accounts. They cannot be expected to view them with the cold objectivity required of auditors. The result is that accountants are understandably lukewarm towards forward-looking approaches to the reporting of business results. The future is not verifiable.

That is the main plot. On many of the sub-plots the economists are on weaker ground. Economists tend to criticize the rather perfunctory role assigned by accounts to the balance sheet. There is a strong case for making the balance sheet meaningful, but the income statement is surely more important to investors. Accountants are criticized for the accrual principle, but sheer cash accounting would be far more misleading and far more manipulable. Transactions and liabilities have to be allocated to their correct periods as long as accounts are produced at annual intervals. Investors need to see the results fairly attributable to the period under review.

The view that the stock market sees through accounting conventions does not rest on robust foundations. Academic research shows that when a well advertised change in an accounting standard begins to feed through into published results, share prices are not significantly affected by the change: the market had seen through it. Surely the market had seen through and discounted the change from the much earlier date when it was published. Analysts and others had adjusted their analysis for what was known to be a non-change in the value of the business. All this is at best the tip of the iceberg.

Over a very wide field the accounting conventions permit a great deal of latitude in presenting results, simply because business is too complex to be reduced to a simple reporting code. The way companies use that latitude is not transparent to the analyst or investor, but is bound to command the attention of managers and accountants.

Is that not reprehensible? What is reprehensible is any deliberate action to mislead the investing public. What cannot be reprehensible is a certain degree of respect shown by managers for the format in which they are legally bound to account for their stewardship, and which acts as the measure of their borrowing powers and the company's solvency. It would be reprehensible if they treated their annual report in the cavalier fashion in which some commentators refer to the process. Nor should we overlook the fact that accounting results form the basis from which taxable profits are derived.

Chapter 13 contains some criticism of currency translation standards. The state of accounting is far from satisfactory, but it cannot be cured by neglect. The cure will involve a fundamental change in the education and culture of those who prepare, audit and read financial statements.

Accounting conventions are not a good basis for taking currency risk management decisions, but prudent managers will normally check the likely accounting effect of their decisions, and at times this review will modify those decisions. We return to this in chapter 9, section 9.7.

7.11 The influence of organization structures

One controversy in the field of currency risk management is that between centralized and decentralized management. A prominent modern issue is how much value the head office adds. It concerns the usefulness of a central staff. Companies whose management style seeks to minimize the size of the head office will be more reluctant to centralize any management of currency risk.

We shall see in chapter 17 that this issue is of considerable practical importance in the currency risk field. We shall see that some degree of centralization opens up a number of currency risk management opportunities and obtains considerable economies in the use of scarce skills and in dealing costs. Moreover, the one thing that even the most complex multinational group cannot decentralize is its credit status in the financial markets, which may benefit from visibly firm and strong handling of currency matters.

Against this, a commercialist company is much more effectively managed if its main profit centres are truly accountable for their commercial performance, which can be powerfully affected by currency matters. Moreover, many currency decisions can only be effectively taken by people close to the affected commercial operations.

In this chapter, which seeks to give a framework to management priorities in currency risk management, we can only draw provisional attention to this conflict. The choice between centralizing and decentralizing structures must of course to some extent derive from a company's management style, but we should not underestimate the extent to which both style and structures are dictated by the nature of the business or businesses conducted by the company. A monolithic single-product company gains much more from centralization than a conglomerate.

7.12 Pragmatic structures

There is another humbler pattern at work. If the running of a business is to be manageable at all, then the effort must be broken down into a hierarchy of tasks each of which must be manageable in its own right. For example in the business of a contractor the critical unity of management must be each tender and contract. Each must be the responsibility of a particular manager. It is he who must ensure that the contract is profitable; it will only be profitable if that aim is single-mindedly pursued at all stages, of which those before signature of contract are often the most critical. All the various risks, including currency risk, must clearly be managed by that manager as subordinate parts of that task. He will of course need help and guidance from the currency manager and from other experts, but the purpose of that part of the currency risk task is to make *that contract* profitable. The eye must firmly be on that ball, at ground level, not on the stratospheric concept of maximizing the value of the company. This is a practical necessity, not a deep issue about the purpose of business activity.

The principle may of course be challenged at a higher conceptual level. Why not take a lofty portfolio approach to the currency risk in all contracts? Why not release the manager of the contract from the complexity of currency risk and judge him on the strength of management reports which hold the initial exchange rate steady, discharging the currency risk management elsewhere, in the finance department?

The case against this view is quite formidable:

1 In the typical contract business the risks in each contract are too large a part of total activity to be managed as part of a portfolio: the size of individual risks is intolerable (see chapter 6, section 6.5).
2 Risks are only too likely to be correlated rather than diversified between contracts. Contracts taken over a period of several years during which the principal currency of cost is following a longer-term trend, will not have diversified outcomes.
3 Each currency risk in this type of business is caused by the specific tender or contract. Decisions about whether and at what price to undertake a given contract, must take account of the currency risk.

Again, managers need to know whether a particular product, division or subsidiary is adequately profitable. Whenever that business unit has a different currency profile from other parts of the business, the currency risk generated by that unit must be part of the essential assessment. Its manager would not like to see it closed down on the grounds of its currency profile, or its past currency losses, if he has had no share in managing that aspect of the business.

These practical needs have their influence on what is practicable in the field of managing currency risks.

7.13 Oxelheim and Wihlborg's framework

Oxelheim and Wihlborg (1987) tackle the whole subject rather more systematically than many other writers. Their conceptual framework inclines towards the integrated approach preferred by financial theory, but their application of the framework takes note of the diversity of practice and of the fragmented views taken by practitioners, and helps practitioners to apply the writers' framework to these fragmented approaches.

Oxelheim and Wihlborg, in one important respect, go one better than other writers. They refuse to treat currency risk as an isolated phenomenon. Exchange rates are an integral part of the macroeconomic environment, which also includes inflation, interest rates, money supply, upswings and downswings in economic activity and so on. Indeed the title of their book *Macroeconomic Uncertainty* does not mention exchange rates, even though the text devotes a great deal of attention to currency risk. We saw one application of this approach in section 7.4.

This integrated approach to all macroeconomic risk is obviously an important and helpful perception, but it is not easy to see managers of *all* kinds of businesses adopting it. There will be some that do. The case of RTZ (chapter 9 and its appendix) shows that the approach suits a company which mines and sells primary commodities. However, for most companies, macroeconomic risks are part of the planning environment in which all major commercial decisions are taken. Managers in the 1980s appear to regard currency risk as something special, more difficult to manage than, for example, interest rate risk, and as a more destabilizing influence on business management. Moreover, this perception is justified to some extent by the different degrees of volatility noted in chapter 4. Spot rates between the major floating currencies are much more volatile than, for example, relative inflation rates or interest rates.

One important perception which is common to Oxelheim and Wihlborg and a number of other academic texts is that, of course, the company's cost of capital is determined in real terms, so that, for example, a hedge which merely compensates for nominal exchange losses may not be adequate. Managers find it much easier, however, to target a nominal rate of return which allows for inflation, than to manage all aspects of the business in real terms. They have to manage, report and monitor performance in money terms. Managers are bound to treat inflation and the rest of the macroeconomic environment as a more fundamental environmental factor than exchange rates. Indeed the most acute volatility of exchange rates, volatility in the very short term, is not predominantly macroeconomic in origin.

7.14 Summary

Alternative approaches seem to make three different assumptions. The financial management or 'financialist' assumption treats currency risk as a purely financial management task. The commercial/financial or 'commercialist' assumption treats currency risk as frequently subordinate to commercial management objectives. The shareholder's portfolio assumption treats it as a single correlation coefficient which either the shareholder or the company on his behalf can manage by a single portfolio hedge.

The portfolio and single lump risk assumptions are rejected because they do not take a realistic view of currency risk, or of the pace of microeconomic change, or of the task of the manager.

A purely financial hedge may not necessarily give adequate protection against commercial setbacks like a loss of market share. This is another reason why some currency risks require management in the commercial markets. The conflict between the 'financialist' and 'commercialist' approaches is ascribed to differences between different businesses' cost profiles and the consequent difference between the priorities given by them to pricing decisions. Many businesses, for good reasons, regard their commercial performance as the key to satisfactory financial performance.

Another relevant determinant is the model of the business which dominates the minds of its top managers. One such model which cannot be ignored, but should not predominate, is the accounting model.

Centralization or decentralization is a particularly important issue in currency risk management. The choice depends not only on the company's management style, but also on the nature of its business. In any case, the logistics of management influence the handling of currency risk in a variety of other ways.

Finally, the chapter discusses the suggestion by Oxelheim and Wihlborg that currency risk should be managed not as a separate phenomenon, but as an integral part of overall macroeconomic risk. The difficulty in applying that perception is mainly practical, but where the fully integrated approach is followed by companies like RTZ, they are managing macroeconomic risk as a whole rather than currency risk as a separate phenomenon.

8

Defining and Classifying Currency Risks

8.1 Introduction

Currency risk has been headline news ever since currencies began to float in 1971–3. Currency losses were blamed for the demise of the famous J. Lyons with its teashops and of Laker Airways. Comment on company results often highlights the effect of currency gains and losses.

All agree it is important. What is not agreed, is the definition of currency risk or of its various classes.

8.2 General business risk

More fundamentally, there is quite a lot of ambiguity about the word 'risk' itself. Risk is of course a common concept outside business, but in this book we restrict our own discussion to business risks. However, even in this narrower context the word 'risk' is used in a variety of senses as noted in chapter 6. They include:

1 an external, uncontrollable feared **event** like a flood or a war or an economic recession, which can damage the business,
2 an expected **variability** or dispersion of possible outcomes in what is known to be a fluctuating market price or state of a market, where the outcomes can be either good or bad, gains or losses for the business,
3 the worst feared **outcome** of 1 or 2,
4 the **probability** of any given outcome of 1 or 2,
5 the **degree** of variability of 2.

We must above all note the distinction between the outward-looking use of the word risk in items 1 and 2 as an external event or state of the world, and its inward-directed use in 3–5 concerned with how a risk looks from the viewpoint of the business.

8.3 One-way and two-way risks

Item 1 concerns one-way risks: there are no negative floods; whereas 2 concerns two-way risks. One-way and two-way risks were discussed in chapter 6, section 6.2. In that chapter we also noted the divergent ways in which risk has at times been treated by financial and insurance theory.

8.4 Intolerable risks

Sections 6.2 and 6.5 also introduced the concept of intolerable levels of risk, which can arise from two-way as well as one-way risks. Bankruptcy could result not only from a disastrous fire, but also from a shock movement in commodity prices or exchange rates. The manager has every incentive to see bankruptcy in terms of 'yes or no' rather than 'how much', regardless of whether the cause was a one-way or two-way risk.

It has been pointed out, e.g. by Hertz and Thomas (1983) that probability (item 4) and severity (item 5) are different dimensions of risk often identified by businessmen. A risk increases not only with the probability of loss, but also with the magnitude or severity of the potential loss, but this distinction is not always explicit (Rothkopf, 1975).

8.5 Existing classifications of currency risks

Many have written about currency risks and their definition and classification. Shapiro (1989) gives a series of definitions which form a good starting point. He describes

- **currency risk in general** as the degree to which a company is affected by exchange rate changes,
- **accounting exposure** as arising from the need to convert the financial statements of foreign operations from local currencies to home currency; the restatement of assets, liabilities, revenues and expenses at new exchange rates will result in exchange gains and losses,
- **economic exposure** as based on the extent to which the value of the company – as measured by the present value of its expected future cash flows – will change when exchange rates change.

Shapiro subdivides economic exposure into

1 **transaction exposure**, which is the possibility of incurring gains or losses, upon settlement at a future date, on transactions already entered into and denominated in a foreign currency, and
2 **real operating exposure**, which arises because currency fluctuations *together with price changes* can alter the amounts and riskiness of a company's future revenue and cost streams, i.e. its operating cash flows.

Shapiro explains that this last type of exposure, real operating exposure, requires detailed knowledge of the company's sensitivity to exchange rate movements, and a long-term perspective. To clarify the discussion, he refers to the concept of the **real exchange rate** which measures changes in the nominal exchange rate adjusted for changes in the relative inflation rates of the two currencies concerned over the period under review. The distinction between the real and the nominal exchange rate is important 'because of their vastly different implications for exchange risk'.

Buckley (1986) classifies currency risks into

- transaction exposure,
- translation (= accounting) exposure,
- economic exposure.

Buckley defines the three concepts in terms similar to Shapiro's, but for practical reasons restricts economic exposure to what Shapiro calls real operating exposures. Buckley describes both transaction and economic exposures as concerned with cash flows. Buckley does not go as far as Shapiro in identifying economic exposure with deviations from purchasing power parity, However, he discusses the test-tube case where a country's exchange parity moves in line with relative inflation rates. It the company's costs were rising at exactly the same rate as the general inflation rate in the country, its exposure would be neutral. If on the other hand its costs do not move in line with general inflation, economic exposure 'will matter' to the company. So if purchasing power parity holds for the company, Buckley's (company-based) economic exposure still exists, but fails to matter. In Shapiro's model it does not exist.

Apparently the first writer to use the expressions translation, transaction and economic risks was Ankrom (1974). Ankrom recognizes only

1 items already on an accounting balance sheet, which he classifies as **translation** risks,

2 future sales and purchases *certain to take place,* but *before the company will be able to adjust prices* in line with exchange rate movements, which he classifies as **transaction** risks.

Ankrom defines **economic** risk as the sum of 1 and 2 after eliminating any double counting, e.g. in inventory. Ankrom's analysis does not cover threats from real exchange rate movements.

Other writers such as Walker (1978) and Wihlborg (1980) use definitions broadly similar to those used by Shapiro and Buckley. Adler and Dumas (1984) by contrast use a very different model, which explicitly analyses currency risk through the eyes of *the shareholder, not the corporate manager*. This model sees all currency risk in terms of the real purchasing power value of the relevant financial asset, such as the ordinary shares. In this model even a holding in a single-country utility is exposed to currency risk if the customers and suppliers of the utility in a zero-inflation economy are exposed to macroeconomic repercussions of exchange rate movements: this model treats currency risk as a regression coefficient which isolates the currency element from all other causes of changes in the value of that financial asset.

Kenyon's (1981) primary distinction was between economic and financial currency risk:

1 **Economic** currency risk was defined as the risk to competitiveness from changes in the real exchange rate – i.e. Shapiro's real operating exposure.
2 **Financial** currency risks were defined as risks from changes in nominal exchange rates to the values of the company's existing assets, liabilities and other commercial commitments. Financial risks were subdivided into
   (a) **trading** risk = mismatch between currencies of cost and of sale, and
   (b) **balance sheet** risk = mismatch between assets and liabilities in a given currency.

Kenyon further suggested that any of these financial risks could be viewed and managed either in accounting terms, i.e. as **accounting or translation** risk, or in cash terms, i.e. as **transaction** risks, but that these two concepts referred to different ways in which management looks at the *same* risks, rather than to different risks.

One contrast between Shapiro's and Kenyon's (1981) classifications stands out: Shapiro regards the main divide as being between the accounting model and the economic or cash flow model, whereas Kenyon (1981) gives primacy to the contrast between risks from the real and nominal exchange rates, a contrast also stressed by Shapiro.

Kenyon (1981) described **trading risk** as having two important stages, the contingent or 'antenatal' stage at which a price had been quoted to a customer but not yet accepted, and the subsequent (postnatal) stage at which the *contract or sale was certain* and the risk had therefore been 'born'. The latter stage, it was suggested, should be treated and managed as part of the balance sheet exposure. Like Ankrom's (1974), this framework stressed that the exposure did not include future sales or purchases for which prices might yet be changed in response to exchange rate movements.

8.6 Risk and exposure

A **business risk** is generally defined either as a possibility of financial loss from uncertain feared events outside the control of the business, or as the variability of possible deviations from an expected outcome of a market risk.

Exposure, following Dumas (1978), is usually defined as 'what one has on risk', in other words as the *amount* which is exposed.

8.7 Is trading risk a separate risk?

Some writers imply that trading risk is simply part of transaction risk, some that it is part of economic risk, and only Kenyon (1981) explicitly defines it as caused by a mismatch between the currency of cost and the currency of the selling price. The cost v. price mismatch is in contrast to the asset v. liability mismatch of all other financial currency risks. Whether this is a separate risk depends on whether companies make pricing decisions and on how important these decisions are in the management of the companies.

In chapter 7 the view is taken that currency risk management must pay considerable attention to the needs of commercial management. Further, chapter 7 has argued that *pricing decisions* are important in many classes of competitive business. For these reasons the need for a separate category of trading risk must be affirmed.

8.8 Impediments to a clear language

The objective of a conceptual framework must be to give practitioners an insightful set of concepts which helps them to understand the risks.

The current frameworks appear to contain a number of relatively loose ends:

1 What is meant by the expression 'cash flows' (see section 8.9)?
2 What is the *dimension* in which risks should be distinguished? For example, are transaction and translation risks different *risks* or threats, or different ways of viewing the *same* threats (see section 8.10)?
3 What is the role of *time-spans* in distinguishing and defining currency risk? Many writers allocate longer time-horizons to some classes of risks. Thus Ankrom distinguishes transaction risks as applying to post-balance sheet sales and purchases, and Shapiro stresses that his real operating exposures must be viewed with a long-term perspective (see section 8.11).
4 What are the *boundaries* of currency risk, and particularly economic currency risk (see section 8.12)?
5 What is the dividing line between trading risk and other financial risks (see section 8.13)?
6 Are there commercial currency risks which are not economic risks (see section 8.14)?

8.9 The meaning of 'cash flows'

Here, as elsewhere, ambiguities are caused by the different languages used by economists and accountants. Accountants often speak of cash receipts as cash inflows and of payments as cash outflows. The expression 'cash flow' or 'net cash flow' is variously defined in *accounting* terminology as

1 the total of receipts less payments = the total of movement of funds = the change in the net liquid position (short-term liquid assets less short-term debt) over the period,
2 the net profit for the period after adding back the depreciation charge.
3 'a measure of the company's ability to fund its capital expenditure and debt repayment out of its own resources' (Boyadjian and Warren, 1987), i.e. the profit before depreciation plus or minus changes in inventories, receivables and payables.

Economists variously use the expression 'cash flows' to mean

4 the total net dividends and liquidation proceeds available to the owners over future years,
5 the total internal cash flows of the business (i.e. earnings before

depreciation minus capital expenditure minus increases in working capital) *as if* they were available to shareholders in cash,

6 the future earnings of the company defined in such a way as to reflect cash earnings rather than earnings computed on the accrual principle of accountancy – this may be close to 2 above, applied to the entire future,

7 (particularly in the context of currency risk) the future earnings of overseas subsidiaries.

Two sets of ambiguity may have been created by this profusion of usages:

(a) the tendency to see both 'transaction' risks and economic risks as concerned with 'cash flows'.

They are, but with two *different* meanings of 'cash flows'. 'Transaction' risks arise from existing contractually committed receipts and payments: accounting usage 1. Economic risks, however, arise from one or more of the economists' definitions of 'cash flows'. It is just possible that this verbal ambiguity is what has prompted a number of writers to see an affinity between transaction and economic risks.

(b) the definition of 'economic risk' (= Shapiro's real operating exposure).

Some writers regard the exchange rates at which future earnings of overseas subsidiaries become available to parent shareholders as the sole content of economic risk, others restrict 'economic' risk to threats to the company's competitiveness from movements in real exchange rates, others leave room for all commercial hazards from any exchange rate movements, real or nominal. A less ambiguous language would use a vocabulary like that shown in table 8.1.

Table 8.1

Expression	Meaning
Receipts and payments	Cash in- and outflows
Profit before depreciation	(Just that)
Cash returns to shareholders	Dividends plus liquidation payments
Total cash flows	Total internal cash flows of the business = total changes in its net liquid position before dividend payments and changes in long-term debt or equity funding
Total returns from overseas subsidiaries	Total cash dividends plus liquidation payments to the parent from overseas subsidiaries

8.10 In what dimension should currency risks be classified?

This issue is best illustrated from the antithesis between transaction and translation risks. Both can be viewed as a currency mismatch between future nominal receipts and payments. Translation risks are restricted by the writers to *contractually committed* receipts and payments. Uncommitted ones may never appear on financial statements at all. Clearly this category of contractually committed receipts and payments overlaps with a considerable proportion of those included in 'transaction risks'. In fact some writers would treat transaction and translation risks as coterminous, whereas others would wish to extend transaction risk to include a number of *uncommitted* future transactions.

What is common to all of them, however, is that the distinction is not between different *external threats*, i.e. different mismatches. Transaction and translation mismatches arise largely from the same transactions: both threats are from the effect of adverse movements in the same nominal exchange rates on the outcomes of largely the same transactions.

Both concepts include, for example, fixed assets: freehold land has to be regarded in the cash flow view as a cash receipt at the expected end of the asset's useful life in its *present* commercial use (which may be 25 years, but not an infinite time-span away). Both also include committed, but as yet uninvoiced transactions which are not yet on the balance sheet.

The distinction is effectively between two models of the business used by managers (noted in chapter 7, sections 7.9 and 7.10), the accounting model and the future cash flows model. The contrast concerns the *values* (current market or balance sheet values?) and the *time-horizons* which the currency manager has in mind when managing the risks. The distinction is subjective in that it turns on his perceptions: if he is concerned with accounting values and with losses or gains arising in financial reporting periods, then he is managing the translation or accounting risk; if he is concerned with the amount of the future cash receipt or payment on its expected date, then he is managing 'transaction' risk.

This distinction between translation and transaction risk is therefore between management perceptions, not between external threats or risks. This reduces the usefulness of the distinction. It is important, but not of first order importance. The most useful dimension in which to classify risks is external causes or threats of losses. Different classes of risk are best seen as different external threats, not as different perceptions of the same threats.

8.11 The role of time-spans

Shapiro (1989) says real operating exposures need a long-term perspective. Donaldson (1980, 1987) says transaction exposures exist for relatively short periods, whereas translation exposures are in existence for periods in excess of a year (thus all but reversing Ankrom's distinction). Donaldson (1980, 1987) devotes much attention to how far into the future it is advisable to manage trading transactions which are not yet contractual commitments. He regards these as economic rather than transaction exposures, suggesting that his principal criterion is that they are not short term. Donaldson is in fact concerned with future transactions which do not require any pricing decisions. In our framework they are therefore postnatal risks (section 8.5), as long as the *volume* of sales is not in doubt. Donaldson's main difficulties with the longer-dated items are management difficulties.

The time-frame is all-important, but not to the task of classifying risks. What matters in the classification is whether future cash transactions are seen to be

1 certain to occur, and
2 at a price to which the business is committed.

The classification in section 8.17 makes the distinctions shown in table 8.2. **Competitiveness** (economic) **risk** is concerned with threats from changes in *real* exchange rates to the competitiveness of costs. It is not the definition, but the management issues that require a long-term perspective.

Table 8.2

Business committed to price?	Transaction certain?	Class of risk
Yes	No	Antenatal trading risk
Yes	Yes	Position risk (8.15.3)
No	Yes *or* no	Competitiveness risk

8.12 The boundaries of currency risk

All are agreed that economic or competitiveness risk is not restricted to businesses which trade with other countries. If, for example, the business is a single hotel, and the home currency becomes uncompetitive, less tourists will come and the hotel will lose business.

Some authors like Adler and Dumas (1984) and Wihlborg (1980) come close to defining economic exposure as comprising *all* relationships between currency movements and the profitability of a company, irrespective of any causal chain. Oxelheim and Wihlborg (1987) treat currency risk as one element of the wider concept of macroeconomic uncertainty. The concept covers all macroeconomic threats to real (inflation-adjusted) 'cash flows'.

One difficulty with this is that it ignores the difference between threats caused by nominal, as opposed to real, exchange rate movements. At a more fundamental level, however, exchange rates are themselves correlated with, and sometimes caused by, macroeconomic phenomena which affect business profitability directly, as well as indirectly via currency movements. Oxelheim and Wihlborg acknowledge this, not least by calling their book *Macroeconomic Uncertainty,* but in their actual treatment of the risk management issues they give exchange rate movements a very central position. We shall see in chapter 9 and its appendix that some companies, like Rio Tinto-Zinc Corporation (RTZ) focus on this wider concept of macroeconomic exposure.

Macroeconomic changes and shocks do not hit the company just through exchange rates and inflation, and companies manage their impact in a variety of ways which go far outside their perception of currency risk management. Those who want to explore the issues of currency-related risks will serve business better by restricting that topic to the impact of real and nominal exchange rate movements. This more helpful approach is adopted for example by Shapiro (1989). Inflation on its own tends to be a risk in the home currency as well as in other currencies, and has to be managed in wider terms, not just in the context of exchange rates. Nor does the management of inflation risk necessarily require the skills of the currency manager.

The actual management problems of companies suggest that a sharp distinction should be made between external influences on (a) their costs and (b) their selling prices. Real exchange rates tend to have much more dramatic impacts on the competitive costs of a given competitor than on the market price of what he is offering. This is because only in conditions of absolute or near-monopoly will the individual seller set market prices. So if an exchange rate shock makes an individual competitor's costs uncompetitive, this will have a marked effect on that competitor. If it affects selling prices, then this is likely to affect all competitors to varying degrees: the differential impact on any one competitor is likely to be less dramatic. Moreover, selling prices depend on wider forces of demand and supply to which a wider macroeconomic analysis is entirely appropriate. Exchange rates are only one of many factors.

This is why in section 8.14 the concept of economic currency risk will be restricted to *cost*-competitiveness.

8.13 Commercial risks

It is clear that all economic currency risks are commercial problems, but can financial risks also cause commercial problems? Yes, an antenatal trading risk carries a commercial risk if competitors are quoting different currencies. In that case the business that has quoted a currency other than that of cost, faces catch-22: if the quoted currency falls, the company stands to win the sale and suffer an antenatal trading loss; if that currency rises against the currencies in which competitors have quoted, the price can become uncompetitive and the sale can be lost! This last risk is commercial and not economic, because it is not caused by the real exchange rate, and affects the price, instead of the costs.

It is in fact rare for buyers to allow competing suppliers to quote in different currencies.

8.14 Difficulties in classifying financial risks

Our conclusions so far are as follows:

1 The principal distinction is between economic and financial risks. Economic risks come from movements in the real exchange rate and threaten competitive costs, financial risks from those in nominal rates. However, as the term 'economic risk' has been so widely applied to so many other aspects of currency risk, we can serve clarity by labelling this risk 'competitiveness risk'. Even so, no labelling system is perfect. We shall have to stress that this definition is aimed at risks to the competitiveness of costs, not prices. The antenatal commercial threat to a *quoted* price in section 8.13 is not part of this risk.
2 Trading risks, at least antenatal ones, need to be distinguished from other financial currency risks, because they alone result from a cost/price mismatch.

That leaves the problem of how best to describe and classify the remaining financial risks, which have been variously labelled as balance sheet risks or transaction and translation (or accounting) risks.

One issue here is whether it makes sense to include, for example, fixed assets as future cash receipts. Financial theory prefers to treat the present value of future 'cash flows' from those assets, not the assets themselves, as part of the exposure. In the final analysis, this divergence between the accounting and economic models of the company is not as wide as might appear at first sight. The concept of the net present value of the 'cash flows' is effectively a valuation of the assets, and the difference largely disappears if the current cost accounting convention is used. There are possible theoretical differences between the net present value, the 'value to the business', and the market selling price of the asset, but they tend to be small compared with the difference between any of these valuations and historic cost book values.

The practical risk management issue is that it can be hazardous to assume a very long life for this type of exposure. Commercial or financial circumstances can change quite suddenly, the asset may have to be sold for its realizable value long before the end of the assumed life-span.

8.15 Transaction and translation risk

The prevailing language uses these two concepts. Anyone who wishes to change the language must show good reason why such a well-established usage should be abandoned, and why the proposed new language should be preferred. There are two objections to the transaction/translation terminology.

8.15.1 Are they different risks?

The addition of the word 'risk' after 'transaction' or 'translation' tends to convey that 'transaction risk' and 'translation risk' are two different risks, i.e. different external threats. In fact, as explained in section 8.10, they are different ways of looking at and managing the *same* (or at least largely overlapping) external threat. This objection is compounded when the 'transaction' mode of the risk is identified or coupled with the 'economic' category.

8.15.2 How appropriate is the word 'transaction'?

The expression 'transaction exposure' tends to convey a fragmented image of a multitude of cash items. In fact, however, a postnatal financial risk encompasses a company's entire *position* in a currency. It is the total net mismatch of either assets less liabilities, or future receipts less payments in that currency. There is one exposure per currency, not per individual transaction (each position needs to be managed separately for each maturity, but not for each transaction). The semantics of the word 'transaction' do not convey this message.

There is also a semantic tendency to identify the word 'transaction' much more closely with trading sales and purchases than with other business cash transactions which equally contribute to financial currency risks: loan drawdowns and repayments, interest, dividend, royalty payments, wages and salaries, etc.

These points are psychological and semantic, but a conceptual language needs to pay close attention to psychological and semantic factors. A language which distracts from the intended message breeds ambiguity.

So what is the best name for this risk? The expression 'balance sheet risk', used by Kenyon (1981), fails to hit the nail on the head. It leans towards the accounting image and fails to signal that off-balance sheet commitments like postnatal trading items are part of the risk.

The term 'financial' risks would avoid many of these objections, but is too wide. On balance, the expression which best conveys the correct concept is **'position risk'.** It may be unfamiliar in this context, but it conveys all the right signals, and does not appear to mislead. The exposure is a net position in a currency. The cash v. accounting distinction is accurately satisfied by specifying that position risk can be *managed* as either cash or accounting position risk.

8.16 The boundary between trading and other financial risks

The boundary between trading and other financial risks causes a number of problems.

8.16.1 When do trading risks become position risks?

Here the practical dividing line adopted by Kenyon (1981) seems to remain the best solution. Trading risks ultimately become receivables or payables and therefore part of the other financial risks. The currency manager ceases to manage the exposure as a trading risk when he shifts his focus from the price-less-cost margin to optimizing the out-turn of the exposure itself. At that point it ceases to make sense to manage trading exposures against the benchmark of the exchange rate used in the pricing decision, and the best time for that transition is normally at 'birth', when the trading transaction becomes a commercial certainty. The issue here is not classification, but the management approach.

8.16.2 Royalties, dividends and interest

When these and similar items are due from or to external parties outside the group of companies, then they cannot be trading risks because their amounts are not prices offered to, but still awaiting acceptance by, the outside party. Whether they are part of position risk or not yet exposures at all depends on the extent to which the company is certain that they will fall due for payment. If we are certain that dividends or royalties next year will be at least x, then x is part of position risk. The final amounts may be substantially more, but the excess should not yet be managed as a currency risk.

Intragroup dividends, royalties, etc. are discussed in section 14.3 and example 14.1 of chapter 14. They change the external liquid position when they are paid, and therefore change the group currency position, as well as the position of each group member concerned.

8.16.3 Capital expenditure

Capital expenditure cannot give rise to antenatal trading risks because the buyer of a capital asset from abroad can determine the currency in which he will finance the purchase at the time when he makes his buying decision, at which point he accepts the price offered. Once again, this is part of position risk because it is always postnatal.

8.17 Proposed classification

We are now ready to tabulate our suggested conclusions in table 8.3.

Table 8.3 Classification of currency risks

	Financial		Economic
	Antenatal trading	Position	Competitiveness
Threat from FX rate	Nominal	Nominal	Real
Mismatch	Cost v. price	Net position	Irrelevant
Exposure			
transactions	Contingent	Certain[1]	Certain or uncertain[3]
prices	Committed[2]	Committed[2]	Uncommitted[2]
exposed items already on balance sheet?	None	Most	None
One risk per	Pricing decision	Currency	Commercial offering with separate costs
Can be viewed in *cash or accounting* terms?	Yes	Yes	Irrelevant

[1] Exposures are treated as 'certain' if business managers regard them as certain.

[2] They are *position* exposures only if the prices at which they will occur are also 'committed' in the sense that the prices do not depend on a pricing decision yet to be made by the business – otherwise they are part of the competitiveness exposure.

[3] Future sales at prices which we have yet to decide upon, give rise to *competitiveness* risk:

- irrespective of whether they will be invoiced in currencies mismatched with the currency of cost.
- as long as competitors (people offering substitute goods or services) have costs in other currencies.

9

Corporate Objectives and Policies in Currency Risk Management

9.1 Corporate objectives in the literature

Corporate objectives concerning currency risk have received much attention. Here as elsewhere a most helpful text is Oxelheim and Wihlborg (1987).

The following issues are usually discussed:

1 Risk aversion: This is seen as a wish to reduce the variability of the cash flows of the business.
2 The target variable:
   (a) What precisely is the company trying to maximize or stabilize?
   (b) Measurement in accounting or cash flow terms.
   (c) Measurement in nominal or real terms.

9.2 Can there be a single set of corporate objectives about currency risk?

Discussion of corporate objectives tends to assume that a company ought to have a single objective or set of objectives specifically concerned with currency risk. The picture is that of a board of directors agreeing either to be risk averse about currencies, or to treat them as an opportunity for making money.

This does not ring true. There cannot be many boards of companies who have consistently adopted such a simple attitude to currency risk.

The difficulties with a free-standing, monolithic and black and white view of currency risk will be clear to the reader of the previous chapters.

All business managers in free market economies want to maximize the value of their company. That is the single objective. Currency risks were shown in chapters 7 and 8 to be

1 a financial topic which must often be subordinate to commercial and other priority targets; and
2 not a single problem, but a complex set of issues which affect a business in a variety of ways.

In short, the single-set approach to corporate objectives accords a free-standing degree of priority to the topic which is rarely found in the real world of business, not even in company L in the appendix to this chapter.

9.3 Commercial v. financial markets

The ultimate objective of every board of directors is to maximize the value of its company. All companies in commercial competitive businesses primarily pursue this goal by the way they position themselves and then compete in their commercial markets (Mathur, 1988).

Attitudes to issues like currency risk vary with the nature and business of the company and with the nature of the currency risk. If the company is one which has to take its pricing decisions seriously, it will manage trading risk, for example, with the primary aim of promoting its commercial success. On the other hand those currency risks which have no appreciable bearing on important commercial issues will be managed as purely financial matters with the direct aim of maximizing the value of the company. All this we noted in chapter 7.

Competitiveness, on the other hand, is always a commercial issue, and will always be managed with the primary aim of improving or maintaining the company's competitive position.

9.4 Attitudes to risk

In the appendix to this chapter the objectives of 13 UK companies are briefly examined. Very broadly they fall into three generic categories, those wishing to smooth ('smoothers'), those wishing to lock in ('lockers'), and those wishing to manage for gain ('dealers'). Six companies are mainly 'lockers', but also selective 'dealers'. Two are primarily 'dealers' but take care to control open positions at moderate levels, two appear to be fairly pure 'lockers'. One is 'dealer' and 'smoother' at the same time, and one a pure 'smoother'. Finally one company, RTZ, is a 'smoother', but what RTZ seeks to smooth is the impact of macroeconomic risk, a concept wider than currency risk. This small sample is of course not statistically significant.

Interestingly there are some affinities between these three classes of corporate objectives and the three types of assumption noted in section 7.1 of chapter 7. The smoothers evidently adopt the shareholders' portfolio assumption 3.

One dimension of this categorization concerns whether a company sees its objective purely in maximizing future cash flows (or earnings), or whether it also wishes to influence directly the earnings multiple, the value put on the cash flows by the financial market. This last view is certainly taken by the 'smoothers'.

The 'lockers' are risk averse in the usual sense. They want to have certainty in money terms about the outcome of an exposure, and therefore to lock the outcome into the present forward rate. The 'dealers' are aggressive, that is risk neutral.They want to manage the position for gain, even if the chance of failure entails a possible loss. All dealers in our sample control their exposures within tolerable limits as defined in chapter 6.

The 'smoother' company, on the other hand, is expressly concerned with its earnings multiple or investor rating. It makes a distinction between the effect of its actions on its cash flows on the one hand and the market valuation of those cash flows on the other. 'Smoothers' wish to convince the stock market that whatever impact currency movements have on their earnings varies little from year to year.

The attitude of the 'lockers' can be alternatively described as

1 a desire to minimize the variability of possible outcomes of a given transaction or position exposure,
2 a preference for certainty, i.e. for locking the outcome into the present known market rates, over the chance of gain from a better outcome,
3 a defensive, as contrasted with an aggressive attitude,
4 a 'hedge everything' policy.

The four versions differ only in language. The same distinction is sometimes drawn between risk averse and risk neutral companies. Risk averse companies seek to minimize variability of cash flows and therefore prefer to hedge all risks. 'Risk neutral' companies wish to maximize their profits, cash flows, or value (Oxelheim and Wihlborg, 1987).

9.5 Risk attitudes are affected by commercial aims

When these polarized contrasts like 'aggressive v. defensive' are applied to currency risk, they appear to understate the complexity of the choice facing companies. One reason is that companies are faced with potential conflicts between commercial and purely financial objectives.

Example 9.1

British Umbrellas' competitive position in the US market enables it to earn a 10 per cent gross margin, quoting prices in sterling. Now suppose that nothing changes, except that BU's customers switch to a strong preference for quotations in US dollars: this switch forces BU to accept a currency risk. BU now decides that the maximum currency loss that it would accept on average over a given period is 4 per cent: the business obtainable by quoting prices in US dollars would not be worth its while unless the average gross margin over that period was at least (10 – 4% =) 6 per cent. BU will then manage the risk with the aim of containing the overall currency loss (including hedging cost) at 4 per cent. Had BU treated the risk as a purely financial one, it might have decided to accept the chance of a maximum loss either bigger or smaller than 4 per cent. However, BU is not free to treat the risk as a purely financial risk: this is not a free-standing risk, but part and parcel of the commercial decision to sell UK-made umbrellas in US dollars. BU must manage it as part of that commercial decision.

9.6 Are there limits to an aggressive policy?

Again, the aggressive v. defensive dilemma is usually equated with the antithesis between a 'hedge everything' and 'hedge nothing' decision. This equation tacitly implies that a company that wishes to make money out of currency risk is restricted to risks which drop naturally out of its pattern of business. In other words, a company that neither buys from nor sells to Japan cannot make money out of yen exposures. In the absence of exchange controls, this is not the case. A company with special skill in the market for yen, but no trading connection with Japan, can borrow yen, create financial yen assets, buy and sell yen spot and forward, write or buy yen call or put options. In the absence of exchange controls, the mechanics of the market allow the company to do any of these things.

BU's board of directors may decide they are 'here to make umbrellas, not to speculate in the money markets', but if they do not decide that, why stop at leaving 'natural' risks unhedged? Why not 'unnaturally' open up yen risks? Why the distinction? If the company deliberately leaves risks unhedged, then it must believe it can outspeculate the market and make money for its investors. If this belief is well founded, then why stop at 'natural' exposures? Quite a few companies in the appendix do not stop there. On the other hand company D expressly states that it does.

Perhaps the inhibition is due to a sense that the financial markets would be critical of a policy of speculating more widely? If BU concealed its policy to use the currency markets as a source of profit, and then announced shock news of losses on positions taken in yen, it could certainly expect its securities to be down-rated by the market. Rowntree suffered this type of setback in 1972 when it was found to have lost £25 million in speculation by one of its managers on cocoa prices. On the other hand if such an aggressive policy was openly declared, the stock market would no doubt accept currency trading as one of BU's business activities.

Is there some ethical constraint? If there were, then most banks, for example, would fall foul of this ethical code. The reasoning would have to be that no business that uses funds belonging to investors or customers should 'gamble' with such funds in volatile markets. This objection is valid if the speculation is

1 concealed, or
2 conducted by persons who are not responsible experts and answerable to senior management, or
3 conducted on a scale which exposes the company to intolerable concentrations of risk (chapter 6), or
4 less than adequately controlled and monitored by top management.

Provided the speculation passes these criteria, it is hard to think of any reason why the line should be drawn at risks which arise 'naturally' from a company's commercial trade.

9.7 The yardsticks: accounting or economic?

What yardsticks do companies apply to their handling of currency risk? What are they concerned to maximize, smooth or optimize? This is not an easy question to answer. The 13 companies in the appendix are seen to have some contrasting views. The variety also appears to owe much to the variety in their commercial activities.

The target variable must be derived from the objectives. We have found that the objectives of currency risk management are likely to be subordinate to the company's main objective. They are also likely to be a heterogeneous collection of aims. We are unlikely to find a single target variable which is either in fact adopted by all companies or can be recommended to all. Most companies are likely to have more than one.

Perhaps the first issue is whether the variables are seen in accounting or economic terms. Chapter 7 contains a critique of the accounting model of the company. Here we are concerned with the related topic of the accounting framework as a yardstick to be used in framing corporate objectives. Oxelheim and Wihlborg (1987) and many other writers reject the selection of an accounting yardstick or variable, on the grounds that the financial markets, and therefore the investors, learn to see through accounting figures and are concerned with economic values. We saw in chapter 7 that this case is not clear-cut. In any case, however, managers are stuck with the accounting framework for two reasons:

1 The accounting framework is the legally required form in which companies must report results and financial condition to investors, which determines their borrowing powers and solvency, and often defines triggers of ratio covenants in debt instruments. These points are noted by Buckley (1986). A number of companies in the sample in the appendix make this point, especially about gearing. Company K has even gone to the trouble of modifying the formula for the gearing ratio in all these instruments so as to remove a particular anomaly in the accounting conventions. This confirms both points: the accounting framework is unrealistic, and yet a paramount constraint.
2 Due to the legal constraints, companies' information systems have to be cast in the accounting mould.

The first of these points is much more powerful than economists allow. If a manager is accountable in one language, he will find it hard to ignore that language. The second one is decisive for all but the largest companies. It costs money to set up a parallel information system. Current cost accounting ran into resistance because it is so costly: it uses economic values which require a great deal of judgement about the future. Accounting has traditionally focused on the relatively less skilled tasks of recording and analysing the past. The skills needed for current cost valuations are scarce and expensive.

The worst feature of the existing accounting framework is its neglect of inflation and real values. An inflation accounting standard like current purchasing power accounting might have got over most of the difficulties. Accounting might still fail to produce pure economic values, but at least results would have been reported in inflation-corrected terms.

However, whether accounts are useful or not, companies are legally compelled to account to their investors in accounting terms, and it is in those terms that a majority probably see their yardstick for managing currency risk. This is certainly true of the informal sample in the appendix.

9.8 Yardsticks in use

A variety of yardsticks are encountered in companies:

1 Financial accounting yardsticks include
  (a) either maximizing or 'smoothing' the effect of currency movements on annual earnings per share (an after-tax measure), or
  (b) maximizing net worth.

As we have seen, some of the sample companies in the appendix are more concerned with smoothing year-by-year accounting results. This concept is not far removed from the view taken by Adler and Dumas (1984), even if the companies define in accounting terms what they wish to smooth. The belief behind this policy is that the stock market values the company's equity more highly if its earnings appear immune to currency movements than if large gains were seen to arise from time to time from such movements.

2 Cash yardsticks include
  (a) optimizing the cash outcome of particular transactions or classes of transactions,
  (b) maximizing the value of the company, defined as the discounted value of expected future cash flows.

3 Commercial yardsticks are mainly
  (a) market share, or
  (b) turnover, or
  (c) achieved gross margins, or better still a desired combination of margins and volume.

9.9 The yardstick currency

RTZ – one of the companies reviewed in the appendix – rejects a currency risk management objective measured in terms of its reporting currency, sterling. As Lighterness (1987) puts it:

> RTZ is generally held as one stock in a broad portfolio. We assume that portfolio managers hold RTZ as part of a diversified portfolio in which the *purchasing power* [our italics] of funds under their management is

> protected. It would therefore be counterproductive for us to attempt to reduce our currency exposure to pounds sterling. We report in sterling, and our balance sheet shrinks if sterling strengthens, but we protect shareholders' wealth by not hedging currency exposure into sterling.

RTZ is more concerned with the wider concept of macroeconomic uncertainty of Oxelheim and Wihlborg (1987) than with currency risk as such. RTZ believes that investors see through the distortions which may be caused by their reporting currency, and value the company in terms of the purchasing power of its net present value. This must also apply to some companies that are known by the market to have little 'exposure' to their reporting currencies.

This contrasts with the view taken by most companies, and by all other companies in the appendix, who measure their performance in the parent company's reporting currency. This is normally also the currency in which a company's share capital is denominated. Some general exceptions are discussed in chapter 13, section 13.3.

One important exception is international banks or other financial services companies whose market share depends on their net worth. They may measure their performance in a composite currency like the SDR or ECU, so that they can validly compare the ranking of their net worth with that of their international competitors.

The other exception is a currency which is not suitable as a measure of value. This can be a currency with hyperinflation or indeed any heavily overvalued currency. A Brazilian company is much more likely to measure its performance in terms of US dollars than cruzeiros.

9.10 Principal factors determining objectives

We have looked at some important considerations. A fuller list of issues which may be influential in drawing up corporate objectives concerning currency risks might include the following:

1 Does the company's commercial effort require important pricing decisions in currencies mismatched with currencies of cost? Similarly, is currency risk always just a financial issue, or is it sometimes subordinate to commercial objectives?
2 Would an uncompetitive currency of cost cause the company major commercial problems?
3 Do the top management team's skills include an understanding of the currency markets, to the point where the team feels confident that it can control and monitor a speculative policy?
4 Do the top team's workloads leave time to give adequate attention to aggressively managed currency risks?

5 Is the company's portfolio of activities or its geographical spread so diverse or complex that its effective control and management requires a high degree of decentralization, i.e. of delegation of profit responsibility to profit centres?
6 Do different types of currency risk require different sets of objectives in the company's business or businesses?
7 Is there any ethical or market reason why the company should restrict its currency exposures to those arising 'naturally' from its business?
8 What is the company's threshold of tolerable risk?
9 Does the company's corporate culture play a part in shaping its attitudes to currency risk?

9.11 Statement of objectives

As currency risk is in fact an important part of a company's working environment, it would be useful if the board of each company drew up and approved a short summary of the principles which should guide the company in approaching various currency risks. Ideally this should distinguish between the various classes of risk, which we have called competitiveness, trading and position risk. The summary should be drawn up after going through some checklist on the lines of section 9.10. The summary should clarify for each class of risk

1 in what circumstances it is to be managed as a commercial, financial or cross-disciplinary issue,
2 the company's main objectives and attitude: to smooth, to lock exposures in, or to manage for gain?
3 yardsticks and yardstick currency.

9.12 Interim conclusions on currency risk management

We can now take stock of our main conclusions so far.

1 Currency risk is not predominantly a free-standing top priority issue in its own right. It is one part of a complex business environment, subordinate to overriding commercial and organizational issues. Ultimate financial goals must be pursued primarily in competitive commercial markets.
2 Managers have opportunities and duties to change a company's sensitivity to currency risks. Measures open to them concern both external and internal business environments.
3 Currency risk is not a simple monolithic phenomenon. Risks are of

different kinds, exchange rate movements are very different over different time-frames, and above all there are great variations in the commercial profiles of businesses. Each of these variables calls for different types of responses by managers to currency risks.

4 Although currency risk is a two-way market risk, intolerable concentrations of it are possible. Intolerable concentrations have to be managed differently from diversifiable forms of risk.

5 There are possible constraints on aggressive risk management, but no objections in principle, as long as any significantly speculative policy is openly declared to the company's present and potential investors.

6 Once the company decides to manage currency risk for gain, there is no reason why it should restrict itself to 'natural' exposures. With suitable disclosure, it should feel free to open up positions where it feels best able to make gains.

7 Companies should manage their exposures in cash rather than accounting terms, but for practical legal reasons few of them can afford to ignore the accounting effects.

Appendix: Some mini case studies of UK corporate objectives concerning currency risk management

An informal sample survey was undertaken in March to May 1989. Nineteen UK public companies were asked for a statement of their objectives or policies in this field. The request referred in general terms to

- how the company defined and classified risks;
- whether it had definite policies on hedging 100 per cent or not at all, or some intermediate proportion;
- whether it was concerned to take a view on the way exchange rates will go or whether all currency exposures are to be hedged irrespective of any views held;
- to what extent the company saw the risk in terms of its effect on the published accounts, or in terms of future cash outcomes, or perhaps in real (i.e. inflation-adjusted) terms.

Companies were encouraged to supply any relevant statements already in existence, but some respondents replied with a new formulation in response to the request.

Ten written replies were received, two companies were interviewed. RTZ referred to published material. Six companies did not reply.

Company A

Company A is mainly a process manufacturer producing semi-finished and finished goods. Its product range varies from highly competitive low-margin products in which it is a price-taker to much more differentiated quality offerings where pricing decisions are important. It therefore has profit centres of highly varied size and sophistication.

A operates through decentralized operating units. To a large extent, however (entirely in the UK and increasingly overseas), those units do their exchange dealing with the central treasury, which then manages the resulting net group positions.

A is primarily concerned with contractual 'transaction' risks. In its decentralized management structure it strongly discourages any 'speculation' by operating units. 'The objective . . . is to avoid risk by securing a *certain* exchange rate for future receivable or payable amounts, . . . not risking (trading) margins on market fluctuations in exchange rates.' A consciously wants units to lock in current market rates and forego possible future gains compared with those rates. At the same time A instructs operating units not to cover forecast (i.e. uncontracted) cash flows.

Like most respondent companies, A is willing to relax its policies at the centre, for example by using options in suitable cases for sales not yet firmly booked.

In its currency risk management policies, A is highly sensitive to the competitive implications of pricing decisions, and of the distinction in this book between ante- and postnatal sales from price-lists.

A also watches 'translation' risk, but uses only its borrowing policy to manage it: forward contracts or options are not used for this purpose.

Company A does not refer to the distinction between the accounting and cash views of exposure, but this distinction is not significant in its business.

Company B

B produces and markets speciality processed materials. B issues few formal rules and statements. Its guiding principle is risk averse, but it successfully makes exceptions where, in its judgement, it would be better not to stick to a 'cover everything' rule. B used to be preoccupied only with 'transaction' risk, but has lately become concerned with 'translation' risk which it has again managed successfully with a mixture of caution and pragmatism. Pragmatism covers a variety of policies, including occasional partial percentage cover.

Interestingly, B regards it as important for the corporate centre to be informed of all exposures when they are 'born', so as to have the opportunity to lock the rate in at that point. In that important sense B is concerned with selling margins, i.e. selling prices.

Company C

Company C is a processor of paper, which it markets in a variety of forms, some highly finished and customized. The group positions itself in differentiated rather than commodity customer markets.

C is mainly concerned with 'transaction' exposure. Its declared policy is 'to minimize exposure to all foreign currency fluctuations'. Its subsidiaries normally invoice their exports in customers' currencies, which C sells forward for sterling. Foreign currency purchases are bought forward.

C also manages its position exposure, matching debt with foreign currency assets. However, when C judges that an unmatched position is likely to be profitable, it exceptionally (and successfully to date) leaves a position open.

C does not mention pricing and sees its exposures in accounting terms.

Company D

D is a multinational with a large proportion of assets and operations overseas. It makes and markets a variety of fast turnover consumer products.

D's policies are clear and detailed. It is concerned with 'transaction', 'economic' and 'translation' risks. It manages translation risk with the objective of protecting its gearing ratio as well as its shareholders funds. D is explicit in quantifying its exposures in accounting terms because its gearing and loan covenant limits are defined in accounting terms. D also has clear policies about intragroup dividends, profits of overseas subsidiaries and capital expenditure commitments.

D manages 'transaction' risks in terms of 'all forecast receipts and payments in a foreign currency within the forward period covered by a pricing structure to which the company is committed'. This is a very clear reference to what this book calls postnatal exposures.

D declares that it does not take open positions on items which do not naturally arise from its operations. This policy is widely shared, but few companies make this explicit.

The basic policy is conservative, but judicious positions are taken, and options are used both for uncertain amounts of sales and for sales with uncommitted prices ('economic' exposures) where flexibility is needed to deal with competitors' future pricing policies.

Company E

E is a multinational which manufactures and markets a variety of fast-moving consumer goods, and other products. All products are the subject of competitive pricing, but in some products these competitive pricing decisions set prices for long periods.

E implements its currency management policies to some extent by motivating operating units to comply. Part of the motivation is to impress on them that the financial market requires a higher incremental return on risky policies than on risk averse ones.

E defines its exposures in some detail. Transaction exposures arise from firm contractual commitments. Economic exposures are defined as expected transaction exposures. This category is defined to include 'dollar commodities' which are bought at sterling prices. Translation exposures are those which arise on translation of the balance sheet and the profit and loss account. So exposures are quantified in accounting terms. E is concerned to protect the effect of translation exposure on the group's gearing ratio.

E's policy is conservative, but permits the corporate centre to take relatively small open positions. E specifically recognizes that the cost of hedging may be excessive in some currencies which do not float freely.

E directs some of its management effort towards avoiding adverse performance against budget; for example it selectively covers exposures on overseas subsidiaries' budgeted profit for the year.

Company F

Company F is a conglomerate making engineering components for a consumer industry and products bought by Government. It also markets services.

F's basic policy is 'to minimize the effects which can result from making investments in or trading in foreign currencies', which it applies wherever the costs of applying it are justified by the risks. One of the objectives of this policy is to protect the sterling value of prices quoted in non-sterling currencies, so that the sterling outcome is one that the company can live with.

F quantifies exposure in accounting terms.

Company G

Company G is heavily concentrated on one engineering product; it is not a conglomerate.

G's currency risk management objectives are consciously designed to serve its commercial profile. That profile is dominated by the fact that the vast majority of its sales are priced in dollars, and its competitors have their costs in dollars. G has the bulk of its costs in sterling; but for G's important presence, this would be a market in which all competitors' costs and all prices are matched in dollars. Moreover, margins are competitive and tight. G is a company listed in London, with almost all its sales in US dollars. Currency risk thus has a critical influence on G's results.

G's response to this is to cover 80 per cent of all customer orders as soon as they are considered 'firm'. (In our terminology this is exactly the point defined as birth of a trading risk.)

However, each such order includes an option to the customer to purchase, over a number of years, further products at the prices fixed in the order now placed. These further orders are uncertain in volume, but at dollar prices already fixed. In our terminology in this book, the uncertain part of that volume gives rise to antenatal trading exposures. G, like many other companies, defines the entire future orders from this source as economic exposures. G covers these forward as far out as five years: the percentage covered for each year declines with the time to maturity. Cover is taken out evenly throughout the year.

The purpose of this hedging policy is to achieve an average $/£ rate which is a weighted average of the preceding four years' $/£ rates. Achieved rates are thus immunized from day-to-day volatility in the $/£ rate and running fairly evenly from one year to the next. It amounts to a smoothing of future results from these sales, and to greater certainty.

The dilemma between the accounting and cash flow views of exposure does not arise in G, or at least not in this principal source of exchange risk. It should be noted that the emphasis leans towards eliminating discontinuities in future results rather than eliminating all uncertainty. Had the company chosen the latter priority, it would cover forward all postnatal sales, i.e. that part of the future sales at fixed prices which it regards as commercially certain now.

G watches out for 'translation' risks, but has not recently had any significant exposures of this kind. If it had, its policy would be to hedge them.

Company H

H is in two main commercial markets with very different currency risk characteristics. One category is major contracts with long time-spans between tender and order, and then again between contract and delivery and cash collection. The second category concerns capital goods of much smaller individual value, delivered mainly from stock immediately following the receipt of an order.

H's policy is to lock in its foreign currency price in sterling at the earliest practical time. In *large contracts* it does this whenever possible by using ECGD's tender to contract cover; and in other cases by allowing for the risk in. its costing and therefore ultimately as a contingency allowance in its quoted price. These methods are described in chapter 12. As soon as a major contract becomes an order, the receipts are sold forward for sterling.

In the case of capital goods sold from stock, costs and receipts are hedged as to 75 per cent of receipts forecast per quarter for a rolling year ahead. The unhedged 25 per cent is to allow for forecasting error.

H balances out all significant balance sheet exposures (called position risks in this book and 'translation risks' by many others), in line with its general objective of wishing to be certain of the sterling outcomes of its business operations. It is only in this context that a conflict between the accounting and cash views of exposure can arise, and H, like most other companies, takes the accounting view.

Company I

Company I trades mainly in commercial markets with two distinct currency risk characteristics: construction or installation contracts and the manufacture of more or less standardized products for sale to the capital goods and other industries.

I recognizes two types of exposure, 'translation' exposure and cash impact exposures, defined as exposures to fluctuations in exchange rates from normal trading transactions and capital flows between different currencies. Translation exposures are managed under policies reviewed by I's board of directors from time to time.

On cash impact exposures, I has a formal policy 'that the risk of cash losses through exposure to movements in exchange rates must be minimized'. I distinguishes clearly between antenatal ('contingent') and postnatal (firm) exposures. I uses ECGD's tender to contract cover and currency options to manage the former, and forward contracts for the latter. All these methods are discussed in chapter 12.

I broadly aims at matching tangible assets with liabilities in non-sterling currencies, but may borrow more than the amount of the tangible assets in a currency where income is high relative to asset values. This is an explicit recognition of the possible shortcomings of accounting values.

Company J

J has very explicit policies, expressly related to its trading pattern. Like G's, its currency exposure is a critical element in its overall performance, because 85 per cent of its output is sold in a number of non-sterling currencies; yet sterling is its reporting currency in which its performance is measured by the financial markets. On the other hand its sterling costs are a minor feature in its performance. J is not a conglomerate. Its business is heavily concentrated in a single family of products. It markets these mainly to public sector customers, with prices agreed and fixed for years ahead. The price elasticity of its main business is zero over the short and medium term.

Rather like company G (which is in a very different business but with remarkably similar currency characteristics), G's policy is to smooth the impact of exchange risks over the years rather than to eliminate it. J aims to have the pattern of its results barely impacted by currency movements between one year and the next. Unlike G, however, J combines the objective of smoothing the impact of exchange rates with a deliberate optimization (as against risk minimization) policy which aims at making steady currency gains. A very active FX hedging strategy is followed, with all exposures reviewed continuously and with opportunities being taken to hedge at optimum points in time.

J also manages the translation risks on non-sterling profits, simply because it wishes to manage everything that impacts on the group profit and loss account.

To sum up, J's perception of risk is in accounting terms, it manages currency exposures for gain, but successfully aims at continuity between years in the impact of currencies on its reported results.

Company K

Company K is a multinational process manufacturer. It converts primary commodities into materials and products for sale to both consumer and industrial outlets. One important operating unit's market is mainly dominated by public sector customers. K's markets are highly competitive – it is mainly a price-taker, and its costs are dominated by (a) raw materials and (b) the capital cost of its plants. Sales tend to be from price-lists which cannot be amended or withdrawn to take account of short-term movements in exchange rates.

For its business, K needs and has a highly specialized and skilled treasury operation. Its mission is to optimize the impact of currency and interest rate risk – an aggressive posture. This is, however, tempered with a tightly controlled determination to contain exposures within moderate levels.

K centralizes its trading exposures. Operating units sell their receivables and payables to the centre at forward rates of exchange. The centre actively manages its trading exposures against a yardstick of hedging 50 per cent. The trading exposure so managed consists of

1 the contractual receivables and payables sold to the centre by the operating units, plus
2 any further sales, not yet booked, which are expected with commercial certainty.

In chapter 8, section 8.16.1, we introduced 'commercial' certainty as the distinguishing characteristic of antenatal exposure in this type of business. Sales are antenatal if the company regards them as not yet commercially certain, and therefore as speculative.

K expressly declines to call its central operation a profit centre: its absolute profit or loss ignores the 50 per cent hedge benchmark and therefore has no significance. There is a strict rule that exposures may not be deliberately opened up in the course of this task. This rule effectively restricts total exposures to moderate levels.

K manages its much smaller net liquid position a good deal more actively. Exposures are deliberately opened up, and are managed daily for a much shorter time-scale. The aim is to improve the overall cost, if the position consists of debt; or its yield if it consists of surplus funds. This aim is consistently achieved.

K also has a clear policy on translation risk. Like other companies in the sample, it manages the group position with an eye on its gearing ratio. The norm is to keep its position in its three main currency blocs roughly in line with the target gearing ratio for the group as a whole, but K will make controlled departures from this principle when it believes that its view of future exchange rate movements between the three dominant currencies will result in a gain, after allowing for the effect of different interest rates. K here measures its position in accounting terms, after correcting one specific unrealistic feature of the accounting definition, unrealistic in K's particular circumstances.

K subordinates the role of currency risk management to the attainment of commercial objectives. K has devoted some thought to economic, i.e. cost competitiveness, risk. Because the bulk of K's costs are capital investment and raw materials, K recognizes that it cannot switch its costs between currencies. For this reason it has not found a satisfactory tool for managing this risk, which is acute in some of its businesses. K has considered long-term currency swaps or forward contracts as tools for managing this economic risk. If K entered into them, it would account for them not centrally, but in the operating businesses. K is quite clear that such hedges would lock the business concerned into the current market rate structure, irrespective of whether this will end in a gain or a loss. The business would have to accept the risk of losing as a result.

Company L

Company L has its headquarters in the UK, and has operations in other countries. It is, however, unique in this appendix in a number of respects. It has a controlling shareholder outside the UK, and neither it not its parent is listed in London or New York. L's activities are centred on trading in a group of commodities and on distributing those commodities and distributing and manufacturing related products. Its commercial markets require a back-up of financial services which L provides as a separate profit centre, with considerable banking skills. L is unique therefore in that it sees its treasury as one of its main activities. As L's excellence derives partly from its dealing skills, this is a natural extension. From these trading activities, L has also developed the marketing of other related services.

The central treasury has the normal functions of ensuring liquidity, managing interest and currency risks (including translation and economic risk), but it combines these with the mission to contribute to group profits as a profit centre in its own right. Scale apart, it operates much like the treasury of a bank. It supports the other operations of the group, but it also deals for its own account.

The treasury is concerned with translation risk where its priorities are first to protect the group from losses to net worth and gearing, and secondly, to exploit any opportunities to make gains.

Finally, L is conscious of competitiveness risk (as defined in chapter 8) and its treasury has a duty to advise on the best way to manage it.

The RTZ Corporation plc

RTZ's commercial activities concern natural resources, industrial operations and energy. Its currency management policies are discussed in Lighterness (1987).

RTZ has developed strong principles from financial portfolio theory. It explicitly rejects the accounting format as a framework for currency risk management policy, because in RTZ's case it is demonstrably inappropriate.

RTZ's fundamental perception is that its cash flows depend above all on the prices of copper, aluminium, iron ore and commodities it sells, and that academic studies (Chu and Morrison, 1984; Grilli and Yang, 1981) have shown those commodity prices to be determined by baskets of currencies (see also Gilbert, 1989). The baskets are heavily weighted towards the US dollar, the yen, and European currencies represented by the ECU.

RTZ therefore sees its net present value to investors as sensitive to fluctuations in that basket of currencies. In order to minimize that sensitivity, RTZ aims to keep its portfolio of debt close to that basket of currencies. This is a smoothing rather than a (short-term) optimization objective.

RTZ's shares are listed on the International Stock Exchange in London, it reports its results and condition in sterling, and no doubt its gearing, loan covenant and other limits are defined in terms of its sterling consolidated balance sheet. However, RTZ consciously does not manage its 'translation' position. RTZ assumes that investors are concerned with the real purchasing power of their investment, not its nominal sterling value. It therefore does not hedge its exposures against sterling. Its focus is on currencies of determination, not currencies of denomination (Lighterness, 1987).

RTZ at first sight appears to be an exception to all the definitions and classifications of chapter 8, and to the views taken in chapter 9. Moreover, RTZ's approach fits well into the framework put forward by Oxelheim and Wihlborg (1987). The facts and causal framework are also quite close to the Vulcan Materials case in Garner and Shapiro (1984). Vulcan's cash flows too are sensitive to metals prices.

On the other hand the priority placed by RTZ on its trading profile and results is very much in harmony with the view taken in this book. RTZ's results are far more sensitive to the demand and supply and price-levels of the commodities it sells than to any trading or financing transactions captured in the conventional categories like 'transaction' or 'translation' exposure. Its main currency-related risk is truly economic. Currency movements affect RTZ much more in their impact on selling volumes and prices than in how they affect particular contracts or combinations of assets and liabilities. One might expect this to apply to all businesses whose main activity is to produce and sell commodities. However, it is not true of many other industrial businesses: certainly not of the other companies studied in this appendix.

The case of RTZ also raises a linguistic point, well taken by Oxelheim and Wihlborg. The risk which RTZ identifies and manages is wider than the currency risks encountered by most companies. RTZ is concerned with the variability in the demand and supply and prices of the commodities it produces and sells. The determinants of these are micro- and macroeconomic. The macroeconomic determinants include those exchange rate movements which affect the terms of trade of consumer and producer countries. RTZ therefore rightly treats them as determinants. At the same time commodity prices and exchange rates obviously affect one another: causality operates in both directions. RTZ manages an economic risk which is wider than any of our classes of currency risk in this book. What needs to be managed in a business like that of RTZ is wider than just the currency environment.

To sum up, RTZ has a sensitivity to macroeconomic changes partially measured by exchange rates; it manages this risk with the objective of smoothing, of stabilizing its results over the years. It aims to do this not in terms of sterling but in terms of real purchasing power, irrespective of any particular currency.

Part III

The Risks and their Management

10

Competitiveness Risk

10.1 Definition

From the classification in chapter 8, competitiveness risk emerges as the risk to the competitive position of a business from the appreciation in real terms of a currency in which it incurs substantial costs, against the currencies of competitors.

For a clear understanding of this risk we need to bear in mind the following features:

1 The threat is from movements of the real, not the nominal exchange rate.
2 The threat is to the competitiveness of *costs;* it affects the ability of the business to compete, to obtain sales at a remunerative margin of price over cost. A rise in the real rate of exchange erodes either margins or sales volume or a mixture of both.
3 The risk specifically *fails to concern* the currencies in which the business *sells.* Rises and falls in the real exchange rate of selling currencies tend to affect all competitors, and are part of the wider phenomenon of macroeconomic uncertainty which every business must manage; this wider environment is not essentially or primarily a currency risk. All businesses have to watch the forces which affect demand and supply of what they are offering. RTZ (see chapter 9 and its appendix) is a good example of a company concerned with the effect of exchange rate movements on the demand for its sales and its selling prices; however, RTZ's risk is a wider macroeconomic one, and not just a currency risk. Currencies are an important part, but not the whole of the relevant economic environment.

Consequently, if there are only two competing suppliers, one with French and one with German costs, and if the bulk of sales are in the

USA in US dollars, a fall in the real exchange rate of the dollar would not cause competitiveness risk. What could cause it is a change in the real FFr/DM exchange rate.

4 The risk concerns future sales for which prices have not yet been quoted: under the classification in chapter 8, section 8.17, all sales for which prices have been quoted are subject to financial risks, not competitiveness risk. Where prices have already been quoted, the management task is concerned with nominal, not real exchange rates. Competitiveness risk thus excludes all potential sales for which the business has quoted prices, as well as all actual sales, regardless of whether they have reached the balance sheet as receivables or payables.

5 The threat is to the competitive position 'of a business'. Strictly, it is to a business in one or more of its commercial markets, where it incurs appreciable costs in a currency which may become less competitive.

There are two points here. First, a multiproduct company may have competitive offerings (see below) which vary in their cost profiles. Secondly, a higher degree of differentiation results in a steeper slope of the demand curve. Differentiation makes the competitiveness of an offering less vulnerable to a rise in its costs. This is developed in sections 10.3.5 and 10.6.

The word **'offering'** refers to what customers choose in their buying decisions. The word is used by writers on competitive strategy (Mathur, 1988). What determines a customer's choice between say different motor-cars is not just the apparent physical attributes of different models, but also the quality of the instruction book, of the after-sales service, and of the attention to his or her personal needs by the garage, and finally the price; in other words, the whole package, comprising how the buyer sees the item bought, the support and the price.

The name 'competitiveness' risk was preferred in chapter 8 to 'economic' risk (used by Kenyon, 1981) because the expression 'economic risk' has been widely used with too many diverse, often much broader and sometimes incompatible meanings. Competitiveness risk is nevertheless an 'economic' risk. Its cause is a macroeconomic phenomenon, a change in the relative purchasing power of a currency. Many writers like Shapiro (1989) identify this risk as either 'economic' risk or as a subset of economic risk.

10.2 Patterns in real exchange rate movements

The concepts of the real exchange rate and purchasing power parity were explored in chapter 4, sections 4.8–12. Figures 4.2 and 4.3 show that real exchange rates follow irregular courses, but the irregularities do not wholly obliterate some underlying patterns which are instructive to managers.

1 Movements of the real exchange rate against purchasing power parity and against equilibrium can be wide. The rate tends to stay either less or more competitive for long periods. It was noted that the diagrams plot real exchange rates against purchasing power parity, which may vary from competitive equilibrium.
2 Once the real exchange rate crosses its average trend value (chapter 4, sections 4.10–11) it may stay on the other side for a long time.

Real exchange rates tend to move slowly in one direction and then in the other. The business manager needs to watch not whether a movement crosses some *objective* price parity or 'equilibrium' line. What matters *to him* is how the relationship between his and his competitor's costs has changed from whatever *he* had previously regarded as the norm when making his commercial and investment decisions. His *subjective* norm might have been something like an average or regression line introduced into figure 4.3, not the horizontal PPP line. An illustration is given in example 10.1, section 10.8.3. A given currency is likely to have prolonged periods in which it will alternately be above and then below its trend value. The pattern is not reliable, but perhaps more reliable than any pattern in the nominal exchange rate. The theoretical difficulties were discussed in chapter 4.

10.3 The characteristics of competitiveness risk

The characteristics of this class of risk are as follows.

10.3.1 Commercial rather than financial threat

The threat is to the competitive position of the business in its commercial markets. In no immediate sense is it a financial risk. It does not concern the financial outcome of committed transactions. Income statements do not show its effects: they do not show missing sales at all, nor do they analyse shrinking margins by their macroeconomic causes. The effect of a less competitive real exchange rate is either narrower margins or lost sales or a mixture of both. Such a threat goes to the heart of the firm's position in its competitive markets (Porter, 1980; Mathur, 1988).

10.3.2 Changes in competitiveness are slow

They take time to be recognized, and call for medium-term responses. This is discussed in section 10.8.

10.3.3 Shifting major costs takes time

The seriousness of the risk depends on how hard it is to shift costs between currencies. For example, the value added by the contractor for a petrochemical process plant is largely design and management, the hardware is all procured from manufacturers. The largest item, the compressor, can be ordered from manufacturers in a number of countries, and if a high real exchange rate makes the British compressor maker uncompetitive, then the contractor has little difficulty in switching this major cost item to a supplier with costs in a more competitive currency. Procurement costs are seldom locked into a particular currency, whereas labour and capital costs are not easily or rapidly switched. So contractors are better placed than manufacturers to switch costs by switching subcontracts. If the main contractor had been a British compressor manufacturer, it would have found it much harder to purchase the compressor from its Swiss competitor, leaving its own British workforce to face redundancies.

10.3.4 Not restricted to international trade

The risk affects businesses not engaged in international trade. The best example here is a famous historic public house in the English Home Counties, located near a holiday camp and caravan site which in summer attracted European tourists. In the mid-1970s, when the pound sterling was well below its competitive equilibrium, the tourist trade was buoyant and this pub had highly profitable summer seasons. When the advent of North Sea oil and monetarism pushed the pound some way above its competitive equilibrium in 1979–80, the bookings at the holiday camp dropped sharply. It finally had to close down. The pub consequently had some poor seasons and was sold to a large conglomerate. The pub was not an exporter or importer, but its effective competitors for the summer holiday trade were in other countries which took the holiday trade away from the UK when the pound became uncompetitive.

10.3.5 Depends on price sensitivity

The sensitivity of a business to competitiveness risk depends on its elasticity of demand.

This was referred to in item 5 in section 10.1. A competitive strategy of differentiation aims precisely at a more steeply sloping demand curve. The less price-sensitive customers are, the less damaging is a deterioration in cost competitiveness (Wilson, 1988).

10.4 Financial hedges of competitiveness risk

Section 7.8 of chapter 7 discussed the suggestion in some financial theory texts that this class of economic risk can be hedged by means of financial instruments. The models do not single competitiveness risk out as the risk to be hedged, but it would not be unfair to describe it as central to their concern. In chapter 7 we noted that such a hedge sought to compensate a competitive setback with a financial gain: yet we found it hard to see how the open-ended loss of competitive position can be adequately compensated by a one-shot financial indemnity.

We now need to describe the difficulties in this concept with greater precision.

10.4.1 Will it work against a real exchange rate threat?

The hedge would operate against movements in the nominal, not the real, exchange rate. In section 4.12 of chapter 4 we noted that even though real and nominal exchange rate movements are nearly identical in the very short period, they tend on average to diverge quite strongly in the very long term, where the real exchange rate tends to move back towards equilibrium. A nominal hedge is therefore unlikely to be a good match for all periods. The models seek to bypass this particular objection by applying a coefficient to the amount of the hedge which, from past observations, relates the particular company's performance to nominal exchange rate movements. The coefficient would thus cover any *stable* divergence between real and nominal exchange rate movements. However, as that divergence is not stable, the resulting hedge will not be an accurate stabilizer against the effect of real exchange movements over a sufficient range of time-frames.

10.4.2 Does it deal with the competitiveness of costs?

We have identified competitive costs as the Achilles heel vulnerable to changes in real exchange rates. The generalized hedge is only indirectly and partially related to costs.

10.4.3 Managers have to manage competitive costs

A manager whose costs become uncompetitive must either get out of that particular commerical offering in its present form, or seek to make his costs competitive. He can only use a hedge against his costs becoming uncompetitive if he treats the effect of that hedge as part of the cost structure. In other words, if the hedge does its job, i.e. provides a financial gain which offsets his costs, he must look at his costs as reduced by the gain from the hedge. The hedge, like any other hedge, has locked him into the exchange rate structure as it was on the date when the the hedge was taken out.

Conversely, however, if his own currency of cost *falls* in real terms, he must treat the loss from the hedge as an extra cost which denies him the benefit of the improvement in the competitiveness of his own currency. It is not easy to see many managers readily accepting that. It would obviously, for example, be dangerous commercial policy where the company has a local competitor in its own country. With a falling real exchange rate it would lose market share to that competitor unless that competitor had adopted an identical hedging policy. Otherwise the competitor would be free to reduce prices or collect higher margins. More generally, no manager will readily handicap his company when its economic environment is favourable. This dilemma is squarely recognized by Company K in the appendix to chapter 9.

10.4.4 Can real exchange rates never be predicted?

Finally, we must discuss the hypothesis that real exchange rates move in an efficient market which cannot be arbitraged. Free financial markets have a high degree of efficiency, but goods markets are often not efficient, and arbitrage opportunities are common in them. It is fallacious to think of the real exchange rate as governed exclusively or predominantly by the financial markets. This is true only in the very short term, and in the very short term we are not concerned with competitiveness risk.

10.5 Opportunities for managing competitiveness risk

Practical opportunities to manage competitiveness risk occur in two types of circumstances. The first is whenever plans are made. A business can seek to improve its competitive position by arranging, as far as practicable, to incur its costs in currencies expected to be relatively competitive during the critical period. Competitiveness risk and the real exchange rate should be taken into account in all investment and other planning decisions. How decisive a role this consideration will play in the decisions will depend on the circumstances of each case. Often it will only play a minor role. In any event, the planning process will be better informed if trends in the real exchange rate and its effect on costs over the planning period are taken into account.

The second set of circumstances is whenever a deterioration in trading performance is being analysed, or where other evidence comes to hand that the currency of major costs is becoming less competitive. Where trading performance has deteriorated, a rising real exchange rate is of course only one of many possible explanations. However, whenever other explanations have been eliminated and yet market share is being lost to foreign competitors, there must be a strong chance that the real exchange rate has done the damage. Again, the opportunity to manage this development depends on whether there is scope for the actions reviewed in section 10.6.

10.6 How can competitiveness risk be managed?

The management actions that may be available to improve the company's competitive position are:

(a) to shift costs into a more competitive currency, or
(b) to increase the degree of differentiation of the company's competitive offering, so as to make it less price-sensitive (Mathur, 1988; Wilson, 1988).

The former can be used aggressively, the latter is defensive in this context of the real exchange rate. It can of course be used as an aggressive competitive strategy.

Neither of these remedies is always promptly available. Company K, in the appendix to chapter 9, is conscious that it can never shift substantial costs from currency to currency.

Competitiveness risk has to be managed opportunistically. Where there are opportunities, they must be seized. Where they do not exist, they can sometimes be created. In any case it is difficult to believe in effective countermeasures outside the commercial markets. Financial hedges can at best be a temporary palliative, at worst a millstone round the company's own neck. Several companies, in the sample in the appendix to chapter 9, have looked for such an answer without success. The most interesting case is company K.

10.7 The currency of cost portfolio

In section 10.4 it was suggested that competitiveness risk cannot be managed as a financial porfolio. A different portfolio approach has been suggested by Hertzell and Caspar (1988). These authors observe that some automobile and electronics manufacturers have set up manufacturing plants in a number of countries. The more balanced the production is among different currencies of cost, the less the risk of the total portfolio.

The suggestion is that this might become a deliberate policy for managing competitiveness risk, with a two-pronged benefit:

(a) the portfolio is itself a reduction of risk, and
(b) a portfolio of underutilized capacity could be exploited to switch production from less to more competitive currencies when real exchange rates move.

This innovative concept runs into many practical difficulties. It can only be contemplated by very big multinationals. The deliberate creation of spare capacity may not be economic. Labour relations might be difficult if work is shifted as an explicit act of policy rather than as a last resort after a site has become manifestly uneconomic.

Nevertheless the concept might be valid but for one objection of principle. A central theme of this book is that major business decisions, like plant location, are not normally driven by currency considerations. It is hard to believe that BMW or Toshiba have decided their plant locations with competitiveness risk uppermost, let alone exclusively in their minds. Competitiveness risk should be one factor to be taken into account, not the tail wagging the dog.

10.8 Time-spans in competitiveness risk

The important interrelation between nominal and real exchange rate movements over various time-spans was described in chapter 4, section

4.12. The time has come to review the significance of those patterns for the manager.

10.8.1 The very short period

In the very shortest term of a dealing day or two (and leaving aside countries with hyperinflation; see chapter 4, section 4.12) relative price levels change at a negligible pace, whereas spot exchange rates can develop very high volatility, up to 5 per cent movement in one day. In that very short term, therefore, real and nominal exchange rate movements are for practical purposes identical. This contrasts very sharply with that long term in which deviations from purchasing power parity tend towards zero.

10.8.2 The first few months

After the very short period a divergence develops between nominal and real exchange rate movements. How fast this becomes appreciable depends of course on the inflation differential itself. If one currency is inflating at the rate of 6 per cent per annum and the other at 2 per cent, then the differential is ⅓ per cent per month. If the respective inflation rates are 6 per cent and 5 per cent, then the differential is only 1/12 per cent per month. Spot rate volatility is often still several times greater, but as the time-horizon lengthens, there comes a point where it is no longer safe to treat movements in nominal and real exchange rates as approximately equal.

It does not, however, follow that the divergence has any practical significance for the manager in this early period. There are two reasons why it should not.

First, commercial markets have a slower tempo than financial markets. A competitor cannot normally change his offering, his price or his cost structure either frequently or at short notice. Customers often need time to make their choice, and prefer a reasonably stable set of offerings and prices which they can compare. Cost structures cannot be changed at will. Employees cannot be laid off or hired, suppliers cannot be switched at the drop of a hat. Production capacity is not always available elsewhere at short notice. The manager can often only respond to movements in the real exchange rate by switching factors of production. This he can only do sparingly and infrequently, when he can see a clear prospect of a sustained change in the real exchange rate.

Secondly, it can take time before such a change is clearly apparent. Information about recent rates of inflation can take time to become available. More importantly, nominal exchange rates are so volatile in the short term that in those early stages trends are hard to distinguish from blips. To sum this up, a commercial response to a rise in the real exchange rate, that is a deliberate change in the company's marketing or cost profiles, requires strong evidence of the rise in the real exchange rate. Such strong evidence will take time to appear. Any minor change in the real exchange rate is unlikely to justify action.

10.8.3 The medium term

The medium term here is the normal commercial planning period in which companies plan major investments in new competitive offerings or in productive capacity. Over these periods, planners must bear in mind that the real exchange rate is likely to change its competitive status.

If the real exchange rate is now below average level (section 10.2 discussed the benchmark to use), i.e. competitive, then the plans must allow for a deterioration by the time the new product or plant comes on stream. If the real exchange rate is now above its average level, then the possibility of an improvement should be cautiously considered.

Example 10.1

In figure 4.3 the diagram for Germany up to 1980 suggests that an average value of the D-Mark's real exchange rate had been about 5–6 per cent below its price parity. In 1980 it was some 7 per cent above that average level; so when it began to drop, a cautious forecast of a sustained improvement in competitiveness compared with 1978–80 might well have been justified. The grounds for this might have included not just the shape of the graph, but also the visible change in US economic management. Confidence in such a forecast should be cautious and modest, but not without some substance.

In any case, the planners should watch the currencies of their competitors, and consider carefully any options to locate the project in a country whose currency shows the best chance of being competitive in the vital early years of the new product or plant.

Finally, managers should analyse the competitiveness of their currency not only by reference to its average level or trend (see section 10.2), but also by whatever competitive analysis they have been implying in their past decisions. They may have taken either a peak competitive or a peak uncompetitive value of the currency as the norm, or as their base case. In that case they should evaluate the likely future *ranges* of the real exchange rate against their previous assumption. The assumption may have been made consciously or unconsciously. Either way it should be reviewed from time to time. The average value helps us to assess the probability of future trends in the real exchange rate, rather than whether our company is now relatively competitive or uncompetitive.

10.9 Objections from financial theory

Current financial theorists may not regard the line taken in this chapter as consistent with their model of currency risk. Our view differs from that model in the following respects:

1. It fails to apply the 'random walk' view of currency risk. It implies that real exchange rate movements are more predictable than nominal exchange rates in the longer term, due to the slow tempo of adjustment in commercial markets.
2. It fails to advocate the portfolio approach. Financial theory prefers to manage currency risk as some distribution of possible outcomes, rejecting the notion that the manager can exploit favourable and avoid unfavourable developments.
3. It rejects management by means of financial hedges, in favour of actions in the commercial markets. Such divergences as there are, rest on
   (a) some different perceptions of how real exchange rates move,
   (b) the view taken in chapter 7 about the place of currency management in relation to commercial and other management tasks, and
   (c) to a lesser extent, our narrower definition of this risk, restricting it to the effect of the real exchange rate on competitive *costs*.

10.10 A mini-case study

There is plenty of anecdotal evidence of competitiveness risk. The most memorable quotation may have been Mr Michael Edwardes' remark to the annual conference of the Confederation of British Industry in 1980: If North Sea Oil did this to sterling, then why not 'leave the bloody stuff under the ground'?

An unpublished case study concerns Topcloth, a multinational company with subsidiaries in both USA and UK. In the early 1970s it made a textile machine in the United States until the dollar became uncompetitive and the business began to make heavy losses. The US factory was closed down and production switched to the UK plant. This went well until sterling became uncompetitive in 1979/80. At this point the UK factory was closed and the machine subcontracted to a German manufacturer.

Topcloth had twice been forced to switch its cost from an uncompetitive to a competitive currency area. The management were quite unaware of the currency background, but circumstances forced them to react to it. Had Topcloth been quicker to spot the reason for its successive misfortunes, it might have acted faster and avoided some heavy losses, first in the US, then in the UK.

10.11 Summary

Competitiveness risk is a threat to the competitiveness of a company's costs from a rise in real terms of the currency in which those costs are incurred. The cause of the risk is the interaction between commercial and currency markets, in which prices move at very different speeds.

Competitiveness risk is not a short-term phenomenon. It cannot be managed day by day. It takes longer periods to recognize shifts in real exchange rates, and the management actions to deal with the risk are strategic rather than tactical, and can only be taken infrequently.

The risk affects companies in their commercial rather than in their financial markets, and suitable management action should be taken in the commercial markets as opportunities occur. The action can be on the demand side, by repositioning commercial offerings in less competitive submarkets or segments, or on the supply side by shifting costs into a more competitive currency. This last action is possible because real exchange rates are slower to move and more predictable than nominal rates. Financial market hedges are unlikely to provide suitable answers to problems in the commercial markets.

11

Trading Risk: The Problem

11.1 What is trading risk?

The best illustration of the nature of trading risk is a tender for a contract like the following:

Example 11.1
Our company is in the construction business. It tenders for a large contract. Our costs are incurred in sterling and we wish to realize a price of £10 million. However, it is a condition of the customer's that tenderers must quote a firm price in US dollars. We find that the spot rate is \$1.50 = £1, so we quote a price of \$15 million. Our tender is successful and two years later, when we receive the \$15 million, we find that the best rate at which we can sell the \$15 million spot for pounds is \$2.00 = £1. We therefore receive into our sterling bank account £7.5 million instead of the planned £10 million. Our trading currency loss is £2.5 million, 25 per cent of our desired price.

The loss is in fact

$$£15m \times (1/2.00 - 1/1.50) = -£2.5m$$

which is the price multiplied by the difference between the rate used in the pricing decision (\$1.50) and the rate at which the exchange deal was done (\$2.00). The *pricing decision* is at the heart of this risk.

11.2 Formal definition

From the classification in chapter 8, we can define trading risk as the risk to a business which *commits* itself to a quoted selling price in a currency other than the currency of cost. The risk is caused by possible subsequent movements in the exchange rate between the two currencies. The risk arises in the process of tendering for contracts, or the issue of price lists in foreign currencies, or generally whenever a price is quoted with a currency mismatch between selling price and costs.

The amount of the gain or loss is the amount of the mismatch multiplied by the difference between two exchange rates:

1 the rate assumed or used in the pricing decision, and
2 the rate at which the exchange deal is finally done; in example 11.1 it was \$2.00 = £1, the rate at which the US dollar sales proceeds were sold to produce cash in sterling.

Some of the terms used need to be explained in more detail:

Commitment The business has to commit itself to a price. The commitment does not have to be legal or contractual. A commercial or competitive commitment is enough to trigger this risk. If the business were free to amend its quoted price in the light of the subsequent movement in the exchange rate, this risk would not exist.

Mismatch The exposure may be less than the full quoted price, if the costs include elements denominated or determined in the currency of the price. If the \$15m price in example 11.1 contained a \$4m dollar subcontract and perhaps \$2m materials bought in sterling but with a world market price determined in dollars, these cost elements are not mismatched and should be deducted in computing the mismatch, at \$15m − \$4m − \$2m = \$9m.

Gain or loss The gain or loss is calculated against the hypothetical cash outcome, had the deal been done at the exchange rate used in the pricing decision. It follows that the gain or loss is not an absolute outcome, but a deviation from the outcome *intended* in the pricing decision.

11.3 Trading risk in purchasing

Purchasing in a currency other than the currency of sale causes a mismatch which gives rise to trading risk. In the normal case this risk will be postnatal because in the normal case the pricing decision – the decision to accept a purchase price – occurs at the point of birth, when the transaction is firm.

However, antenatal risk can occur in purchasing. Examples will be given in section 11.12.

11.4 Can trading risks be neutralized by forward or spot deals?

11.4.1 The on-line forward hedge

Example 11.2

Suppose I telephone my Italian supplier today and ask him to quote a price for a machine I need. He quotes L110m payable 90 days from now. My video terminal tells me that Midland Bank is now offering a three months forward rate of L2212–2214 = £1. This means that I could buy L110m forward now for L110,000,000/2212 = £49,728.75. Midland's quotation is the most competitive. So while I am on the line to the Italian supplier, I say *'va bene, grazie!'*, ring off and do the forward deal with Midland Bank. The purchase of the machine and the exchange deal have been concluded 'on line' and I have run no risk of a trading currency loss. The sterling cost of the machine is firm.

My action has locked me into today's forward rate. If on day 90 the spot rate is 2200, I have saved money by buying the lire forward; if the rate is then 2220, my action has cost me extra. What the forward purchase has, in any case, achieved is to give me certainty, for if the three months volatility were as much as 15 per cent either way, which is quite possible, I stood to gain or lose some £7,500 – quite a large uncertainty.

11.4.2 The on-line spot hedge

We learned in chapter 2 and chapter 3, sections 3.4 (covered arbitrage) and 3.7.1 (interest parity), that the outcome might have been very similar if, instead of buying the L110m forward, I had bought them spot and deposited them in a 90-day Eurolire deposit. I should have had to pay sterling rates of interest for 90 days on the sterling used to buy lire spot, and received lire rates of interest on the deposited lire: the interest differential should be equal to the forward discount or premium on the lire.

So if trading risk can be hedged so easily by such simple instruments as forward or spot deals, is it really a problem? It all depends on the sequence of events. Prices are not always agreed 'on line' as in this last example.

11.5 Life-cycle of a trading risk

If we look more closely at the biography of the risk in example 11.1, we find it strangely similar to the life-cycle of a human being. The important stages are:

Conception We quote a price, but we have not yet got a sale. Our customer is not yet committed to our price, but we are.

Birth We become commercially certain that we have won the contract.

Anniversaries Annual reporting dates, on which the foreign currency receivables and payables are 'translated' into the reporting currency, and an interim profit or loss taken.

Death The (spot or forward) exchange deal which sells the foreign currency receivables for the currency of cost or buys the foreign currency payables for the currency of sale.

The death of a trading risk can of course occur before some of the anniversaries, if a forward contract is entered into before the date of the customer's payment.

11.6 The critical antenatal period

The critical period for trading risk is the antenatal period between conception and birth. In contracts this is known as the tender period, during which the tenderer is committed to his price, but his customer is not. This asymmetry is what makes it dangerous for the seller to sell his potential future currency receipt forward. Tenders for contracts provide the most dramatic demonstration of this.

Example 11.3

In our $15 million tender we quoted that price because the current *spot* rate was $1.50 =£1, and we knew no better than to convert our desired £10 million price into US dollars at that rate.

Now suppose we had instead decided to use the three-year *forward* rate of $1.40 = £1 to compute a price of $14 million. We chose the three years rate because we expected to receive our cash in month 36 after the date of our tender. We assumed that the contract would be awarded in month 6 and completed and paid for in month 36 after a 30-month construction period. Our idea was that we could neutralize the exchange risk by an immediate forward sale of the $14 million for £10 million, for month 36.

In fact, however, we lost the award to a competitor. We heard this bad news in month 9. By that time the spot rate had moved to $1.20 = £1 and the 27-months forward rate (to month 36) to $1.12 = £1. We no longer expected to receive $14 million from the customer in month 36, but we remained committed to deliver $14 million to the bank at that time. All exchange deals with banks are binding, as we saw in chapter 2.

So in month 9 we bought \$14m 27 months forward for month 36 at the forward rate of \$1.12 = £1 in order to 'close out' our original forward contract. The dollars bought forward in month 9 would pay off the dollars sold forward in month 0, when we tendered.

That forward purchase of \$14 million at \$1.12 cost £12,500,000. The original forward contract will only produce a receipt of £10,000,000. So we have incurred a straight cash loss for month 36 of £2,500,000, and this time without winning our commercial contract!

Example 11.3 conveys a key lesson: antenatal forward cover actually creates a risk which can turn out worse than the one it was intended to hedge: worse because its worst outcome is combined with the loss of the commercial tender. We might well have incurred a similar loss if we had not covered forward, but only if we had won that commercial contract. The fatal error is to lock into an exchange rate before we are certain that we have the risk.

We shall presently discover some better solutions to antenatal risk than antenatal forward cover.

11.7 'Commercial' certainty: tenders

The antenatal period ends with birth. In section 11.5 we said that birth occurs when the seller is 'commercially' certain that he has a sale.

In the case of the tender for a contract, this is not necessarily at the time when a contract is signed. Nor is it necessarily at the time when a contract comes into force, which could be when some prior conditions (for example exchange control consent by the buyer's central bank) have been met. Birth of the risk occurs when the seller feels sufficiently confident that the contract will go ahead, to accept the commitment of selling the mismatched currency receipts forward. This test of 'commercial certainty' may sound a very fine distinction, but it can be of great practical significance. Several companies in the appendix to chapter 9 are concerned with this issue.

Contractors get to know their customers. Some customers can be relied upon to enter into a contract as soon as they informally telex the winning tenderer that he has the contract. This may be months before the detailed contract has been negotiated and signed. Other customers cannot be trusted that far until they have signed a contract. In other cases again, a local authority in, say, Colombia may be the customer. It can only sign a contract subject to legalization or ratification by the central government of its country, and that legalization may not only take years, but may actually in the end be withheld altogether. The prudent contractor will not put work in hand until he is certain of the order, and in the same way he will not treat the trading risk as born or postnatal. He will not sell his future currency receipts forward until he has reached commercial certainty. That may occur well before or well after the contract is signed.

11.8 'Commercial' certainty: price lists

The case of the foreign currency price list raises the same problem in a different way.

Example 11.4

Our company sells British-made hydraulic pumps to Switzerland, issuing a price list in Swiss francs every quarter. It decides its prices for the 1 April to 30 June quarter on 1 March. In deciding those prices we assume an average exchange rate during April–June of SFr2.60 = £1. This decision is taken on 1 March, but in the four months to 30 June that rate could well be expected to move by say 4 per cent to SFr2.70 or SFr2.50.

A 4 per cent swing is not far from an average expectation of volatility for our mean time-lag of 2.5 months from 1 March to the middle of the quarter, 15 May. And 4 per cent is in most businesses a substantial part of the gross margin, and the kind of deviation from intended margins that managers must identify and control. The uncertainty could be eliminated by selling the receipts forward, but are we commercially certain that the receipts will come?

In this case normal sales in the April–June quarter are SFr6 million. Our experience tells us that this year they may be anything from SFr4.5 to SFr7 million. We are commercially certain of SFr4.5 million as a minimum sale. We regard this as postnatal, and SFr2.5 million as antenatal at this stage. We should therefore sell SFr4.5 million forward and treat SFr2.5 million as an antenatal risk. Commercial certainty defines birth and thus the boundary of antenatal risk.

11.9 Management is concerned with gross margins

All the examples of antenatal risk highlight the management objective of controlling gross margins when there are pricing decisions to make. The risks are too big in relation to the immediate management task to permit a detached portfolio attitude. It is gross margins on these major pricing decisions which are the primary focus of commercial management, and therefore of management as a whole. The risk cannot be managed as a purely financial phenomenon. The risk arises from trading decisions, and must be managed as part of trading performance.

11.10 No antenatal risk without a pricing decision before the sale is certain

Some situations have no antenatal phase.

1 The 'on-line' case in example 11.2, where a British manager agrees his lire buying price on the telephone with his Italian supplier, and simultaneously buys the lire forward: here the risk is not antenatal for either side. If the Italian supplier had quoted a sterling price and agreed it simultaneously on the telephone, he could have sold his sterling forward or spot and incurred no antenatal risk.

2 Where prices are fixed by the market and not by the seller, as in commodity trading: here the risk is not trading risk, because the definition of trading risk requires an active pricing decision.

11.11 The asymmetries of antenatal trading risk

The description and illustrations of antenatal risk bring out the essential asymmetry of this risk, which takes two forms.

11.11.1 The customer does not have it

This is because the customer, unlike the seller, is not committed to the price before his buying decision. In the case of the price list, if the competitive position is that a supplier is expected to keep his price list open for three months, any supplier who does amend his prices within that period will become less attractive to the market and risks losing at least some market share.

The customer can, at the time of his buying decision, compare competing prices, using forward rates to compare them in a single currency, and lock the comparison in by buying his currency forward for the chosen offer.

11.11.2 Nor have some competitors

If any competitors happen to have the required tender currency as their currency of cost, then they have a windfall advantage over the remaining ones. In example 11.3 all tenderers were required to tender in

US dollars. This gave some of them a major risk, but not all of them. If any of them were located in the United States with US dollar costs, they had an asymmetrical advantage over their non-US rivals.

11.12 Intragroup trading risk

Chapter 14 deals with intragroup position risk. Trading risk can be complicated where one group member A sells indirectly via a fellow subsidiary B, possibly in another country. What matters is whether the risk is antenatal, and whether the company with the risk knows when birth occurs. We shall only discuss the relatively common cases.

11.12.1 Tender through local group company

This is the common case where S is the effective contractor with management responsibility, but formally acts as subcontractor to its fellow subsidiary B in the buyer's country. B acts as legal letterhead or façade main contractor. The customer either requires or prefers a nominally local supplier. S is effectively in charge, and S's performance triggers the final customer's main payments under the contract. If that customer delays payment for defective or late performance, the fault will in fact be S's, not B's.

In this case there is no problem. The subcontract price between S and B should be in the same currency as the main contract. S now has the exposure, and all the information needed to manage it.

11.12.2 Price list sales: internal sale in buyer's currency

In this case S sells to B (the local subsidiary) in B's currency, and therefore has the exchange risk. The group as a whole has an antenatal trading risk, and this risk is located with S which also took the pricing decision. If stocks are held by S, so that each sale triggers a delivery by S, the risk is as if B were not interposed. If B holds the stock, then it is important that actual orders from that price list are reported to S with zero or minimum delay.

11.12.3 Price list sales: internal sale in supplier's currency

In this case S sells to B in S's currency, and B should be making the pricing decision, i.e. issue the local currency price list. B has the antenatal risk as if it were buying from a non-Group source. B's exposure is identical with that of the Group, provided all S's costs arise in S's home currency. If S has costs in a third purchase currency P, it should manage its P v. S trading risk as a separate risk.

In all these cases

- the group has costs in S's currency and has quoted a price in B's currency,
- the trading risk is best placed with the group company which decides the price to the external customer,
- if so, that company's exposure is identical with that of the group: by managing it in its own self-interest it is managing it in the group's interest.

11.13 Antenatal trading risk in purchasing

Section 11.3 showed that trading risk in purchasing is normally postnatal. Exceptions occur, however, whenever a purchase at an agreed price is contingent upon subsequent sale. In example 11.1, our company with sterling costs quoted its selling price in dollars. The mismatch was in that case caused by the choice of currency of sale. A similar antenatal mismatch would arise in the following cases.

1 In the paper tissue making industry: UK manufacturers negotiate prices in the winter with a supplier in say Finland in markka (the local currency) on a call-off contract. Amounts called off depend on what orders the manufacturer obtains from UK retail chains during the following summer. The manufacturer has a currency mismatch on his purchase; but the amount of his purchases depends on subsequent sales of uncertain volume to his customers.
2 On a large contract, where a subcontract in a mismatched currency is conditional on the main contract being awarded to the contractor. In example 11.1, this would occur if 20 per cent of the contract price consisted of a French subcontract, priced in French francs. The only commercially safe way to deal with this is to obtain a firm price from the French supplier. If for some reason we cannot get a competitive price from that supplier in US dollars or sterling, we have an antenatal buying risk in French francs. We cannot place a firm order nor buy the FFr20m forward, until we are commercially certain that we have won our main contract.

In both cases the company could sustain a trading loss if the markka or French franc appreciated by the time the company secured its own order.

11.14 The two-stage structure of trading risk management

We saw in chapter 8 that there is one trading risk per pricing decision. This means one per contract tender and one per price list in any currency other than the currency of cost. Most businesses make relatively few pricing decisions, dozens in a year rather than hundreds. The task of managing each trading risk separately should not therefore be excessively costly.

The reader will by now have seen that the central issue of trading risk is the antenatal stage, and that the focus of management is on two objectives: (a) winning the business, and (b) controlling the margin of price over cost at which the orders are won.

The problem is that, during the antenatal period, that margin is in the uncontrolled hands of the currency market. If we have quoted $15 million, hoping to obtain £10 million sterling, then if the exchange rate at which we eventually sell the $15m for sterling rises above $1.50, we shall receive less than £10 million, and thus less than our intended margin.

The risk of this increases with every day that we postpone the exchange deal. As we cannot, however, improve our safety by doing an exchange deal before birth, it follows that any risk averse policy will aim at doing the exchange deal precisely at birth – no sooner and no later.

Consequently the structure of the trading risk management problem is a two-stage structure. In the first antenatal stage the manager manages the risk with the best available means. Then at birth he does an exchange deal which will also constitute the death of the risk. So the antenatal stage is a *bridging* operation from conception to birth. Chapter 12 deals with the means by which the risk can be managed at either stage.

The question whether trading risk is managed in accounting or cash terms, does not really arise because the antenatal stage is managed with an eye on birth whenever birth may occur. Annual reporting dates are immaterial. The question affects position risk (chapter 13), but not antenatal trading risk.

11.15 No management for gain? Managing trading risk after birth

This fundamental framework for the management of trading risk is not intended to imply that this or any other currency risk must be managed defensively, or that the sole objective is to avoid a loss. What is being argued here is that during the antenatal stage of trading risk the commercial interest is dominant, and the commercial interest lies in controlling the profit margin.

On the other hand a practical decision has to be taken about trading risk after birth. The currency risk manager may well at birth decide to leave the risk unhedged, if the company's policy permits this. He will leave it unhedged if he makes a positive judgement that this particular exposure should be left open and managed for gain. It would in practice, however, be illogical if from then on he still managed that risk against the benchmark of the exchange rate used in the pricing decision. By the time of birth the spot rate will normally have moved far enough away from that rate to make it unrealistic to go on managing against that benchmark. As a target it has by then become either too demanding or too undemanding.

However, once the management of the exposure has moved away from that benchmark, the risk is no longer being managed as trading risk, as we have defined it. The exposure should therefore be treated as part of the position risk in the currency concerned. We shall pick this point up in chapter 13.

11.16 Summary

In the antenatal period, trading risk should be managed by one of the antenatal measures discussed in chapter 12. At birth the exposure should either be closed out, perhaps by means of a spot, swap, forward or futures deal; or reclassified as part of the positon risk. The outcome of the trading risk as such would in that latter case be the rate at which the exposure could have been closed out at birth. The primary aim of trading risk management is to achieve an exchange rate no worse than was used in the pricing decision. Position risk on the hand is a dominantly financial management problem, and lends itself to policies designed to gain from currency movements.

12

Managing Trading Risk: The Mechanisms

12.1 Introduction

Chapter 11, sections 11.14–15 explained why trading risks need to be managed in two stages. The normal business objective is to do no worse than the exchange rate used in the pricing decision. As long as this is the objective, the task of managing the antenatal stage of trading risk is inherently defensive. From birth onwards the company is of course free to manage it aggressively for gain, though by that time it is no longer being managed as a trading risk, but as part of position risk.

12.2 Mechanisms available to manage trading risk

Trading risk can be managed by a variety of market instruments and other measures. The most important distinction here is between those which can be used after and before birth (table 12.1). These will now be reviewed.

Table 12.1

Antenatal	Section	Postnatal	Section
avoidance	12.3	spot deal	12.7
ECGD's TTC cover	12.4	forward deal	12.7
currency options	12.5	swap deal	12.8
costing the risk	12.6	futures deal	12.9

12.3 Avoiding the antenatal risk

This is the first of the measures open to the company at the point of conception. It is an attempt to quote the currency of cost without losing the tender to competitors. At first sight it sounds unattractive, boring, simplistic and uncompetitive. In fact, however, it has been used very effectively and competitively. There are broadly three types of situations:

1 formal competitive tenders, where the currency of the tender is formally specified in the invitation to tender,
2 negotiated contracts, where the tender is discussed with the customer while it is being prepared,
3 the issue of price lists.

12.3.1 Where dialogue is possible with buyers

The critical point is whether communication is possible with buyers. This occurs in negotiated contracts and in those price list cases where the buyers are few and professional, so that the seller can contact them and explain the benefit of looking at prices in the currency of cost.

The following attractions of avoidance can be stressed to buyers:

1 The cost of the risk is saved. Every risk is a cost. Antenatal trading risk is a large risk and therefore a large cost. The buyer can expect to be offered a lower price if our business does not have to bear this large risk. Whether the buyer chooses to buy from us or not, his choice must be more attractive if lower prices are offered.
2 In fact the two-way nature of the risk can turn out to the buyer's *further* advantage. It the buyer allows us to quote the currency of our cost, this currency can either fall or rise against the buyer's currency between now and when the buyer makes his choice. If it falls, the buyer gains. If it rises, he remains free to choose a cheaper supplier.
3 In any case the buyer need not bear the risk: at birth, when he makes his choice, he can compare the competing offers at the current forward rates, choose the cheapest and buy his currency forward – the buyer will know exactly what our offer will cost him in his own currency. The buyer cannot lose!

In the special case where the buyer's reason for needing a quotation in, say, rupees is exchange control, we can achieve avoidance by quoting in rupees subject to a currency adjustment clause. This quotes a rupee price, but specifies that the rupee price will be adjusted down or up pro rata to the change in the London closing spot rate of the two currencies between today's rate (date of tender) and the rate on the day he accepts our offer. The price remains a rupee price, but it is in effect fixed in the currency of cost. Antenatal risk is avoided.

Finally, avoidance has been successful even with a multicurrency tender! Where a tender price contained major cost elements in four currencies (say 25 per cent each in dollars, sterling, D-Marks and rurals, the Ruritanian buyer's local currency), the buyer accepted an offer broken down by currency elements, because he was impressed by the cost saving described in item 1 above.

12.3.2 No dialogue possible with buyer

Avoidance is unlikely to be practicable with a price list. However, in the case of the formal tender, it should often be possible to give the buyer a two-tier quotation with two prices.

Example 12.1

The buyer requires a dollar price and our costs are in sterling. As in example 11.3 in chapter 11, we quote a fixed dollar price of $14 million, which at the forward rate is intended to produce £10 million sterling. This fixed dollar price contains a loading of £800,000 for the antenatal risk. We also quote an optional alternative sterling price of £9.2 million, which has not been loaded with that cost. When the buyer comes to make his choice, he takes whichever of these prices, at the then ruling exchange rates, gives him the lower dollar cost, i.e. the first price of $14 million or the £9.2 million bought forward for the estimated forward dates of payment. If sterling falls against the dollar in the antenatal period, the buyer stands to make a substantial saving on the £9.2 million price, compared with a single compliant quotation of $14 million. The second price has, in that case, saved him not only £800,000, but also the fall in the $/£ exchange rate. We have avoided the antenatal risk *and* made ourselves more competitive!

This device has been used successfully. Care must, however, be taken to scrutinize the invitation to tender for any clause that might disqualify the tender if it contains such a 'non-compliant' alternative offer.

Avoidance may well be boring. But it can be a formidable competitive weapon.

12.4 ECGD's tender to contract (TTC) cover

This cover was introduced by the UK Government in 1977 because at that time the Government itself had effectively forced UK exporters to arrange export credits for capital goods contracts in non-sterling currencies. With credits in other currencies, customers were unlikely to accept tenders priced in sterling. The Government had created a trading risk for exporters against which it then felt obliged to offer a form of state-backed insurance. This took the form of the Export Credits Guarantee Department's (ECGD's) tender to contract (TTC) cover. ECGD's normal function is to insure export credit risks for UK exporters.

ECGD's TTC cover is of course for British exporters, but the concept of governmental insurance against antenatal trading risk is not just a British phenomenon. ECGD's French counterpart, COFACE, for example, also offers cover against antenatal currency risk.

When it was first available, the TTC cover made heavy losses for ECGD and the taxpayer, which made it very popular with exporters. In the early 1980s access to sterling export credits was restored, and the terms of the cover were greatly stiffened. It is instructive to compare TTC cover with the currency option (section 12.5). It is significant that TTC cover officially recognizes the special problems of antenatal risk.

In 1990 the conditions of TTC cover are as follows.

- The tender must contain a minimum of £10m UK export content.
- The credit risk in the contract must be covered by one of ECGD's normal facilities for cash or credit contracts (specific guarantee, short-term guarantee or buyer credit).
- TTC cover fails to protect a tender price which cannot be revised after nine months.
- It is offered only for UK exports quoted in US dollars, Canadian dollars, D-Marks, Swiss francs or yen, but other currencies have been approved case by case.
- The premium is 0.1 per cent of insured receipts (i.e. the UK export content) for each tender, plus 2.5–4 per cent (depending on length of insured tender period) for each contract won.
- The insured foreign currency contract receipts *must* be sold forward for sterling when the contract is signed.
- 'Claims' are calculated on the cumulative difference between (a) the outcome of these actual forward contracts, and (b) a benchmark schedule of market forward rates issued by ECGD at the time of tender. ECGD takes the *whole* of any resulting gain, and pays out any loss up to 25 per cent of insured receipts, after deducting the first 1 per cent. Its maximum liability is thus 24 per cent.

The TTC cover's main attraction is the low cost of 0.1 per cent for lost tenders. Its worst drawback is the absolute restriction to nine months' protection. A detailed comparison with the currency option is found in section 12.5.5.

12.5 The currency option

The currency option became a widely traded instrument only in December 1982. It is traded on a number of formal open outcry exchanges, especially the Philadelphia Stock Exchange, and also 'over the counter' (OTC) by many banks.

The currency option is a true 'yes/no' option, and akin to insurance. The hedger pays a premium to the option-writer. In return for this he obtains the right, but *not* the obligation, to buy ('call') or sell ('put') a specified amount of one currency against another on a specified future 'exercise date' and at a stated 'strike price'.

European options can only be exercised on the exercise date, **American** ones at any time up to that date.

Example 12.2

On 1 September in year 1 we could buy an OTC option to sell dollars for sterling at the rate of $1.55 (strike price) on 20 January of year 2 (exercise date). Suppose that on 20 January of year 2 the spot rate turns out to be *either* $1.65 *or* $1.45. If it is $1.65, the option at $1.55 gives us a better rate than spot, we shall exercise it. If it is $1.45, we do better to sell dollars spot: so we allow the option to lapse. Our worst loss is the (with hindsight wasted) cost of the premium, but our potential gain is unlimited.

12.5.1 Option as antenatal currency hedge

If we have used the option to hedge the risk of an antenatal loss, that loss too is potentially unlimited, and is compensated by the gain on the option, less the cost of the premium. In fact, the antenatal offer of a commercial US dollar price representing sterling costs could be described as a currency option that we have written for our customer.

Here is an example of the neatness of the option as a hedge against antenatal risk. A tenderer with sterling costs tenders a US dollar price and buys an option to sell dollars for sterling. The simplified matrix of possible outcomes is shown in table 12.2. In cases 1A and 1B the option itself turns out to be unprofitable, not worth exercising: 1A results in antenatal gain less premium; 1B is the disastrous case in example 11.3 of chapter 11, where the dollar tender price was sold forward for sterling at

Table 12.2

The commercial tender is	Between tender and contract the tender currency	
	1 rises	2 falls
A Won	Option lapsed Antenatal gain realized *less* premium cost	Option exercised Antenatal loss offset by option gain *less* premium cost
B Lost	Option lapsed Loss restricted to premium cost	Option exercised Option gain realized *less* premium cost

birth, the tender was lost and dollar then rose sharply. The option restricts the cost to that of the premium.

In cases 2A and 2B the option turns out to be profitable in its own right. In 2A the option does the job for which it was taken out: in return for the premium cost it compensates for the antenatal loss. In 2B it yields a sheer financial gain (less premium), with no commercial contract won.

12.5.2 Options can look expensive

Options, if correctly priced, look expensive to those companies who underestimate the cost of the risk of quoting for business in a mismatched currency. The premium is of course the measure of the valuable right which the option confers on its buyer. It is determined by the current relationship between the spot rate and the exercise price, by the expected volatility of the spot rate, and by the time to expiry. An option market is essentially a market in the volatility of the underlying instrument, in this case exchange rates.

The theory of option pricing is centred on the Black–Scholes model. A full account of options, trading strategies and hedging strategies for option writers is found in BIS (1986). Excellent introductions are in Heywood (1984b), Back (1988) and Cooper (1985, 1987). We shall here cover the currency management principles only.

Whether the option is economic for the antenatal tenderer, therefore depends on the size of the premium and on his chance of winning his commercial contract. Premium rates began very low in December 1982. When exchange rate volatility rose sharply in 1984, some option writers burned their fingers. They had underestimated volatility. Since then

OTC premiums have seen peak levels of 3 per cent for three months and 6 per cent for six months, declining by 1987 to around 2.5 per cent for three months and around 4.5 per cent for six to nine months for US dollar/sterling options. Even these reduced levels represent a heavy cost for traders who issue tenders or currency price lists. A cost of 4.5 per cent for a tender with a nine months' validity is high in relation to margins in this class of business. A contractor who can expect to win one tender in ten and uses options whenever costs and price are mismatched, bears a 45 per cent loading on his successful currency tenders, less a suitable allowance for the purely financial gains in box 2B in table 12.2.

A contractor therefore needs to use options selectively. His alternatives are

- not to use options, e.g. if TTC cover solves the problem;
- greater selectivity in tendering: some contractors waste far too much tendering expense (which they may well underestimate) on contracts they have very little hope of winning;
- to cut the cost of options by reducing the degree of protection; for example by buying 'out of the money' options (i.e. options at exercise prices which represent a loss against the current market price of 'underlying' instrument, the forward contract maturing at the exercise date: out of the money options are cheaper); alternatively, option 'derivatives' like 'knock-in options' can be constructed for almost any desired risk profile, at costs appropriate to that profile (Duker, 1989; Ducros, 1989);
- buying an option on an option;
- to construct synthetic do-it-yourself options, using the delta hedging technique described in BIS (1986) and Cooper (1985); it is not free from other risks and burdens, and involves holding a portfolio of market assets or liabilities in the currency concerned.

12.5.3 Traded v. OTC options

Currency option trading began in earnest when the Philadelphia Stock Exchange began to trade them in 1982. Options are now also traded on a number of exchanges other than Philadelphia, including the International Stock Exchange and LIFFE in London. The markets in London are much less liquid. However, by 1988 the great majority of option dealing was in the OTC or bank market.

Competition from Philadelphia is very strong, especially since Philadelphia rearranged its trading hours to cover those of the London markets despite the time difference. Philadelphia is now open 0430 to 1430 Philadelphia time for D-Mark, yen, sterling, Swiss franc, Australian dollar, Canadian dollar, French franc and ECU options.

To make trading on formal markets possible, instruments have to be standardized commodities, and therefore of limited variety. Traded currency options are available only in a few currencies like the eight just listed, against the US dollar, and of standard

- unit amounts
- exercise dates
- strike prices
- strike price intervals

For example, on the Philadelphia Stock Exchange, sterling options are in £31,250 units, strike prices are traded at 2.5 US cent intervals. There are four quarterly exercise dates in March, June, September and December, plus the two nearest-term months. The exercise date is the Saturday before the third Wednesday of the month. The exercise cycles (maturity periods) are 1, 2, 3, 6, 9 and 12 months. Philadelphia traded about 10 million contracts in 1988, 33.6 per cent in D-Marks, 29 per cent in yen, 13.6 per cent in sterling, 12.4 per cent in Swiss francs.

The rigidities of the traded option markets can be inconvenient. In any case they reduce the accuracy of a hedge. OTC options are tailored to the bank customer's requirements. On the other hand, as tailored options are harder for banks to hedge, they cost more. Whether a corporate hedger is better off with a cheaper traded option depends above all on the internal cost to the hedger of the formal system of margin calls and other paperwork.

Currency options are limited in their maturity reach (usually 6, 9 or at most 12 months) and in the amounts in which single trades can be done. This may limit their usefulness for large tenders.

12.5.4 Option derivatives

In the mid-1980s a great many new instruments have been marketed, mainly by banks. Many of them are derived from options, futures, swaps and some more traditional instruments like forward contracts. A few are discussed here because they illustrate what is and is not an effective hedge against antenatal trading risk. (Good texts here are Sarwal (1989), also Duker (1989) and Ducros (1989) in *The Treasurer*.)

(*a*) *The break forward (Midland Bank) or forward with optional exit (FOX, marketed by Hambros)*

The bank's customer enters into a forward contract, say to sell US dollars for sterling on day 180 at a special forward rate f, with an option to reverse that contract at exit rate x.

Technically, this is a binding forward contract to *sell* dollars for sterling at f and an option under which the customer can *buy* dollars for sterling at x.

Exit rate x values dollars at a 'spread' $x-m$ above the market forward rate m. The rate f values dollars below m, so that m lies between x and f. The rates might for example be

$$f = \$1.62 \text{ per } £1 = 61.73\text{p per } \$1$$
$$m = \$1.61 \text{ per } £1 = 62.11\text{p per } \$1$$
$$x = \$1.59 \text{ per } £1 = 62.89\text{p per } \$1$$

It is usual to choose x and f so that no further premium is payable to the bank for the option. As the bank's customer is or would be buying dollars at x and selling them at f, both x and f are less favourable to the customer than the market forward rate m. *The option spread $x-m$ or the forward loading $m-f$ take the place of the up-front premium charged in the straight option.*

The customer incurs *either* the option spread, if he uses his exit option, *or* the forward loading if he does not. If the spot rate s on the exercise date values the dollar above x, then it is obviously profitable for the customer to exit. However, the customer is also better off exiting as long as s puts the dollar below x, but by not more than the forward loading. In other words, the customer's break-even point for using the exit is where $s = x - m + f$; in our example, 62.51p.

A UK exporter could use this break forward or FOX to hedge his antenatal risk. He too would exit above the break-even point $s = x - m + f$, but not if s is below that rate. As the option spread and the forward loading may well be of different sizes, the costs which replace the premium can vary according to where s turns out to be.

We assume in what follows that the exporter used m as the rate for his pricing decision. He will therefore calculate his antenatal gains and losses against m. With the above rates assumed for x, m and f, the exporter's cost is $f - m = 0.38$p per dollar if the exit option is lapsed, or $x - m = 0.78$p if it is exercised.

The effect can be illustrated from the example in section 12.5.1, using the above rates for x, m and f, as in table 12.3.

Compared with the straight option in section 12.5.1, the exporter

- pays no up-front premium;
- pays the forward loading of maximum $f - m$ if the spot value of the dollar on maturity falls short of break-even;
- pays the 'spread' of $m - x$ if it exceeds break-even (see figure 12.1).

In the table and in figure 12.1, the 'effect of FOX' represents the overall difference (including the cost of FOX) between the unhedged

Table 12.3

Commercial tender	On the forward contract date the spot value s of the \$ (tender currency) is	
	Above $x - m + f$ *exit used* effect of FOX: $m - x$	Below $x - m + f$ *exit unused* effect of FOX: $f - s$
A Won	Unlimited AG $= s - m$ Cost: $m - x$	Unlimited AL $= s - m$ matched by FG Cost: $f - m$
B Lost	No forward Cost: $m - x$	Unlimited FG Cost: $f - m$

AG = antenatal gain $= s - m$; AL = antenatal loss $= s - m$; FG = gain on forward contract $= m - s$.

As the break-even point between gain and loss is m, and the break-even for exit is $x - m + f$, AG, AL and FG can all have small negative values between m and $x - m + f$. With the values assumed in this example the break-even for exit ($x - m + f = 62.51$p) values the dollar above $m = 62.11$p. When s is in this 0.30p range, then for example the AL in the right-hand column is in fact an AG and the FG an FL (loss on forward).

effect and the effect with FOX. In the right-hand column, this is $f - s = (f - m) - (s - m)$.

How economic the break forward or FOX is, must depend on where the bank sets f and x. Rates need to be competitive because the active exporter can otherwise replicate the transaction by shopping around for his own forward and straight option at market rates, with deferred terms for the straight option premium.

(*b*) *The cylinder or collar option*

Here the bank's customer buys an option to sell, say, US dollars for sterling at x and writes an option for the bank under which the bank can sell the same amount of dollars for sterling at y; x values dollars below the current forward rate f, y above it. The customer will use his option if the spot value of the dollar is below x, the bank if it is above y. Between x and y neither option will be exercised, so that within that range the customer will deal at the spot rate. The customer obtains complete protection at low values of the dollar, but not at values above y.

An exporter who has issued a tender in US dollars needs protection against both very high and very low values of the dollar, low if he wins his tender and high if he loses it; for in that last case the bank can call upon him to deliver dollars at y, which he may have to buy at the market spot rate at a potentially unlimited loss.

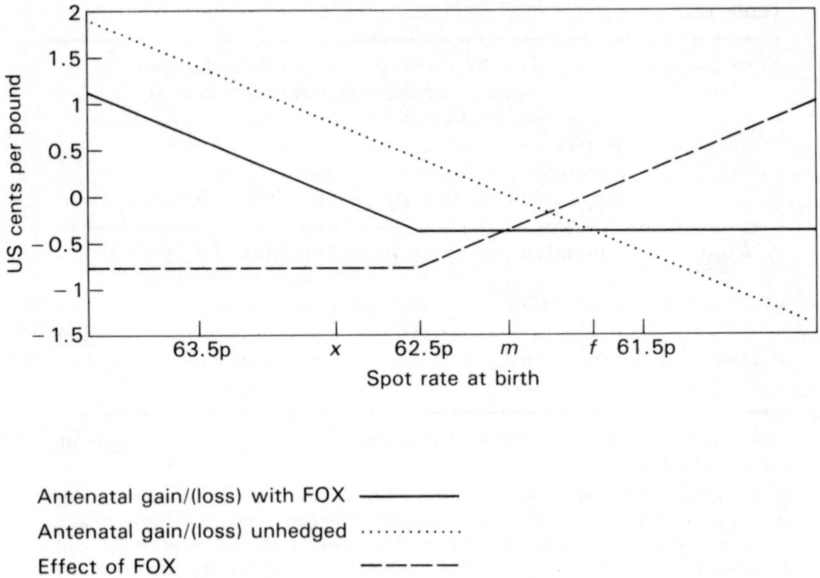

Figure 12.1 Effect of FOX on antenatal exposure ($x = 62.89$, $f = 61.73$, exit break-even at $x + f - m$)

The collar option and the break forward are thus opposites. The break forward protects the open-ended risk of a worst outcome beyond *x* or *f*, but not any outcome within the inner range between *x* and *f*. On the other hand the collar option protects within a finite range up to *y*, but not against the open-ended risk above *y*. An exporter with antenatal risk would therefore find the break forward appropriate and the collar option inappropriate to his needs.

(*c*) *The participating forward*

The bank's customer here

1 buys an option from the bank at rate *f* and
2 simultaneously writes an option for the bank at the same rate *f*, but for a lower amount, say 25 per cent of the amount of the option bought.

Both options are for the sale (or both for the purchase) of say US dollars for sterling. The effect here is a straight-line reduction in the gain or loss from a simple option by 25 per cent. The bank's customer has 75 per cent, the bank 25 per cent of that gain or loss. Once again if the percentage is struck at a point where the bank is exactly remunerated for the option it is writing, the premium cost is zero.

This instrument is suitable as a hedge against antenatal risk in the sense that it protects the downside absolutely at the exporter's option strike price *f*. It also gives him an unlimited upside potential, but he is left with a risk of losing 25 per cent of the potentially unlimited rise in the spot rate, whereas the straight option and the break forward or FOX give him 100 per cent protection against that risk. However, the zero premium version again gives the exporter an outright saving of the option premium, as does the zero premium collar.

To sum up, the straight option and the break forward or FOX act as hedges against antenatal risk, the collar and the participating forward do not.

Figure 12.2 shows the comparative profiles of the above three derivatives.

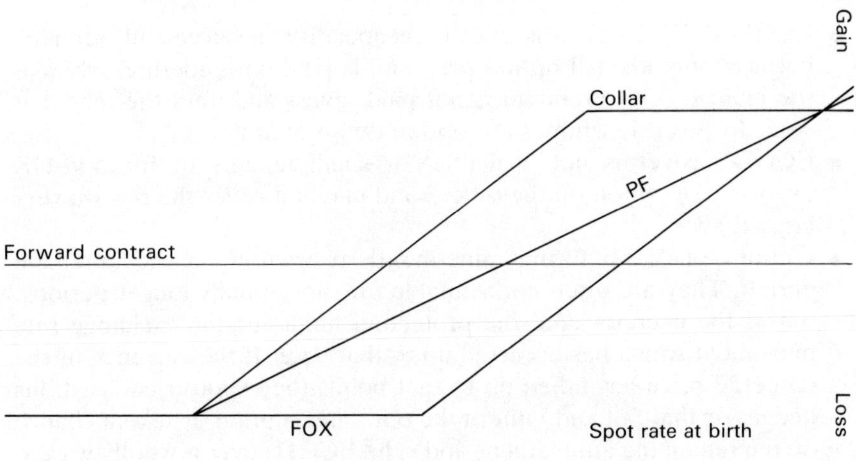

Figure 12.2 Profiles of collar, FOX and participating forward (PF)

(*d*) *Shared currency option under tender (SCOUT)*

This very different instrument is a straight currency option to protect a mismatched tender price, but taken out by the *customer* who has invited tenders. That customer then allocates the cost and the benefit of the option to as many tenderers as have their costs in the currency which can be *bought* in the option. If there are three such tenderers and the option costs 3 per cent, then each pays only 1 per cent and saves 2 per cent. SCOUT is unfortunately useful only where there are a number of tenderers with the same currency of cost (Sarwal, 1989).

(e) Hambros' Tender Risk Avoidance (EXTRA)

EXTRA is available to exporters with sterling costs tendering a US dollar price of up to $2.5 million, subject to some restrictions, but at a premium rate below the market option premium.

There are several other option derivatives to deal with the tender to contract problem. Some leave the exporter with a first loss; others restrict or eliminate gains on unsuccessful tenders, and take account in the premium of an agreed chance of success of the tender.

12.5.5 Comparing straight options with TTC cover

The overall cost of TTC cover and the straight option has come to be broadly comparable for successful tenders, but their profiles differ significantly:

- ECGD's TTC cover is much cheaper for unsuccessful tenders, because only a small option premium is paid on tendering, whereas the main ECGD premium is not paid unless and until the tender is won. In this it resembles the option on an option.
- ECGD's cover is not available for small tenders or for non-UK exports; the option on the other hand may not cover the risk on very large tenders.
- Options place no formal nine-month restriction on the antenatal period. They are often not available for substantially longer periods, but at the exercise date the protection holds for the exchange rate movement which has occurred up to that date. If the currency of the tendered price has fallen up to that point, the exporter can cash his hedge for that fall and either take out a new option or take a chance on the remaining antenatal period. The ECGD cover is wholly wasted after nine months.
- Options do not have ECGD's restrictions on the settlement. The option purchaser has no first loss of 1 per cent, no ceiling claim of 25 per cent, and he can cash his gains on a lost tender if the option is profitable.

The upshot is that where both instruments are available, the choice may well depend on the tenderer's chances of winning his contract. If they are poor, the TTC cover should be taken.

12.6 Costing the risk

In many situations, insurance schemes like ECGD's TTC cover and currency options may be either unavailable or inappropriate, or just uneconomic. The contract might be too small for TTC cover, or too large for currency options, or in a currency in which neither is available, or the antenatal risk might arise from a price list where the cost of options is felt to be uneconomic. Avoidance is not always practicable.

In such situations the company has no alternative but to cost the risk. This process is similar to self-insurance. Self-insurance can, however, cost more than external insurance, especially for intolerable concentrations of risk. If an intolerable risk is properly quantified, it is only too likely to make the tender uncompetitive.

This has misled some companies into thinking that the very recognition of the risk as a cost is in some sense optional and potentially uncompetitive. Antenatal risk is itself a cost, and a handicap *vis-à-vis* a lucky competitor who happens to have his costs in the required currency. This owes nothing to how we manage the risk. The fortunate competitor will not have any cost at all, irrespective of whether our cost takes the form of an option or TTC premium or an internal contingency. The contingency cost allowance replaces the cost of TTC or the option, and will be less competitive only to the extent that the risk is of intolerable size.

Quantifying the cost of an antenatal risk is in fact technically difficult. The correct evaluation of the cost depends on whether the potential size of the loss is intolerable or not. If not, then the cost is equal to the appropriate actual or hypothetical currency option premium. If yes, then the cost is higher, and needs to be derived from the realistically worst currency outcome of the antenatal risk. In other words, if the most that the exchange rate can reasonably be expected to move in nine months is 25 per cent, then that is the 'worst case' rate to use in the calculation. This cost is then built into the cost estimate. This, however, means quantifying the cost of the risk at a level substantially higher than the option or TTC premium. Unfortunately this will be far from uncommon, as many antenatal risks are of intolerable size, even in price-list business.

What does not automatically follow is the need to add the cost of the risk to the selling price. Whether the price can be raised depends on whether this will make it uncompetitive. If it cannot be raised, the company has to work out its rock bottom margin, below which it would prefer not to quote for the business at all.

Example 12.3

For a tender the original cost estimate was £9 million, and the commercial manager's minimum selling price £10 million. The cost of the antenatal risk is assessed at £1.5 million, making the total cost £10.5 million and the corresponding sterling equivalent price £11.5 million. The commercial manager believes that a competitive price is $15 million. The period from contract to average date of receipt of cash is 3 years, and the current 3-year forward rate is $1.40 = £1. $15 million at 1.40 gives an expected out-turn of around £10,714,000. Can the company live with a price which is a mere £214,000 above the adjusted cost? That is the decision to be taken. (This is of course a short-cut calculation using the forward rate for a single average future date. In practice a separate calculation would be made for the various forward dates when dollars are to be received.)

The decision process is complex and above all *multidisciplinary*. The currency manager has to evaluate the cost of the risk, the commercial manager has to assess the competitive price and the minimum profit which his trading account can stand. Both have an interest in getting their judgements right, because neither will have a job if the company either makes an unsustainable loss or fails to win contracts.

This process of costing the risk brings us to the heart of the problem of antenatal risk. If an unwelcome cost emerges, the team must review again whether one of the other tools, and especially avoidance, is not less painful in the circumstances. Yet none of the other tools may in fact be available, and the final decision must be whether to abandon this tender altogether.

The principles of managing antenatal risk are well illustrated by the case of mismatched sales from price lists.

Example 12.4

Bendydinks Inc. sells bendy toys to Japan. Its costs are in US dollars, its prices quoted in price lists issued to its Japanese distributors for each calendar quarter a week before the quarter begins. The list in force from 1 April to 30 June is issued on 24 March, and the price calculations and commercial decisions are made using forward yen/dollar rates as they stood on 17 March. The average forward rate, weighted by the expected pattern of yen receipts over the period 1 July to 30 September (after 90 days effective credit) is Y125 = $1.

Bendydinks' managers are commercially certain that they will achieve minimum sales of Y200 million from this price list, and regard a maximum of Y300 million as possible. This implies that Y200 million are postnatal, and can therefore be sold forward.

The remaining Y100 million are antenatal, and the risk should be managed by means of either options or costing the risk. Avoidance is excluded for commercial reasons and TTC cover is not available. The choice will take into account the probability distribution of the uncertain Y100 million sales and the cost of options or option derivatives. Many companies in Bendydinks' shoes would buy yen put options for a percentage (say 75 per cent) of the Y100 million. The percentage would depend on the probabilities and costs.

12.7 Spot and forward hedges

We are now ready to review the *postnatal* tools for managing trading risk. We saw in chapter 11, section 11.14 that the management of trading risk is a two-stage affair. All the devices for managing antenatal risk serve to bridge the antenatal period. All presuppose that the risk will be closed out at birth by an exchange deal or a futures contract. TTC cover in fact makes forward contracts obligatory.

Chapter 3 showed how interest parity ensures that spot and forward hedges have very similar financial effects. This is because the forward premium or discount tends to be equal to the Eurocurrency interest differential.

Example 12.5

Super Alloys Inc. with US dollar costs wishes to hedge the receipt of L300 million from an Italian customer three months from today. The most competitive quotations obtained by its London treasury operation are:

Three months Eurocurrency deposits (% per annum)	
Lire	12½–12
Dollars	7¹⁄₁₆–6¹⁵⁄₁₆

Foreign exchange rates	
Spot	L1359¼–1359¾ = $1
3 months forward	15.00–18.00 dis

Super Alloys could sell the L300 million forward at the rate of (1359.75 + 18 =) 1377.75, producing $217,746.32

Alternatively, it could borrow L300 million at 12.5 per cent, and simultaneously sell them spot for dollars at the rate of L1359.75. This would produce $220,628.79. If Super Alloys then used that receipt to repay an existing Eurodollar borrowing, it would during the three months pay 12½ per cent per annum for the lire, and save 7¹⁄₁₆ per cent per annum on the dollars. That is a difference per annum of 5⁷⁄₁₆ per cent. The extra interest cost is therefore $3/12 \times 5.4375 \times 1/100 \times$ \$220,628.79 = \$2,999.17. The net total dollar proceeds from this hedge are therefore \$220,628.79 − \$2,999.17 = \$217,629.62, just \$116.70 or 0.017 per cent less than from the forward hedge. When the L300 million are duly received on day 91, Super Alloys uses that receipt to repay the borrowing.

The example illustrates the similarity between the financial outcomes of spot and forward hedges. There are, however, some important practical differences between them:

1 The outcome will vary to the extent that the marginal interest rates which the company incurs or saves are not Eurocurrency interest rates. If, in the above example, Super Alloys had repaid domestic dollar instead of Eurodollar borrowings, then its interest gain would be at the domestic rate of interest, which is likely to differ from the Eurodollar interest rate.
2 In any case, if the spot hedge had caused Super Alloys to *deposit* dollars (instead of repaying debt) and receive Eurodollar interest, it would save less dollar interest due to the bid–offer spread between deposit and borrowing rates.
3 Through interest parity, the forward contract is the equivalent of a *fixed* interest borrowing and deposit. If our actual interest terms arising from the spot deal are at *variable* rates, differences will arise from that cause.
4 The spot hedge is particularly convenient if the currency sold is borrowed on overdraft. The forward contract causes some administrative burdens and inconvenience because it has to be actioned on maturity. An overdraft can simply be continued, for example if the customer's dollars in example 12.3 arrive late.
5 For many currencies, forwards are only available for relatively short periods like 6 or 12 months, because the reach of the forward market tends to be limited to the reach of the fixed interest market in any currency. Consequently, for these currencies spot deals with borrowings/deposits at variable interest rates (rollovers) can be arranged for much longer periods. The short maturity stretch applies more to minor currencies. For major traded foreign exchange rates, like dollar/sterling, maturities of up to 5 or even 15 years are often available.
6 Spot and forward deals both require credit limits with the banks concerned, but forward deals take up less limit than borrowings.
7 Forward contracts are a wholesale instrument, and are not normally available in amounts of less than, say, £100,000, nor for customers

with inadequate credit limits (futures are another solution for this, see section 12.9).

8 The most important difference between the outright forward and the spot hedge is that the forward deal does not change assets or liabilites during the period of the hedge and therefore cannot have a gearing effect, whereas a spot deal can result in extra debt and therefore gearing.

In example 12.5, if Super Alloys has to borrow the lire for the spot deal, this could on the face of it add to the debt on the balance sheet. However, if the dollars for which the lire are sold are immediately used to repay $217,629.62 debt, as was in fact done, then one debt has replaced another and there will be no gearing effect.

Example 12.6: using set-off letters

On the other hand, let us suppose a British company with sterling costs and a sterling overdraft contracts in dollars, but this time with costs incurred in Swiss francs. For its spot hedge it must sell dollars for Swiss francs. The company needs to deposit the Swiss francs because it has no debt to repay in that currency. This would on the face of it increase the gearing, because it creates overlapping assets and liabilities. However, the company can avoid that effect by exchanging set-off letters with the bank providing the overdraft and depositing the francs with that bank. Its balance sheet will show only the net amount of the overdraft balance less the sterling value of the Swiss francs. Once again a spot hedge has been achieved without increasing the company's gearing.

The use of this set-off technique can be expensive where it causes banks to widen their bid–offer spreads. This will occur where the cross-currency set-off is set aside for the purpose of the supervisory authority's calculation of capital adequacy. The Bank of England, for example, does not permit such netting on the balance sheets of banks supervised by it.

12.8 Using the interbank swap as a hedge

The interbank swap was described in chapter 2, section 2.7. It has to be distinguished from the (bilateral) currency swap, which tends to be longer term, can be between non-bank parties, and will be described in chapter 15.

Example 12.7

Intraders Inc. swaps $100,000 into D-Marks for three months. The spot rate is DM1.90 = $1 and the three months swap rate is 2.00pf. Intraders on day 2 receives DM190,000 for \$100,000, and on day 91 receives (190,000/1.88 =) \$101,063.83 in return for the DM190,000.

The swap consists of two offsetting deals, whose two spot rate elements (\$100,000 in example 12.7) cancel out on maturity. The other element (\$1063.83) – the swap rate – represents the interest rate differential for the intervening period during which the user's currency position has been transferred from one currency (\$) to another (DM). It should be balanced out by the different rates of interest incurred or saved on the two currencies during the period of the swap.

In total and on its own, the swap as such is therefore not a hedge at all. It can act as a hedge only for the period to maturity. It can, however, become a hedge if the spot leg is neutralized by an offsetting spot deal.

Example 12.8: a synthetic forward hedge

Intraders expects a DM190,000 receipt on day 91. So it enters into the swap in example 12.7 and a simultaneous spot sale of D-Marks for dollars. As both deals are done in much more liquid markets than the outright forward, the combined spreads may be less than that of the alternative outright forward.

The combined swap and spot deals will be the exact equivalent of an outright forward, with no balance sheet and gearing effect.

12.9 Futures contracts as a hedge

Futures contracts were described in chapter 2. If a futures contract exactly (in amount and maturity date) hedges a crystallized postnatal exposure, it should within narrow limits counteract the currency result of the exposure, just like a forward contract. It too locks the hedger into the market rate structure at the time the hedge is established. As the futures market and the 'cash' foreign exchange market are arbitraged against each other, the futures price should be close to the forward rate.

So what are the criteria by which we should choose between the futures and the forward market?

1 The futures market is more accessible to the small business, too small to have exposures or credit limits big enough for the wholesale forward market.
2 Businesses large enough to use the wholesale markets do not generally use currency futures; they find the margin procedures with their frequent small cash transactions administratively burdensome. Overall, futures markets tend to be more expensive to use for that

reason. Corporates do of course use the futures markets for interest rate hedging.

3 On the other hand the margin system does eliminate counterparty credit risk. Bank failures do occur, and business customers are not always protected against loss.

12.10 Timing uncertainty

A major problem in managing trading risk is to assess accurately the maturity date for which the risk should be hedged at birth. Problems can be due to errors in cash forecasting, customers paying late, and uncertain sales volumes.

The uncertainty is a major feature of *price list* business. On the other hand price list business tends to consist of large numbers of small transactions which in modern conditions can be averaged and hedged for peak dates each month. Predictable patterns are common. All this arises even more acutely in position risk (chapter 16, section 16.3). However, the sheer size of some large, irregular contract receipts makes the control and handling of that problem more critical.

12.10.1 Currency bank accounts

Currency bank accounts are the most convenient solution. It is often best to use a domestic bank with which we have an overdraft, so as to make set-off arrangements easier (see example 12.6). Where such an account is overdrawn, it is a currency overdraft, referred to in item 4 of the list in section 12.7. Where such an account is in credit, it can be used like the Swiss franc deposit in item 8 (section 12.7). Whenever the customer's payment reaches an interest-bearing account which is not a time-deposit or a term borrowing, it effortlessly accommodates any elasticity in the timing of the customer's remittance, as part of the process of operating a spot hedge.

Currency bank accounts can also be used to deal with original hedges in the forms of swaps, outright forwards or futures deals. The benefit of these accounts is always to take the strain of the time difference between the unknown actual date of arrival of the customer's funds and the committed maturity date of the original forward, swap or futures hedge. As long as we are free to have the currency account overdrawn or in credit, it makes little difference whether the buyer's payment arrives before or after the maturity date of the hedge.

12.10.2 Forward options

Forward options are not 'yes/no', but 'when' options. They are ordinary forward contracts with a bank, except that they mature on whatever date the bank's client chooses during an agreed option period of say 15 days. Forward options have become less popular: they are costly and they do not protect against arrival of the funds after the end of the option period. They are costly because the forward rate quoted by the bank is the one for the first or last day of the option period, whichever gives the bank the best rate. So the longer the option period, the greater the cost.

12.10.3 Rolling forward contracts over

A forward contract is rolled over by entering into a further foward contract at the time of settling the original one. The transaction is in fact an interbank swap. Rolling over has lost some of its popularity to the use of currency bank accounts. The reason is that rolling over is administratively burdensome, and subject to further uncertainty at the end of each new forward contract as to when the customer's remittance will finally arrive. A whole series of further forward contracts may be needed before the buyer's funds finally arrive.

12.11 Conclusions on hedging at birth

Generally, currency accounts should be used to deal with timing differences, where the amounts are relatively small. For the original hedge, the use of futures contracts is most favourable for the small business. Corporates should look at the relative costs of spot-and-swaps and spot hedges, coupled with simple set-off arrangements, before assuming that forward contracts are the best answer.

12.12 Summary

The antenatal hedging problem is the most difficult one. Avoidance is so much more economic than other solutions that it should always receive serious consideration. Where available, the ECGD TTC cover – or its equivalents outside the UK – should be considered, especially by exporters with a poor strike rate of successful tenders. For many others the currency option is the most economic solution. Derivatives like break forward or FOX, or knock-in options, or options on options should be considered as variants of the straight option. Where none of these are feasible or economic, the risk must be costed.

At birth the risk should be closed out by one of the hedges reviewed unless control of the intended margin is not a major objective of the business.

13
Position Risk

13.1 Introduction and definition

Many academic writers regard economic risk as the only currency risk to be managed. Many managers on the other hand seem to recognize only the risk that we call position risk. This chapter discusses what is a zero position exposure. In chapter 8 the exposure was described as a mismatch of committed future cash inflows and outflows in a 'foreign' currency: cash inflows and outflows which the business regards as certain to occur at prices or amounts that it regards as committed, in the sense that they do not depend on future commercial choices of the company or its customers or suppliers. The threat which causes position risk, it will be recalled, is from changes in the nominal, not the real exchange rate. Trading risk causes one exposure per pricing decision. Position risk causes one per currency; each position exposure must, however, be subdivided by maturity dates. We have used some expressions which need a closer look.

13.1.1 'Mismatch . . . in a currency'

This simply means a net position which is not zero.

13.1.2 'Future cash inflows and outflows'

This expression is equivalent to assets and liabilities, plus any committed items which are not yet on the balance sheet, such as uninvoiced postnatal trading risks, or items like dividends and royalties which are certain but not yet accrued (see section 13.2.1).

There is an important choice. Non-monetary transactions, mainly fixed assets or inventories, can be valued at their market values or at their book values; the choice depends on whether the company wishes to manage its position risk in cash or in accounting terms.

13.1.3 'Foreign' currency

In most companies this will be any currency other than the reporting currency; but strictly it is any currency other than a company's yardstick currency (chapter 9, section 9.9) in which it monitors its net worth and operating performance.

13.1.4 Flows regarded as 'certain'

Certainty here means commercial rather than contractual certainty: managers must feel confident enough to act on it (chapter 11, sections 11.7–8).

13.1.5 Distinguishing position risk from other currency risks

'Certain to occur' distinguishes position risk from antenatal trading risk; 'committed prices' distinguish position risk from competitiveness risk: 'committed' here means that prices do not depend on a pricing decision which the business has yet to make.

So if Highland Essentials plc has issued a price list in US dollars for its sales to the USA of Scotch whisky, and if its managers are commercially certain that at least $300,000 sales will result at those prices, but think it possible that the total will come to $380,000, then the $300,000 are part of its US dollar position, but the extra $80,000 has to be managed as antenatal trading, not position risk (chapter 11, section 11.8).

13.2 Quantifying the position exposure

Exposure is the amount at risk. To measure the amount, we need to choose between the accounting and cash flow views of position risk (section 13.4).

The economic view, which values the *business* at the present value of its prospective future cash flows, is not relevant: we are not here trying to value the *business* as such. Position risk is the risk from nominal currency movements to transactions which are known to face the company in the future, at prices which are already known and do not require future commercial pricing decisions by the company.

Financial theory does not recognize this risk as one to be managed in this form and against fluctuations in nominal exchange rates. Most managers, however, do regard this as something they ought to manage, no doubt because they need to give priority to commercial and other intermediate objectives, and because the exposure can powerfully affect the financial gearing. These management priorities were discussed in chapters 7 and 9.

13.2.1 Position risk includes all committed *items*

The position in a given currency includes items which are not yet on an accounting balance sheet. Transactions only enter the accounting system when they are invoiced or implemented, not at the earlier stage at which they become contractual or commercial commitments. So a contractual delivery of goods, in or out, will not enter the balance sheet until it has occurred.

Chapter 11, section 11.15, suggested that trading risks left unhedged at birth should from birth onwards be managed as part of the position exposure in the currency concerned. This is because after birth it is no longer sensible or realistic to manage trading risks against the benchmark of the exchange rate used in the pricing decision. The dividing line depends on the management intention.

Similarly items like dividends, royalties or interest charges which are bound to fall due, are part of the position irrespective of whether they are already on the balance sheet.

13.2.2 Treatment of hedged items

The treatment of existing hedges evidently gives some people conceptual problems. The effect of all specific hedges is

1 to fix the value of the hedged transaction in the currency for which it has been hedged. e.g. covered forward, and
2 to remove it from the company's position in the currency in which it was originally denominated; the DM10,000 which have been sold forward for US dollars are now part of the company's US dollar, not its D-Mark position.

Where a forward contract is *not* earmarked as a hedge against a *specific* exposure, financial managers who take the cash flow view of position exposure, should value it at its market value (the difference between the rate in the forward contract and the current forward rate for the same maturity date: that difference may be a gain or a loss). Similarly currency options should be valued at market value, if any. The treatment of *interbank swaps* and bilateral *currency swaps* should be analogous to that of forward contracts.

None of these questions arise with the *spot hedge*. As the hedge is an immediate currency deal, all the items are already on the balance sheet in their correct currencies.

We have looked at the valuation of hedged items or hedges from the point of view of the currency manager. The applicable accounting conventions are another matter, and must be kept distinct. Interestingly, the US accounting standard SFAS 52 recognizes the ambivalence of forward contracts by using different language when describing forward contracts which are not specifically earmarked. SFAS 52 treats a forward contract, which is initiated as a specific hedge, as an integral part of the item hedged. If a US company enters into a forward contract specifically in order to hedge a DM10,000 receivable, SFAS 52 requires the gain or loss on the forward contract to 'be deferred and included in the measurement of the basis of' the DM10,000 receivable.

However, where the forward contract is not entered into as a specific hedge, SFAS 52 detaches that forward contract as a separate transaction, and values it as an instrument in its own right:

1 Where it is an *unspecific hedge,* the forward premium or discount must be valued separately from the spot rate element of the forward rate, and apportioned over the period of the contract. This recognizes the premium or discount as the equivalent of an interest transaction (see chapter 16, example 16.3).
2 Where, on the other hand, the forward contract is *not entered into as a hedge* at all, it must be valued at its market value on the reporting date.

The UK standard SSAP 20 treats the specific hedge in the same way as SFAS 52, but does not discuss the other two cases.

13.3 The yardstick currency

The yardstick currency was briefly referred to in chapter 9, section 9.9. We take a simple case where International Traders plc has positions in only three non-sterling currencies, D-Mark, Swiss francs and US dollars.

The net total positions are then ascertained as shown in table 13.1. Sterling is the company's reporting currency, but also the currency of its capital. The balance sheet shows capital plus reserves of £4.5 million, consequently its net sterling liabilities included in the last column are (6.64 – 4.5 =) £2.14m. For the purpose of ascertaining its position in sterling, the figure is nevertheless –£6.64 million. For position exposure measurement the capital and reserves count as just another liablility.

Table 13.1 (Amounts in £ million)

	Per balance sheet	Other committed items	Total
DM	6.27	−0.39	5.88
SFr	2.90	0.41	3.31
$	−1.60	−0.95	−2.55
£	−7.57	0.93	−6.64

Most UK companies like International Traders would treat sterling as their yardstick currency, mainly because it is in sterling terms and on the London International Stock Exchange that International Traders has to raise capital and meet the performance critieria of its investors.

There are, however, exceptions. The most common exception has already been mentioned in chapter 9, section 9.9. It concerns an international financial institution whose market share depends on its capital. It therefore measures its performance in terms of the relative sizes of its own and its international competitors' net worth. It might adopt as its yardstick currency an international currency like the dollar, or a basket of currencies like the Special Drawing Rights (SDR) or European Currency Unit (ECU), or a weighted average of its particular competitors' currencies.

Another very interesting exception is the case of the Scandinavian Bank plc in London which has adopted a multicurrency share capital in response to its position risk.

The commonest form of the dilemma faces overseas subsidiaries (see chapter 14). In practically all countries they are required to file financial statements, and to satisfy domestic solvency criteria, in their local currencies. Nevertheless many of them, especially those controlled by US parent companies, measure their performance in the currency of the parent. The only safe path for such a subsidiary to tread is to meet both sets of criteria. In any event the choice of yardstick currency powerfully affects the motivation in managing position risk.

13.4 Accounting v. future cash flow views of position risk

We must now turn to this conflict, because it colours many of the issues to be reviewed. Many commentators are disappointed that this conflict has remained alive. In earlier decades there was much support for the view that financial markets were primarily concerned with accounting performance in valuing companies' securities. By the late 1980s there was much wider agreement that stock markets are aware of the shortcomings of financial accounting statements. So why do so many managers persist in paying attention to accounting effects in the way they manage currency risk? The answers were given in chapter 9, section 9.7: gearing and borrowing limits are defined in accounting terms, managers are legally accountable to shareholders in those terms, and their expensive information systems are geared to that task. The pressures to use the same format for management information are strong.

13.5 The accounting issue is mainly about fixed assets

Why and where does the dispute matter? Position risk can be seen in terms of either

- assets and liabilities, as defined and valued in conventional accounts, or
- future committed cash inflows and outflows, i.e. receipts and payments.

The two views do not conflict in what items they cover, because committed items are included on either view (section 13.2.1). That leaves two areas of conflict: (a) valuation, and (b) the time perspective.

The valuation of *monetary* items causes no conflict; they are on either view valued in money terms. This effectively leaves fixed assets and inventories. However, inventories are seldom in practice a material problem: they are not usually held for long periods. Moreover when they are held for longer periods and possibly obsolescent, the accounting rules require them to be written down to the lower of cost or net realizable values. It is therefore a good practical approximation to assume that conflicting valuations mainly concern fixed assets.

The time perspective is a matter of the maturity dates at which the items are seen to be at risk: in other words whether position risk is managed with an eye on the next reporting date, or on when the various transactions are expected to become cash inflows or outflows. This is discussed in section 13.8.

13.6 The future cash flow view

Position risk management treats all assets and liabilities, including fixed and other non-monetary assets, as committed future receipts and payments. The cash flow view assumes that at some future time all the liabilities will be discharged in cash, that all monetary assets will be collected in cash, and that non-monetary assets will cease to be used in their present commercial use and realized in cash. Land owned by the business may be physically indestructible, but the commercial effort which it now accommodates has a finite life.

This view treats fixed assets as future cash receipts at the end of their finite life, in their present commercial use, but at their present market value. The present market value has to be used, because zero exposure means zero now.

Example 13.1

Multidrinks plc has just two assets outside its reporting currency, sterling. One asset is US land with an estimated commercial life in its present business use of 15 years, a net book value of $1 million and a market value of $2 million. The $1 million net book value, represents $1.05 million original cost less $50,000 depreciation provided. The other asset is $300,000 receivables maturing approximately 90 days from now. The position would be at a theoretical zero risk position in *cash* terms if these assets were matched with a $2 million 15-year borrowing and a 90-day borrowing of $300,000.

Had the *accounting* view been taken, then the $2 million borrowing would be only $1 million, and probably repayable at the next balance sheet date.

We are not at this stage concerned to recommend a financing policy which matches the cash flows with this precision. We are merely defining a zero position exposure. The definition follows from the fact that position risk is caused by *nominal* exchange rate movements.

The differences between this view and those of financial theory were discussed in chapter 8, section 8.14.

13.7 The accounting view: fixed asset values

The appendix to this chapter is a summary of SSAP 20, the UK accounting standard on foreign currency translation. 'Translation' means the restatement in the reporting currency of items denominated in other currencies. The standard is closely harmonized with SFAS 52, the US standard. The impact of accounting conventions depends just as much, however, on the underlying local currency accounts as on the translation process.

The historical cost (HC) accounting convention values fixed assets at their original money cost, and amortizes this cost over their estimated life, by reducing (depreciating) their balance sheet value over that period. The HC convention pretends that a 1970 pound sterling equals a 1988 or 1995 pound sterling, no matter what inflation may have done to the purchasing power of the pound in the interval. If there has been appreciable inflation, then the depreciation process aggravates the undervaluation of the resulting balance sheet value, compared with current market values.

From the point of view of both financial theory and ordinary logic, the HC convention does not set out to provide any very useful valuation of fixed assets. This criticism would not apply to current cost (CCA) or current purchasing power (CPP) accounting, or any other accounting convention which aims to show fixed assets at current values. The various suggested conventions may differ substantially among themselves, but by nothing like the chasm that gapes between them on the one hand and the HC convention on the other. The big issue is the effect of inflation.

Example 13.2

World Holidays plc (WH) in year 0 bought an Italian hotel for L3.0 billion, buying that sum spot at L1500 = £1 for £2 million. In year 12 the hotel still stands in the local books at L3.0 billion, but WH now translates it at the closing rate of L2400 = £1, producing an HC book value of £1.25 million. Assuming that the current replacement cost of the asset is L4.8 billion = £2 million, should WH value its exposure at £1.25 million or at £2 million? To achieve a zero exposure in lire, does it borrow L4.8 billion or L3.0 billion? The dilemma of fixed asset values is most acute in the combination where

- they appear at HC values in local financial statements,
- local inflation since their acquisition has been substantially higher than inflation of the reporting currency, and
- the accounting standard requires their translation at the closing rate.

In a nutshell, the mischief is caused by the combination of obsolete HC values with a new closing exchange rate.

Example 13.3

If World Holidays takes the cash flow view of the Italian hotel and borrows the current value of L4.8bn (=£2m), it will have a substantial 'short' position in lire in its HC accounts. If the lira were then to rise substantially, a large accounting loss would appear in its next annual report. Now suppose World Holidays took the accounting view, and restricted its lire borrowing to the HC value of L3.0 billion; and suppose that the lira then fell to L3000 = £1, and further that the company then needs to sell the hotel, realizing L4.8 billion. The hedge falls short of the cash exposure by L1.8 billion, leaving a cash currency loss of

$$1.8 \text{ billion}/3000 - 1.8 \text{ billion}/2400 = -£150{,}000$$

13.8 When does position risk end?

This question is about the currency manager's time-horizon (see section 13.5). Here too the accounting and cash flow views are in conflict.

Example 13.4

In June of year 0 we borrow DM2 million for repayment in June of year 5. We have no D-Mark assets. Do we look upon this risk as one which now concerns us only up to our next annual reporting date on 31 March of year 1, or up to the maturity of the loan in June of year 5?

The accounting view often restricts its time-horizon to the next reporting date. It is in that case concerned with the effect only on the next set of reported results. In the 1970s a large US multinational *every* quarter sold £1 billion forward for the three months to its next quarterly reporting date. Its bank agonized whether it was acting ethically in accepting this lucrative business without pointing out to its customer that there were better ways to handle its exposure.

There is of course no practical need to take such a myopic view of an exposure which is clearly seen to have a longer life. If the multinational had originally sold the £1 billion forward for several years, the sterling assets would still effectively have been translated at the forward rate at the end of each successive quarter. The forward rate would admittedly have differed a little, due to the longer forward period, but the objective would still have been achieved: the sterling position would still have been locked in at the original market rate structure for dollar/sterling. Considerable spreads and dealing costs would have been saved.

This is not therefore a real practical dilemma. Hedges can be built for any reasonable forward period, and dismantled again if the asset life has been overestimated: we shall see in chapter 15 that the markets are quite flexible enough to give corporate hedgers all the latitude they need. The issue nevertheless serves to remind us how widely corporate preoccupations can differ, and how powerfully accounting conventions can influence managers. It reinforces the need for explicit and clearly thought out objectives for position risk management.

We can recapitulate the two views of when position risk ends as follows:

On the *cash* view, where the business has many assets and/or liabilities in a given currency, the total net imbalance must be subdivided by maturities. Even properties do not have an infinite life in a given business, and can be allotted realistic lives. It is usual to subdivide by months for the first year, then by quarters, then by years, and finally by 2½- and 5-year groupings.

In the extreme form of the *accounting* view, all risks mature at the next reporting date or at their earlier contractual payment date. Here too this shorter period to maturity may need to be subdivided into perhaps monthly maturities for the purpose of management.

13.9 Other accounting issues

13.9.1 Where are gains or losses shown?

The summary of SSAP 20 in the appendix brings out one other issue which preoccupies companies. It is whether gains or losses from currency movements are dealt with in the reserves or in the income statement as part of the ordinary results of the business. In the former case they bypass the income statement and therefore the reported results altogether.

Perversely SSAP 20 often has the effect of separate disclosure only for those currency gains and losses which are dealt with in the reserves. Those which go through the income statement are an undifferentiated part of the ordinary result for the period.

In fact companies and financial markets are more interested in the income statement than in the balance sheet. However, as only currency effects on reserve movements are disclosed, it is these which receive disproportionate attention. Broadly, the reserves deal with those gains and losses which arise purely in the process of consolidating subsidiaries into the group accounts. Gains and losses that arise in any single company, e.g. the parent or a subsidiary, are lost from view as part of the ordinary result, irrespective of whether they are of a capital or revenue nature.

These rules tend to distort companies' motivation. Managers probably do not pay enough attention to the group balance sheet, and probably too much to position risk within a single company. This is because success or failure in managing currency positions in the single company affects the ordinary reported results on which their minds are focused.

13.9.2 Does the accounting treatment undo hedges?

A very important feature of SSAP 20 and SFAS 52 is the cover method. Its purpose is to ensure that a spot hedge, i.e. a foreign currency borrowing to finance a foreign currency asset, has the intended hedging effect in the financial acounts. This was by no means the case under the previous US accounting standard, the notorious SFAS 8. Under SSAP 20 the cover method (see point 7 in section A1 and point 4 in section A2 of the appendix) is the main exception to the rule that all currency gains and losses in a single company must be treated as part of the ordinary results. However, the standard is not particularly careful to ensure that financial statements give full effect to spot hedges. On the one hand SSAP 20 permits the hedge to be in a non-matching currency; on the other it restricts the cover method to the 'carrying cost' (book value) of the foreign currency asset, which can be a mere fraction of its market value.

SFAS 52 at least is nevertheless a spectacular advance on its predecessor, SFAS 8.

13.10 Which of the two views is to be preferred? Cash or accounting?

Our analysis of the two main issues, valuation and time-frame, suggests a strong balance in favour of the cash view. The accounting view tends to be unrealistic in both cases. The case for the accounting view does not rest on its realism or its intrinsic merit, but on the legal force of the accounting format, and on the high cost of a more relevant parallel management information system. These points were noted in chapter 9, section 9.7.

Yet it is easier to make this analytical choice than to make the decision to ignore the accounting model in the management process. We return to this point in chapter 16, section 16.4.

13.11 When does a position exposure begin?

In trading risk we found that the origination of each exposure was vital to its recognition, analysis and its correct management. In position risk the question is less critical. It nevertheless decides the benchmark exchange rate for measuring gains and losses.

It is less critical because in position risk we do not normally need to distinguish between the two stages of conception and birth. An antenatal stage is exceptional in position risk. Major investments, loan repayments or capital issues are not usually decided upon without a simultaneous determination of the prices or values. The antenatal exception is where a company makes an offer or take-over bid which may not be successful. Other kinds of investment decisions can be synchronized with the financing decision. If we propose to acquire a company in Canada, we are free to finance the acquisition with

Canadian dollar debt if we wish. Conception and birth coincide in most cases.

In practice, however, position risk is very often perceived for the first time not when a major change in the balance sheet is contemplated, but on an *ad hoc* or routine review of the net position in each currency. If so, that perception becomes the starting point or birth, and the spot and forward rates of exchange at that time become the benchmark against which gains, losses and risks should be measured from then on.

13.12 Are fixed assets at risk at all?

Donaldson (1980, 1987) eloquently argues that fixed assets are not a source of exposure. His argument rests largely on purchasing power parity, and is thus close to the objections of financial theory. The argument goes to the root of the whole concept of position risk as a risk from *nominal* currency movements.

We could restate Donaldson's point in terms of examples 13.2 and 13.3 about World Holidays' Italian hotel. It is quite likely that the movement of the lira/sterling exchange rate from L1500 to L2400 was close to the change in the two countries' relative price levels over the same period. So if World Holidays plc had originally borrowed L3.0 billion when it bought the hotel, then the hedge would have gradually declined to near 1500/2400 or ⅝ of the market value of the hotel, along with the purchasing power of the lira against sterling. Donaldson points out that a monetary hedge is unprofitable against a weak currency, but profitable against a strong currency. However, this point is valid without any foreign currency investment at all. A weak currency liability is profitable in its own right and a strong currency liability is unprofitable in its own right. The difficulty lies in the advance identification of weak and strong currencies.

One assumption here is of course that we can ignore interest rates (see chapter 16, example 16.3). Moreover, UK corporates should give less weight to interest rates because the UK tax system asymmetrically makes capital differences in liabilities bigger after tax than equivalent differences in interest rates. In the Swedish system the reverse applies.

How should this matter be viewed? There are many points to be made.

13.12.1 What issue?

The focus of this chapter is on defining zero exposure. The issue raised by Donaldson is whether fixed assets present a currency exposure worth hedging.

13.12.2 Weak and strong

It is increasingly difficult to call the major world currencies 'weak' or 'strong'. Until 1973 under the Bretton Woods system, the words were entirely appropriate. Each currency was either weak or strong, i.e. likely to either fall or rise. From 1973 to the end of the decade countries still pursued sufficiently different economic policies to have very different inflation rates. So some currencies continued to be considerably stronger than others. But since 1980 there has been so much convergence in the major countries' economic policies that it is more and more difficult to be confident about these categories.

Minor and especially hyperinflation currencies are of course a very different matter.

13.12.3 Deviations from purchasing power parity

Figures 4.2 and 4.3 in chapter 4 show that currencies diverge from their purchasing power parity values by considerable margins for relatively long periods. Moreover, it can be shown that the parity itself tends to have a long-term upward or downward trend, depending on whether the country concerned has relatively high or low growth in productivity.

First of all therefore it is not correct to think of purchasing power parity itself as a static quantity. In the long run the inflation differential between two currencies will be either more or less than the trend in their exchange rate. Secondly, although purchasing power equilibrium may be attained and crossed every so often, most of the time the exchange rate will deviate from that equilibrium, often by considerable margins. (Equilibrium means current account equilibrium which may diverge from price level parity.)

In the light of these facts we can strictly only regard fixed assets as unexposed to position risk if two propositions hold:

- that we regard the currencies which concern us as having a static purchasing power equilibrium,
- that we can safely regard the assets as permanent for the planning period, i.e. that World Holdays' Italian hotel may not suddenly have to be sold for commercial or other reasons.

13.12.4 Zero exposure is not static

If the managers of World Holidays (examples 13.2 and 13.3) had always recognized position risk as we are defining it, and wished to have zero exposure on their Italian hotel property, they would originally have borrowed L3 billion for the acquisition. They would not, however, have been able to forget about the exposure for the intervening 12 years. Every 6 or 12 months they should have topped the loan up (or reduced it) to the current market value and exchange rate. Position risk management of this defensive kind needs to readjust positions to zero from time to time. This is because nominal rates are by their nature more volatile than real rates of exchange.

As Donaldson reminds us, if we wish to look at this in practical management terms instead of merely defining zero exposure, the point would have been more persuasive over that particular 12-year period for Vacanze Globali SpA of Milan and its hotel in Stratford-upon-Avon than for its competitor World Holidays and its hotel on Lake Garda.

We conclude that fixed assets cannot normally be regarded as immune to position risk. That immunity would apply only in very special circumstances. It is quite another matter whether the exposure should be hedged.

13.13 Are subsidiaries 'islands'?

The 'island' view treats an overseas subsidiary as a single asset with a single long-term life-span, normally in the local currency. This view can be very useful, and has been incorporated in the US and UK currency translation standards SFAS 52 and SSAP 20 (see appendix, section A2, point 1) as the 'net investment' view.

13.13.1 The perceived time horizon of the exposure

In many cases the island view is a useful and time-saving approximation. More than that, it has often greater validity than the alternative view, which treats the overseas subsidiary as a collection of individual assets and liabilities. The advantage of the island view is its greater realism about the duration for which the currency position will be with the company. Our German subsidiary's receivables may all be due in 30 days' time, but as an investment by the parent company it may well be sensible to treat them as part of a single investment of much longer duration. If all the receivables are in D-Marks, then they are much more usefully regarded as a revolving long-term D-Mark position for the group.

13.13.2 Subsidiaries with one-off business

The island view is not appropriate where a subsidiary's business consists of a few relatively large contracts, contracts which will vary in their currency characteristics. If the German subsidiary is now engaged on a contract in Saudi Arabia, to be followed by a large one in Hong Kong and a smaller one in Iceland, then as a currency asset it has no continuity, for its assets will largely consist of work in progress and receivables in different successive currencies.

13.13.3 Subsidiaries with stable currency patterns

Nor will the island view give us a useful quantification of the exposure if the subsidiary consistently has material assets and liabilities in different currencies.

Example 13.5

The UK parent has an Italian subsidiary with the following position in current values of L millions:

Shareholders funds	5000	US dollar receivables	3400
Yen bond	2400	Net lire assets	4000
	7400		7400

The island approach is appropriate, but the group's net lire investment is L4000 million, not L5000 million. The net assets in US dollars and yen of L3400m – L2400m = L1000 million need to be excluded, and treated as part of the positions in those two currencies. Either the subsidiary or the parent must manage these non-lire exposures.

13.14 The effect of taxation

No topic needs stressing more in currency risk management than the effect of tax on currency gains and losses, on their management, and on the instruments used in that management process. Unfortunately it is a subject of such complexity and uncertainty that it takes a tax specialist to do it justice. The reader is referred to Chown (1986a, 1986b, 1988a, 1988b, 1990), Chown and Evans (1987) and Sarwal (1989)

Asymmetry and uncertainty are the key words. Many transactions in this field are treated asymmetrically for tax

- in the two countries to a cross-border transaction,
- between a gain and a loss outcome,

- in the two dimensions in which they are linked by an arbitrage relationship, such as capital and interest in the case of interest parity (see chapter 3).

The main practical point is that when it is known that a currency movement will have a tax effect on some of the components of a position, but not others, then the net position must be recalculated after tax for the purpose of ascertaining the appropriate hedge.

Example 13.6
The only asset to be hedged by a UK company with a marginal tax rate of 35 per cent is a French franc receivable of FFr100,000. Any currency gain or loss on this would be reduced by tax to the sterling equivalent of a gain or loss on FFr65,000. Whether we should hedge this by borrowing FFr65,000 or FFr100,000, depends on whether we can satisfy the UK Inland Revenue that the borrowing was undertaken for a trading purpose.

Tax legislation tends to lag market developments by several decades. Many new instruments which were mushrooming in the mid-1980s, like options, swaps and their derivatives, are still quite unknown to tax laws. Taxing authorities tend to tax such transactions *ad hoc*, usually to the taxpayer's disadvantage.

Finally, even at the ordinary level of aggregating a net currency position in a currency, the currency manager must keep an eye open for any items which are or are not tax-effective (i.e. taxable or tax-deductible), and make sure that his hedges are effective after tax. As gains are often taxed asymmetrically from losses, this is not always achievable!

13.15 Summary

Position exposures can be defined either in accounting terms or in future cash inflow and outflow terms. The position in a given currency includes all those future sales, purchases and other transactions which are either committed or commercially certain. Many of these, like uninvoiced postnatal trading risks, will not yet be included in an accounting balance sheet. The position includes items which have been bought or sold forward for the currency, and excludes those covered forward for other currencies. The position is measured in the yardstick currency in which the company monitors its performance and net worth. The problematical effect of taxation on exposures must be carefully taken into account.

The dilemma between the accounting and cash flow views mainly concerns the valuation of fixed assets; if accounts were presented in current values, the dilemma would lose much of its practical importance. As historical cost values can be very unrealistic, companies should manage their positions in cash flow terms, but they cannot afford to ignore the accounting view as long as it governs legal definitions of solvency and borrowing powers and contractual definitions of ratio covenants in loan agreements.

Fixed assets should be treated as part of the exposure because unexpected early disposals are a feature of business life. The 'island' view of overseas subsidiaries is a useful insight, but it cannot be applied in all circumstances.

Appendix: Summary of SSAP 20, the UK currency translation standard

SSAP 20 became effective on 1 April 1983. It is broadly in harmony with the US SFAS 52. There is therefore less need to describe the features of earlier accounting standards which have been influential in the field of currency risk management. Here is a brief summary of the main features of SSAP 20:

A1 In individual companies

1 Foreign currency items should be *recorded* at the spot rate on the date of the transaction (the transaction date of a receivable is the date of its invoice).
2 Non-monetary items will normally stay at the local currency (LC) value thus translated and recorded.
3 At each balance sheet date *monetary* items in foreign currencies are translated into LC at the closing rate. However, if trading items have been specifically covered forward, they may be translated at the rates of the forward contracts.
4 Gains and losses, realized or unrealized, on monetary items, should be disclosed in the profit and loss account as part of the result of the year from ordinary activities, subject to the exceptions set out in 5–7 below.
5 If the gains or losses on monetary items stem from transactions which themselves are extraordinary items, they must be disclosed as part of extraordinary items.
6 Where the monetary items are long term, it may be imprudent to allow them to create gains or net gains in the profit and loss account if the convertibility of the currency is in doubt.
7 Forward contracts are only briefly covered in para 46: 'Where a

trading transaction is covered by a related or matching forward contract, the rate of exchange specified in that contract may be used.' So apparently a dividend (not being a trading transaction) would have to be valued at the spot rate, whereas a hedged trade receivable could be valued at either the spot or the forward rate, but in the latter case there is no provision for apportioning the premium or discount over the forward period, if it overlaps a reporting date. (The treatment of forward contracts by US standard SFAS 52 is discussed in chapter 13, section 13.2.2 and example 16.3 in chapter 16.)

8 The important 'cover method' rule is not restricted to monetary items: this rule lays down that on certain conditions exchange differences on matching assets and liabilities may be taken to reserve and there netted. It applies where the company has borrowed 'foreign' currency to finance or to hedge its 'foreign' equity investments. 'Foreign' here means 'other than the parent's currency and country': the loans do not have to be in the local currency of the investment. The exchange differences on borrowings which can be so treated must not exceed the exchange differences on the carrying amount (book value) of the equity investments. The equity investments are defined as the net assets of the investee company plus, in appropriate circumstances, any intragroup borrowings. The foreign currency borrowings to which the cover method is applied, must not exceed the total cash (including profits) expected to be generated by the investments concerned.

The intended effect of the 'cover' rule is to prevent the accounting rules from undoing hedging actions taken by companies.

A2 In consolidated financial statements

1 The normal method of translation is the closing rate/net investment method. The investment in a subsidiary is viewed not as a collection of different assets and liabilities of the parent company, but as a single long-term investment or 'island'.

(Exceptionally, the closing rate/net investment method may be replaced by the temporal method, provided that the subsidiary is viewed not as a separate entity but as an extension of the parent company's operations so that the parent currency is also the functional currency of the subsidiary – we shall not describe this unusual case further.)

2 Exchange differences arising from the retranslation of the opening net investment are treated as reserve movements, and therefore not as part of the profit and loss account or income statement.

3 The foreign subsidiary's profit and loss account should be translated at the closing rate or at an average rate for the period. In the latter case the difference arising from the discrepancy between those two rates is treated as another movement on the reserves.
4 The 'cover' method applies subject to the same restrictions as for the individual company. The loans do not have to be liabilities of the same group company which holds the investments.

14

Position Risk in the Group of Companies

14.1 Does a group structure affect position risk?

This chapter examines the extent to which currency risk in a group structure needs to be managed differently from currency risk in a single company. The main issues are as follows:

- Do intragroup transactions cause currency risk to the group?
- The possible overlap between the group's collective exposure and the exposures of the individual subsidiaries.
- Centralization of currency risk management in a group.

One of the many services rendered by Donaldson (1980, 1987) to this literature is his stress on the need to distinguish between the way currency risk affects the group of companies on the one hand and its individual member companies on the other. The US and UK accounting standards also make the distinction, but are not looking at the management issues.

The issues of **group trading risk** were discussed in chapter 11, section 11.12. This chapter first defines zero position exposure in the group context and then reviews the policy issues.

Generally this chapter assumes that all the group companies concerned are wholly owned. Where subsidiaries are partly owned, they should almost certainly be treated as external and autonomous parties. Unless all transactions with such partly owned subsidiaries are conducted at arm's length, it is at least a very onerous and tedious task to hold the scales evenly between the interests of the parent company's and the subsidiary's non-group shareholders.

This chapter is only concerned with operating units of the group. So-called 'vehicle companies' are effectively extensions of the parent and discussed in chapter 15, section 15.9.6.

Throughout this chapter we shall adopt the cash flow view of position risk, except where the accounting exposure is expressly addressed.

14.2 Whose exposure?

Where there is an intragroup transaction between two group members, S (the internal seller) and B (the internal buyer), we have to examine the interests and the exposure of each of them and that of the group as a whole.

14.3 Do intragroup transactions create position risk for the group as a whole?

This question needs two clarifications:

1 The answer can be 'yes' only if the group's net position in one or more currencies is changed by the intragroup transaction. A net position of zero is immune to changes in nominal exchange rates.
2 If the intragroup transaction is incidental to an external transaction, and if it is that external transaction which has changed the group exposure, then the internal transaction as such has created no exposure. If it does not modify the group exposure *in its own right,* then it has created no position risk.

In this narrow sense, only those intragroup transactions create risks which modify the external net liquid position of the group. These are

- internal profit transfers like intragroup dividends, royalties, interest or management charges,
- leading and lagging,
- internal sales not closely linked to an external sale (see section 14.6.3).

Intragroup dividends and profit transfers shift net positions from the payer's to the payee's currency. In the case of dividends, that means from the subsidiary's local currency to the parent's.

Example 14.1: intragroup dividend

To simplify, we assume that both US parent and Canadian subsidiary are net borrowers. The dividend payment therefore increases the group's Canadian dollar debt and reduces its US dollar debt, and modifies the group's position exposure. This effect was not inevitable: the Canadian subsidiary could have funded its dividend by borrowing

US dollars, but that is a hedging response, not a natural consequence of a dividend payment.

Leading and lagging is the deliberate modification of intragroup credit periods within a multinational group. It is an extremely effective method for temporarily shifting group liquidity between different countries.

Example 14.2: leading and lagging

Group company B in Austria is a regular buyer of goods from group company S in Belgium. B has a steady monthly volume of payments to make to S after after taking its normal intragroup credit of 30 days. The monthly average is the equivalent of $2 million. Now suppose the US parent company takes the view that the Belgian franc will be devalued within the EMS against the D-Mark, and therefore against the Austrian schilling, by 5 per cent. So the parent instructs B to pay after 90 instead of 30 days for the time being. This shifts $4 million liquidity from B to S. The parent wants B to borrow extra Belgian francs worth $4 million from local banks and S to repay Austrian schilling debt also worth $4 million. If the EMS realignment takes place, and the Belgian franc falls 5 per cent against the schilling (which tends to be firmly fixed to the D-Mark), the group will have made a cash gain of $200,000. That gain will almost certainly not be taxable. After the realignment the credit period can revert to 30 days.

14.4 The effect of intragroup trading on position exposures: with internal seller commercially responsible

To make this example simple, we assume that

- all exposures are postnatal,
- internal seller S (the Belgian subsidiary) commercially prices and obtains the sale to external customer C in Austria,
- goods are physically shipped by S to C,
- but are invoiced by S to the Austrian subsidiary B, which instantly reinvoices without mark-up to C, in Austrian schillings (ASch),
- the goods are at no time in B's stock,
- the internal sale from S to B can be in either Belgian francs or Austrian schillings.

The *group* position is unaffected by making the sale indirect, and the individual positions of S and B are only affected if the intragroup transfer is in the seller's currency. When the goods are invoiced to C, B acquires a schilling asset: first a receivable, then cash. S acquires an internal receivable and B an internal payable, both in the internal transfer currency.

14.4.1 *Internal sale in* seller's *currency*

S sells to B in BFr (see table 14.1). Making the sale indirect has made no difference to the group position, but has in this case transferred the position exposure from S to B.

Table 14.1

	Effect on S (Belgium)	Effect on B (Austria)	Effect on group
Indirect sale	+ BFr	− BFr + ASch	+ ASch
If direct	+ ASch		+ ASch
Incremental effect of indirect sale	+ BFr −ASch	−BFr + ASch	—

14.4.2 *Internal sale in* buyer's *currency*

S sells to B in ASch (see table 14.2). Making the sale indirect has in this second case made no difference to either internal party, nor of course to the group position.

Table 14.2

	Effect on S (Belgium)	Effect on B (Austria)	Effect on group
Indirect sale	+ ASch	− ASch + ASch	+ ASch
If direct	+ ASch		+ ASch
Incremental effect of indirect sale	—	—	—

Which is the better internal transfer currency? In this case it is Austrian schillings, because it gives the exposure to B, the party in commercial control. Unless B is instantly aware of exchange rate movements, B may not respond promptly to its commercial problems or opportunities. For example, a drop in the Belgium franc presents the group with a choice between

1 reducing prices to gain market share, and
2 collecting a higher margin at unchanged prices.

If the currency exposure is left with S, the group may be slow to adapt its pricing policy to the changed currency environment.

14.5 The effect of intragroup trading on position exposures: with internal *buyer* commercially responsible

If B rather than S is in commercial charge, but all other assumptions remain unchanged, it is better to give the position exposure to B, for the same reasons. B is now the party which has to take any pricing action. The internal transfer currency should be the BFr.

14.6 The effect of intragroup trading on position exposures: removing other assumptions in section 14.4

14.6.1 B temporarily holds the goods in stock

Here the reinvoicing sale by B to C occurs, say, 7 days after S has invoiced B. This makes no important difference, except that in the interval the accounting rules treat the stock as an ASch asset instead of a BFr asset; if there were a reporting date during that period and the exchange rate had moved, a temporary accounting gain or loss would be shown. After reinvoicing by B to C, the position would again be as in sections 14.4 and 14.5.

14.6.2 B buys at a discount from S

This is likely, as B needs to cover its expenses. This simply reduces the size of the positions (and thus the mismatch) by the amount of the discount.

14.6.3 B buys for stock, before selling to C

This is a very common case. There may well be considerable value added in Austria, so that the purchase from Belgium may only be components or materials. The internal credit period will be independent of the due date of C's payment: B must pay S irrespective of whether B has made a sale to C. This is no longer an indirect sale: the exposure from the internal sale has to be managed as a separate transaction, as in section 14.3.

14.6.4 The exposure is antenatal

If the exposure is antenatal, this is not position risk, but trading risk. It is dealt with in chapter 11, section 11.12.

14.7 Management issues of the group structure

The illustrations show that any one transaction can cause an exposure in one group company, which then also becomes an exposure of the combined group. However, position risk is defined as a single collective phenomenon in each currency, so that exposures from individual transactions can either increase or reduce the mismatched net position. A wide variety of patterns is possible.

This raises a number of questions:

- In an international group is it enough to manage position risk for the group as a whole, or must it be managed for each subsidiary?
- How much centralization of position risk management is desirable? For example, how undesirable is it for the Austrian subsidiary to be selling dollars forward while the UK parent is buying them forward? Should the group have a single monolithic hedging activity?

14.8 Is the *group* position risk all that needs to be managed?

Does a group of companies need to manage only the group's exposures? Can it afford to ignore currency exposures in the subsidiaries? We are here concerned only with exchange risk, i.e. with the risk of loss due to exchange rate movements, not with risks from exchange controls.

Where a subsidiary's local currency is inconvertible, there is a risk of piling up unremittable local currency liquid assets. These cash balances cannot be made available to the parent company's shareholders: this is exchange control risk rather than exchange risk. We therefore begin this discussion by assuming all the currencies to be freely tradable.

The question is best tackled with the following illustration:

Example 14.3

The group treasurer of Universal Saxophones plc takes an inventory of all world-wide net currency positions of the group. Suppose he finds that there is a net short (liability) position of SFr16 million with a maturity of 12 months, and the company's policy requires a zero position in Swiss francs. He can reduce his group position to zero by buying SFr16 million forward for 12 months.

However, SFr4 million out of that total is in the Italian subsidiary, and the other SFr12 million in the US subsidiary, and he has bought SFr16 million forward for the parent company. The Swiss franc positions are now

Parent	+ SFr16m
Sassofoni Italia	− SFr4m
Universal Sax Inc	− SFr12m
Group	zero

If the Swiss franc moves up or down against any currency, the *group* will have no position gains or losses. It has zero exposure, as long as all three positions have the same tax status.

Can the treasurer safely ignore the individual exposures of the two subsidiaries? He can, in the sense that the stock market in London pays little attention to the positions of overseas subsidiaries: indeed it may be unaware of these positions. He is not therefore jeopardizing the shareholders' wealth in terms of the share price.

However, a 10 per cent rise of the Swiss franc against the Italian lira would result in a SFr400,000 loss in the Italian company. If this was large enough to wipe out the Italian company's local currency net worth, that subsidiary would be technically insolvent and would probably, under Italian law, have to cease trading. The consequent disruption of its Italian business could considerably damage Universal Saxophones' competitive position in Italy. In certain circumstances it could also damage the group's international financial standing.

Currency imbalances in an overseas subsidiary can therefore be neglected only as long as they are small enough to constitute no threat to the legal solvency of the subsidiary. As there is a general tendency for wholly owned overseas subsidiaries to be thinly capitalized, there may well be many subsidiaries whose positions must be managed separately, and in addition to that of the group as a whole.

14.9 How much centralization of currency risk management is desirable?

Although this issue is closely linked to the group structure, it is left to be dealt with in chapter 17, section 17.1.

14.10 Summary

The main conclusions are these:

Partly owned subsidiaries must be treated as external parties because there is conflict of interest between different sets of shareholders, parent and minority.

Intragroup transactions, as such, affect the currency exposure of the group as a whole only where they shift liquid balances between countries and therefore currencies. This is true mainly of intragroup dividends, royalties, interest payments and the like, and of leading and lagging. Typically these reduce the group's net liquid position at the paying end and boost it at the receiving end. Indirect sales, invoiced via an overseas subsidiary, do not normally affect the group's currency position.

For indirect sales the best internal transfer currency is the one that gives the exposure to *the group company in commercial control,* which decides selling prices to external customers.

To manage only the group's exposures and to ignore exposures in overseas subsidiaries is safe only where potential currency losses in those subsidiaries are too small to jeopardize their net worth and thus their solvency. As many wholly owned subsidiaries are thinly capitalized, there are relatively few groups which can safely adopt such a policy.

15

Managing Position Risk: The Mechanisms

15.1 Introduction

Position risk management calls for some complex policy decisions, which will be discussed in chapter 16. Trading risk causes many a painful dilemma when a company badly needs business; but the issues of position risk management do not fit into a simple conceptual framework. Chapter 13 dealt with those issues which affect the definitions of position risk and exposure, and chapter 14 with those arising from the group structure. This chapter focuses on the techniques and issues of risk management.

15.2 The techniques of position risk management

By techniques we mean methods and market instruments which can be used to modify an exposure. When a position is changed to zero, then the technique has been used as a hedge. Techniques can, however, be used to adjust a position to any other position. The exposure can be eliminated, reduced, increased or reversed. The currency manager now has a multiplicity of methods and instruments to use, but the basic building bricks are shown in table 15.1.

15.3 Hedging by spot deal

Table 15.2 reproduces table 13.1, showing International Traders plc (IT) with imbalances in only three currencies other than sterling. The last column of table 15.2 displays IT's overall imbalances. It could reduce all these to zero by doing the following spot deals:

Table 15.1

Market instruments	'Internal' measures
Spot deal	Matching
Forward deal	Netting
Interbank swap	Leading and lagging
Futures contract	
Currency option	
Currency swap	

- sell £5.88m worth of D-Marks for sterling,
- sell £0.76m worth of Swiss francs for sterling,
- sell £2.55m worth of Swiss francs for dollars.

Some important complications have so far been ignored.

Table 15.2 (Amounts in £ million)

	Per balance sheet	Other committed items	Total
DM	6.27	−0.39	5.88
SFr	2.90	0.41	3.31
$	−1.60	−0.95	−2.55
£	−7.57	0.93	−6.64

15.3.1 Are borrowings needed for the deals?

First, does the company need to borrow D-Marks and Swiss francs in order to sell them spot? If it does, then it needs debt capacity and credit limits with headroom for these new borrowings; yet it may have earmarked its headroom for other operational needs.

Whether IT needs to borrow depends on whether its existing D-Mark and Swiss franc assets are liquid, like overnight deposits which can be sold off without breaking covenants. For example, if the assets are fixed assets or inventories, then they cannot be instantly realized; and in any case not in time to fund a spot deal. If they are term deposits with Credit Suisse with one month to run to maturity, then again it may cost a stiff penalty to realize them ahead of the due date. However, in that last case IT might be able to borrow Swiss francs and D-Marks from Credit Suisse for one month under a right of set-off. The effect would be that its positions with Credit Suisse would net out to zero, and IT would require no credit limit and would not increase its gearing or use up its debt capacity.

Most texts describe this spot deal mechanism as a 'foreign currency borrowing' or a 'money market hedge'. These expressions miss the central point. What nets out the position is not the borrowing as such, but the spot deal. If the borrowed Swiss francs were left on Swiss franc deposit with a bank, IT would simply have doubled up its Swiss franc assets and added a further Swiss franc liability, leaving its net long position undiminished. In any case, the mechanism can work without a borrowing, for example if IT can simply sell a Swiss franc deposit for one in another currency.

15.3.2 Different maturities

Suppose International Traders' short position in dollars of the equivalent of net £2.55 million = $4.5 million consisted of a loan maturing in month 15 of $5 million and receivables due to IT of $150,000 in month 3 and $350,000 in month 6. How can IT ensure that it has no exposure?

The only difficulty here is to choose between a profusion of alternatives. A few illustrations will make this clear. Let us assume that IT does not wish to enter into an immediate spot purchase of dollars so as to avoid possible gearing effects. IT can alternatively

- buy $5m forward for 15 months, and sell forward $150,000 for month 3 and $350,000 for month 6;
- buy $15m forward for 15 months, sell $500,000 spot, repaying the borrowed $500,000 in two instalments, $150,000 in month 3 and $350,000 in month 6;
- buy $4.5m forward for month 15, in month 3 swap $150,000 for sterling for month 15, in month 6 swap $350,000 for sterling for month 15.

The choice will largely be governed by administrative convenience and to a minor extent by spreads. The last option accepts a minor exposure to a shift in the swap rate (i.e. the interest differential) between now and months 3 and 6, but not to changes in the spot rate.

15.4 Forward and interbank swap hedges

These instruments, and their respective advantages and disadvantages have been discussed in chapter 12, sections 12.7 and 12.8. The techniques of managing postnatal trading and position risk are largely identical.

15.5 Hedging by futures contracts

Futures contracts are described in chapter 2, and compared with forward contracts in chapter 12, section 12.9. Where futures markets are true alternatives to forward hedges, they have a very similar effect: they lock the hedger into the current set of market rates.

Their usefulness in hedging position risk is likely to be restricted by the administrative effort involved, by the relatively short maturity stretch of the futures market – it seldom exceeds 12 months – and to a lesser extent by its inflexible amounts and maturity dates. On the other hand futures markets are far better at accommodating small amounts and small companies who can only command relatively low credit limits with banks.

15.6 Hedging by currency option

Currency options are described in chapter 12, section 12.5.

There is a wide difference between the use of currency options to hedge antenatal trading risk on the one hand and postnatal or position risks on the other. The mismatched antenatal price quotation, with price in one currency and cost in another, is itself a kind of currency option written by the seller to the customer. The exporter's customer may or may not buy from him if he can get a better bargain elsewhere. The currency option is in that sense very close to an exact hedge against antenatal risk, an option *bought* against an option *'written'* by the exporter.

Against position risk, however, the currency option buys something better, something more valuable than a hedge. The option buys at worst an outcome at the strike price, but it has a 50 per cent chance (if at the money) of producing something better than that outcome, something better than a mere hedge. It is wrong therefore to regard the option as a very expensive alternative to the forward contract. If the option is correctly and competitively priced, it buys extra value, at a premium which should no more than match that extra value.

Expressed in currency management terms, the currency option enables the hedger to manage his risk both defensively and aggressively. It limits the downside without restricting the upside.

Some companies with large numbers of variable small transactions derive an additional benefit from currency options. Options enable them to hedge unknown volumes of short-term transactions in different currencies without running the risk of having to close out forward contracts at a loss. Elements of antenatal and postnatal risks are here combined. The risks are in principle postnatal – they do not depend on the outcome of quotations to customers. They acquire an antenatal or uncertain element because the company finds it uneconomic to capture in its data system, and then to hedge, every postnatal risk when it is incurred. The company finds the option premium cheaper, bearing in mind that surplus options have a good chance of ending in gains. The example illustrates rather well the need to weigh administrative costs against the benefits of hedging with great precision.

Modern derivatives from options are often worth considering in managing position risk. This is particularly the case with option combinations in which the hedger reduces or eliminates the cost of the premium, in return for a restriction or customized reshaping of his risk profile. A good introduction is in Duker (1989) and Ducros (1989). Chapter 12, section 12.5.4 discussed the cylinder or collar option and some of those derivatives which are combined with forward contracts, like Hambros' 'forward with optional exit' (FOX).

Example 15.1: FOX

On day 91 Traders Inc. owes SFr1,420,000. At today's forward rate of SFr1.42 = $1, this would cost $1,000,000. Under a FOX, Traders Inc. would accept a loaded forward rate of, say, SFr1.4059. This buys Traders Inc. the right to reverse the forward deal at the agreed exit rate of SFr1.44. It will pay Traders Inc. to exercise that right if it can then buy the SFr1,420,000 at a spot rate which is better than SFr1.44. The comparative US dollar cost of SFr1,420,000 is then as shown in table 15.3.

Table 15.3 (Amounts in US dollars)

Spot day 91	If unhedged	With forward deal	With FOX
1.35	1,051,852	1,000,000	1,010,029[1]
1.375	1,032,727	1,000,000	1,010,029[1]
1.40	1,014,286	1,000,000	1,010,029[1]
1.4059	1,010,029	1,000,000	1,010,029[1]
1.425	996,491	1,000,000	1,010,029[1]
1.45	979,310	1,000,000	1,003,228[2]
1.4548	976,079	1,000,000	999,997[2]
1.475	962,712	1,000,000	986,630[2]
1.50	946,667	1,000,000	970,585[2]

[1] 1420000/1.4059
[2] 1420000/1.4059 − 1420000/1.44 + 1420000/spot

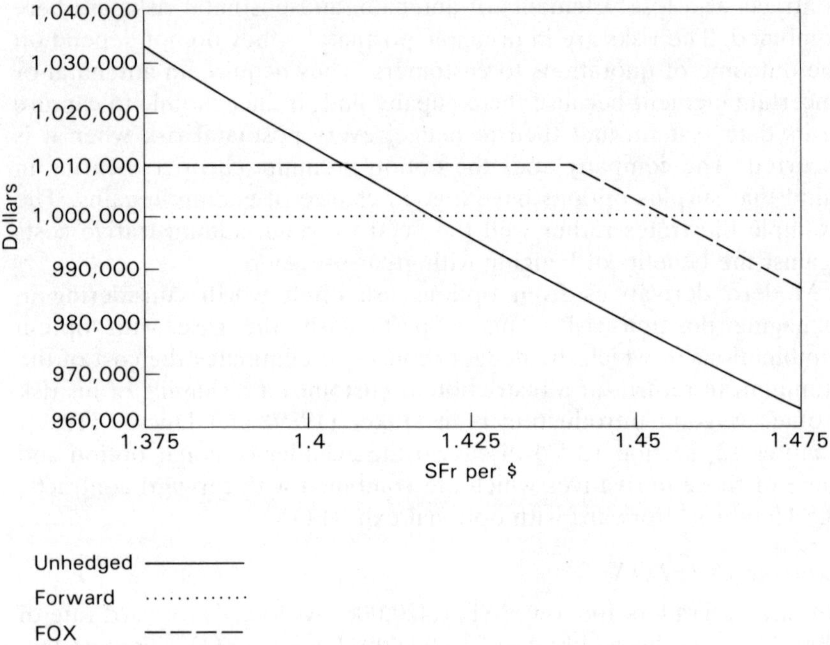

Figure 15.1 FOX v. unhedged and forward

As figure 15.1 shows, the result of FOX is better than an unhedged position if the spot rate on day 91 is less than SFr1.4059, and better than a forward contract if it is more than SFr1.4548. Between those two points it turns out to be more profitable than both the other alternatives.

15.7 Hedging with currency swaps

Currency and interest rate swaps are one of the great innovations of the 1980s. We are here only concerned with currency swaps. Currency swaps need to be distinguished from the interbank swaps to which we have referred especially in chapters 2, 3, 12 and in this chapter. A currency swap differs from an interbank swap mainly in that it

1 does not need banks as principal parties,
2 tends to be for longer maturities,
3 usually requires annual mutual interest payments, and
4 in that case applies the same exchange rate to both the spot and the reverse forward leg of the deal,

5 can sometimes be arranged without the initial spot deal (which brings it closer to a longer-term forward contract).

A currency swap is thus normally an agreement between two parties A and B to exchange agreed amounts of two currencies spot, and to reverse that exchange at an agreed future maturity, usually at the same original rate of exchange, and to pay each other interest or equivalent compensation on the respective amounts owed to each other at the future date. It has now sometimes been done without the initial spot deal, and occasionally with a swap rate substituted for the periodical interest settlements.

Currency swaps have developed from, and largely superseded, a series of bilateral hedging or financing instruments like reciprocal and parallel loans. Banks pioneered these swaps. At first, acting like marriage brokers, they put parties with equal and opposite needs together. The market did not grow strongly at that stage.This was partly because it was hard to find two counterparties with equal and opposite needs, and partly because two non-bank counterparties did not always wish to accept one another's credit risk for large amounts and long maturities. The swap market only took off when the banks became market-makers instead of marriage brokers, and back-to-back principals so as to act as credit guarantors to both non-bank parties.

Currency swaps are particularly useful as a tool to manage position risk for large amounts and long maturities, because under current accounting conventions they have no balance sheet gearing effects. Moreover a swap can normally be terminated or neutralized if circumstances change, for example by another swap in the opposite direction.

When a currency swap is used to hedge a position exposure, the principles in chapter 12, section 12.8 apply. Suppose a US dollar-based company wishes to hedge a long-term short position in yen with a swap. It must then in its currency swap sell yen spot for dollars, and agree to re-exchange them in, say, 12 years' time, but take care to neutralize the spot leg of that swap with a simultaneous spot sale of dollars for yen, to ensure that the two spot deals cancel out. The company has thus taken out a hedge similar to a long-term forward purchase of yen. The total cost of the hedge includes the relatively small cost of the offsetting spot sale of yen. Caution is, however, needed concerning the accounting and tax effects of currency swaps. These are very uncertain within and between countries and need to be checked with very great care.

15.8 Currency matching

Currency matching and netting are often mistaken for being the same thing. Matching is the financing of capital expenditure or acquisitions in the same currency, so as to leave the company's net currency positions unchanged.

Whether this device makes sense as a risk averse measure depends on how the company defines its zero risk position. For example, does it take interest rates or inflation into account for longer-term risks? Or is its policy to manage the position in accounting terms?

The benefit of matching also depends on the tax environment. If we assume for the moment that the international Fisher effect holds, then a company in the UK can in some circumstances expect to be better off after tax if it gives priority to the effect on the principal, not the interest. In Sweden the effect of tax is the exact reverse: it pays to give priority to the effect on interest income or expense. In many other countries like USA and Brazil the tax effect is neutral.

15.9 Netting

Netting is an adjunct to risk management tools, not a tool in its own right. Its function is to ease the mechanics of managing a position in a currency. There is one position exposure per currency, subdivided by maturities. Netting is merely the process of assembling all the inflows and outflows at a given maturity, netting them so as to become a single net amount receivable or payable at that date. Then if we wish to have a zero risk in cash terms at that date, we enter, say, into a forward contract which brings the exposure down to zero.

Example 15.2

On day 180 we must pay a bill of exchange of Y250 million. We also have export receipts due that date totalling Y228 million. As we want to take no chance on the outcome, we net this to a short position of Y22 million, and buy Y22 million forward for day 180 against sterling, our yardstick currency.

If on the other hand the company had a policy of managing its yen exposure aggressively, and expected the yen to appreciate against sterling over the period, it might choose to buy Y72 million forward, giving it a long position of Y50 million. If the expectation turned out correct and the spot rate on day 180 was 10 per cent better than the forward rate, the company would make a gain of Y5 million, amounting to £22,727 if Y220 = £1. Netting has simplified the decision and the action.

Netting appears a very simple concept. However, there are some problems.

15.9.1 Netting date or period?

In simple examples the receipts and payments are all due on the same day. In practice where the business has large numbers of transactions, the task of netting has to be simplified by netting for periods like a week or a month, so that the French franc position might be subdivided by 12 months a year rather than some 255 dealing days. So if in March we have thousands of French franc transactions due, netting out as a payment of FFr750,000, we buy forward FFr750,000 for, say, 15 March. This may balance out the month as a whole, but not the individual 22 dealing days. There are nowadays many ways of managing the intra-month swings, but by far the most convenient is the EuroFrench franc current account which we can have, for example, in New York, London, Frankfurt or Zurich, with any international bank. This account can be in credit or overdrawn, and can carry interest if in credit. For a large company with other accounts at the same bank, and a set-off letter, there is no separate problem of credit limits; it can have a single credit limit covering all its accounts. A debit balance on the EuroFrench franc account will be offset by any credit balances elsewhere. The forward purchase of FFr750,000 is credited to this account. If the forecast was correct, the transactions for the month will balance out by the end of the month. The use of set-off letters may, however, incur extra cost, as explained at the end of section 12.7 of chapter 12.

15.9.2 What period patterns?

Many companies use an exposure statement which subdivides the total position in a currency by maturities. Typically this is done monthly for the first one or two years, then quarterly, next annually, and finally in 2½- and 5-year periods (see example 13.4, chapter 13) if the position runs that far into the future. Within each period the format separately shows receipts and payments, forward contracts already entered into, net position and a space for action now decided upon. In different businesses much shorter periods are needed, with groupings by weeks followed by months, rather than months followed by periods of several years. Each such exposure position is for one currency only. An excellent format of an exposure statement is found in Donaldson (1987, page 61).

15.9.3 How wide? Company or group?

Chapter 14 discusses intragroup issues and chapter 17 the question of centralization v. decentralization of management and dealing. Different structures suit different businesses, but the netting system as such can accommodate them all. Where intragroup remittances are part of the total position, it is best to separate them out if the group wishes to use leading and lagging (section 15.10) as a management option.

15.9.4 Zero risk or what?

Netting is a mere implement. The use, however, to which it is put is a matter of company policy. It can be used to reduce exposure to zero; or to increase exposure away from zero, if the company believes it can outperform the market forward rate in predicting the future spot rate. It can also be used to shade the degree of exposure to a fraction, say 25, 50 or 75 per cent of its original size by taking out forward contracts for the rest of the net imbalance.

15.9.5 Netting is an aid, not an instrument

Finally, in the examples we have assumed that the instrument used on the strength of the exposure statement is a forward contract. In fact of course it can be a spot deal or an interbank swap or a currency swap or a currency option. Netting is not an instrument in its own right, merely a sorting and marshalling routine to define the exposure that needs to be managed.

15.9.6 Netting and reinvoicing vehicles

Some multinational groups set up special vehicle companies, often but not invariably in a low tax environment like Switzerland, to which all internal exports are invoiced, and which then reinvoices them to the other group companies. Settlement is then effected globally and net. The advantages of such a reinvoicing vehicle include economies of scale (fewer transactions at lower spreads), reduced transaction volumes from netting, expert management by the central specialists, disengagement of non-financial managers from financial complexities and the opportunity to take central currency positions by leading and lagging (section 15.10), to accumulate central liquidity in a convenient place free from exchange controls and high taxes, and generally to manage the currency positions arising from ordinary trade flows actively and centrally. The vehicle normally accepts transfers at forward rates for normal intragroup credit periods. The internal parties are insulated from financial currency risks.

The concept can be extended to embrace external sales and purchases, and even to manipulate transfer prices, i.e. to take a slice of profit in the vehicle where it incurs zero or low tax. This last use is outside the scope of this book because it is more concerned with taxation than currency risk.

All the advantages are in the field of pure financial management, often at the expense of commercial management. The drawback is that the netting vehicle insulates the internal suppliers from their ultimate external customer markets. It can result in suboptimal pricing and other commercial decisions because the commercial units do not have any direct experience of the effect of exchange rate movements on their competitive positions in their markets. The benefit of these vehicles is therefore greatest in those companies whose market offerings are relatively undifferentiated from those of competitors, so that they are price-takers with few pricing decisions to take.

15.10 Leading and lagging

Leading and lagging is shortening or lengthening the period of credit, usually within a group of companies.

Example 15.3 (see also example 14.2)

Harps International plc has a subsidiary in Milan. The only lire position in the whole group is in that subsidiary, which has net lire assets of L40 billion. Due to unsettled conditions in the European Monetary System Eurolire interest rates are abnormally high and the forward market in lire temporarily very thin and expensive. The subsidiary has undrawn credit lines from the local banks of L20 billion. Fearing a major devaluation of the lira, the parent instructs the subsidiary to speed up intragroup invoices from the normal credit period of 120 days to 30 days. This depletes the cash position of the subsidiary by L20 billion, improves the cash position of the group outside Italy by L20 billion, so that the lire long position has been cut from L40 billion to L20 billion. If the lira is then devalued by 10 per cent, the group has reduced its loss by L2 billion, say £1 million if L2000 = £1. After the devaluation the intragroup credit is restored to 120 days.

Leading and lagging is thus a device which adjusts the group position in one or more currencies, by shifting liquidity between countries. The group raises its external debt in Italy, reducing it by the same amount in the rest of the world. In fact, leading and lagging is most effective in doing just that: shifting liquidity.

Leading and lagging is a hedge only in very special conditions: when it happens to produce a net zero position in one currency. Its function in currency risk management is almost invariably to shift the group position away from a weak and towards stronger currencies. This, however, begs the familiar question how we can distinguish weak from strong currencies. Unless we know better than the market and the international Fisher effect, we do best to assume that the future spot rate will be the present forward rate. In the example that was so, for within the artificial constraints of the European Monetary System we know that in the short term currencies are subject to the constraints in its rules: when one of the intervention limits is reached, the central banks must intervene. Currency managers can exploit these rules and make gains at the central banks' expense, much as they could under the Bretton Woods system.

In fact leading and lagging was more appropriate to the old world of Bretton Woods or to the artificial EMS than to the freely floating system of the major currencies. Under Bretton Woods everyone knew which currencies were weak and strong. Since 1973 and for freely floating currencies we do not normally know that.

In any case, leading and lagging is subject to some other important constraints:

1 the amount of outstanding intragroup credit: it is difficult to achieve a negative credit period;
2 the unused credit limits or cash resources of those subsidiaries from which liquidity is to be withdrawn;
3 possible exchange and other controls restricting maximum intragroup credit periods and similar matters in various countries.

However, where leading and lagging is used, it changes the liquidity of each participating subsidiary. As the modern tendency is to monitor the cash flow performance of managers, leading and lagging has come to be seen as central interference and as demotivating delegated management responsibilities. This is another powerful reason for the evident decline of leading and lagging as a currency risk management device.

15.11 Summary

A position exposure can be managed defensively by bringing it to zero; aggressively by adjusting it to a desired level of profitable imbalance. It can, by management action, be eliminated, reduced, increased or reversed.

Market instruments available to perform these tasks are spot, forward and interbank swap deals, futures, options and currency swaps. Companies can also use internal measures: matching, netting, and leading and lagging.

The currency option is always something both dearer and better than a mere hedging instrument, because it limits the downside without restricting the upside.

Netting is not an instrument, but an adjunct to other instruments. Its function is to reduce the amounts to be managed by the other instruments to a single net sum, usually for a period like a week or a month. Currency bank accounts are the most flexible instrument for dealing with imbalances within the period.

The netting technique is at its most developed where group trading and other transactions are transferred to a reinvoicing vehicle company, which then manages the group's net exposure. This arrangement tends to insulate commercial operations from the currency environment of their markets, and can have adverse commercial effects in businesses which need to take pricing decisions.

16

Policy Decisions in Position Risk Management

16.1 Introduction

Position risk management calls for complex policy decisions. Many of these go to the heart of corporate objectives in this field, and were in that context reviewed in chapter 9.

Chapter 13 set out to define zero position exposure. Chapter 14 dealt with issues arising from a group structure. Chapter 15 reviewed the mechanisms for managing position risk. We now address the main management issues, taking as our starting point some conclusions of chapter 9, section 9.12, which were particularly concerned with position risk:

5 There are some constraints on aggressive risk management, but no objections in principle, as long as any significantly speculative policy is openly declared to the company's present and potential investors.
6 Once the company decides to manage currency risk for gain, there is no reason why it should restrict itself to 'natural' exposures. It should feel free to open up positions where it feels best able to make gains, as long as its policy is adequately disclosed to the financial markets.
7 Companies should manage their exposures in cash rather than accounting terms, but cannot afford to ignore the accounting effects. Position risk is of concern to management because fluctuations in nominal exchange rates cause gains and losses in cash or accounting terms. For the most part these overlap. In the short term these gains and losses can be important. Once a cash gain or loss has occurred, it is irreversible.

We single out four main issues:

- Aggressive or defensive approach (section 16.2)?

- The timing dilemma (section 16.3).
- How much attention to accounting effects (section 16.4)?
- Relationship with other financial policies (section 16.5).

16.2 Aggressive or defensive?

The view taken in this book is that a company needs internal controls which enable it to manage at a zero risk level when desired, even though there are no objections in principle to a disclosed policy of aggressive management. If managers wish to make departures from zero exposure, these must be *controlled* departures. These speculative efforts do not, however, need to be confined to 'natural' exposures: there is no plausible reason why managers should not deliberately open up exposures for gain (chapter 9, section 9.6).

The practical case for opening exposures up deliberately is the scarcity of currency expertise. Moreover, those few who can consistently speculate for gain are not universal geniuses. An expert may be good at discovering certain types of misalignment, or his home ground may be a particular currency like the yen or the Swiss franc, or a particular controlled environment like the European Monetary System. The company that wants him to make gains, must give him a chance to play on his home ground, irrespective of whether the company's 'natural' pattern of business produces exposures on his home ground. It would make a lot of sense if he and his team were allowed to hedge all the time-consuming 'natural' exposures, and to concentrate their rare skills on their chosen expert area of currency risk.

In view, however, of the difficulties reviewed in chapters 3–5, much scepticism is in order about the possibility of making systematic gains in the currency markets. Over much of the range of currencies and maturities the forward rate expresses as good a view of the future spot rate for given future dates as any expert can hope to obtain.

Before we believe claims of superior expertise, we should therefore highlight the places and situations where opportunities have a good chance of occurring. The exploration in chapters 4 and 5 suggests that they are as follows.

16.2.1 Very short maturities

Over very short periods, mainly intraday mismatches, net gains can consistently be made by those well placed to spot bandwagons and the extent to which they have run their course. These opportunities are open mainly to those who are interbank parties in the Eurocurrency and foreign exchange market, or are big enough non-bank players to be accepted as interbank participants.

16.2.2 Tax arbitrage

A company can expect on a balance of probabilities to gain rather than lose if it exploits a mismatch between its own tax position and the tax neutral position normally assumed by an arbitrage relationship in the market like the international Fisher effect. The most obvious case is where a company has a backlog of tax losses to use up.

16.2.3 Absence of time-constraints

A company which diagnoses a fundamental misalignment, say an overvalued dollar in the early 1980s, can take an open position against that misalignment, provided it can afford to wait indefinitely, even for years, for that misalignment to be corrected. The company must also consciously justify its dissent from the international Fisher effect. In other words, it must either have clear reasons for disbelieving the view currently presented by the international Fisher effect, or operate in a tax environment in which interest differentials and currency gains or losses are taxed differently, as in the UK and Sweden. In the latter case it is exploiting a tax arbitrage opportunity as much as taking a position against the market.

16.2.4 Central bank intervention rules

The early years of the European Monetary System are the obvious example here, but there have been successes in speculating, for example, with Scandinavian currencies, or in the past with currencies like the Australian dollar. The essence of the opportunity is that in some situations a currency can only move in one direction, because its central bank is obliged by the rules to deal at a loss to counteract those speculating against it. Sooner or later there must be a substantial devaluation or realignment. If it comes while the speculator's position is open, he makes a handsome gain. If not, his worst outcome will be a very small loss. The asymmetry is caused by the rules which force central banks to be ready to intervene at a loss: the adroit speculator ensures that their loss becomes his gain.

16.2.5 Long periods

Over very long periods the financial markets are often misaligned with inflation expectations, so that both the Fisher effect and purchasing power parity give opportunities for arbitrage. Companies need to judge to what extent the international Fisher relationship is weaker in the long run than the two inflation-related ones: Fisher effect and purchasing power parity. They also need to judge where the present spot rate is in relation to the present appropriate norm (see chapter 10, section 10.2). This form of speculation is hazardous, especially for the company which needs to get its timing right with any precision, but it does give the trained economist an advantage over other market participants. If relative inflation rates are likely to be more influential than relative interest rates, then it may well be possible to beat the market.

These five opportunities in sections 16.2.1–5 are important, but they represent exceptions. Over most of the field an aggressive policy is unlikely to result in a systematic tendency to gain rather than lose. For the most part, therefore, the corporate currency manager should adopt a defensive stance. Yet there is room for rational aggressive management for those who have the will, the skill and the confidence to disclose this policy to investors.

16.3 The timing dilemma

The **timing** of hedging action can be one of the worst dilemmas in managing position risk.

Example 16.1

Universal Music Inc., whose reporting currency is US dollars, noticed in June 1978 when the dollar/sterling spot rate was $1.82=£1 that it had a long-term surplus of sterling assets over liabilities amounting to £40 million. It looked upon its British subsidiary as an island (see chapter 13, section 13.13), i.e. as a single net asset with an assumed life (maturity) of 25 years. Corporate policy was risk averse, and required the risk to be hedged by raising long-term sterling debt. Nevertheless the sterling exposure had been there unnoticed for many years.

Figure 4.1 in chapter 4 shows the monthly average $/£ exchange rates over the period since currencies began to float.

In June 1978 it was open to the company to realize $72.8 million by doing an instant spot deal at the rate of $1.82. Had it taken the action in March 1975 at $2.42, it could have realized $96.8 million. However, it had not then been aware of the sterling mismatch. With hindsight we know that in January 1981 it would have been able to realize $96 million at the rate of $2.40, but Universal Music could not have predicted this in June 1978 (see table 16.1).

Table 16.1 Summary of possible outcomes, with benefit of hindsight

Month	Spot Rate per £1 ($)	Cash result ($ million)
March 1975	2.42	96.8
June 1978	1.82	72.8
January 1981	2.40	96.0

Without the benefit of hindsight, what was the right thing to do in June 1978, and what yardsticks should Universal Music apply to its decision?

There seem to be two broad alternative approaches:

1 Take a doctrinal stand on the declared policy that every risk must be hedged *instantly*. In this case Universal Music must instantly in June 1978 sell £40 million spot for $72.8 million. As there was not yet in 1978 a liquid market in currency swaps, the company would probably borrow £40m for a short period from the banks or in the commercial paper market whilst mounting a Eurosterling bond issue.
2 Identify the dilemma as an exception to normal company disciplines. Top managers might think it unwise to take a blind doctrinal approach after negligently ignoring the exposure for some years. They might reflect that Universal Music's stockholders could be critical if their sterling asset was locked into a $72.8m cash outcome, when it might with better timing have crystallized at $96.8m in March 1975. With hindsight, we know that the investors might have felt even more critical in January 1981, when it appeared that as much as $96m could again have been realized if only the management had waited until then, instead of dealing at $1.82 in June 1978.

This major sterling asset had been there for many years. It has little in common with a receivable due in three months; to such a receivable, both stockholders and managers would have to apply a much shorter time-scale. Major issues are not best decided by a blind or mechanistic approach. The managers of Universal Music should reflect, perhaps with expert advice, on whether waiting could reasonably be regarded as a better policy. In fact, there appear to be no time constraints, an opportunity noted in section 16.2.3. The question was whether a rise of sterling above $1.82 was on the cards at *some* time in the future. If the managers reach the conclusion that there are no good grounds for expecting that rise in sterling, then they should of course deal spot at $1.82. That decision is justifiable as long as it was not taken blindly.

A greater difficulty for the managers is to formulate a precise and practical decision if their considered view leans the other way, i.e. to the belief that sterling will at some time rise above $1.82 again. If the worst loss is not potentially intolerable (chapter 6, section 6.5), then some alternative decisions like the following can be considered:

1 To sell £20m spot for dollars now, and the remaining £20m when sterling reaches $2.00 (a 10 per cent rise) or $1.73 (stop-loss for a 5 per cent fall).
2 To sell the entire £40 million if sterling should either rise to $2.00 or fall to $1.73.

If the worst loss is of intolerable proportions (chapter 6), then the position must now be closed out (i.e. sold for dollars) to the extent needed to reduce the worst loss to tolerable proportions.

In any case, as long as any part of the position is left open, the company should hold regular monthly reviews of the outlook for the dollar/sterling rate of exchange. There should be no blind policy of keeping it open.

This dilemma is one of the worst in currency risk; there are no easy decisions. Exposures which represent an important part of a company's net worth should only be managed by people with strong nerves.

The timing dilemma also occurs on a smaller scale every time a currency manager has to deal in the market. The foreign exchange market is so volatile from minute to minute that it is unusual for the same rate to be available for minutes at a time. The market is always getting either better or worse from the currency manager's viewpoint. He may be free to deal up to 4 pm today, or perhaps up to 4 pm this Friday. If he can see the rate improving, how long does he delay before he deals?

16.4 How much attention to accounting effects?

Our position in chapters 9 (section 9.7) and 13 (section 13.10) was that companies should give preference to managing exposures in cash terms, without ignoring the accounting effects altogether. Reasons for paying at least some attention to accounting effects are that under the laws of most countries the accounting framework determines

- how managers account to investors for their stewardship,
- the borrowing powers of the company,
- the company's solvency and its ability to trade.

It also tends to determine gearing limits under the terms of loan agreements and other debt instruments.

Example 16.2: fixed asset values

In example 13.3 in chapter 13, section 13.7, we took the view that World Holidays should certainly hedge the Italian hotel asset at the cash view level of L4.8 billion rather than the accounting value of L3.0 billion. This preference for the cash view protects World Holidays against a substantial unexpected cash loss in the event of an early disposal of the hotel after a major fall in the lira. In historical cost accounting terms, however, this gives the company a significant short position in lira. The company needs to consider this carefully. The consideration should include these steps:

1 The short position would lead to an accounting loss if the lira were to rise against sterling between now and the next reporting date. What is the maximum rise that can be contemplated? If this were 10 per cent, the loss could be of the order of £200,000.
2 Even an accounting exposure can have intolerable effects, for example if it can cause the company to exceed its borrowing powers, loan covenants or solvency criterion. So is £200,000 intolerable or catastrophic? If yes, then that loss must not be given a chance to occur. In that case World Holidays should perhaps revalue the asset in the accounts so as to preclude a short position being shown in historical cost accounts. This revaluation may not be possible in isolation from other group assets, but must be considered. An alternative is a currency option, possibly at a strike price 'out of the money' so as to minimize the cost. Several companies in the appendix to chapter 9 are concerned with this point. Company K is particularly interesting.
3 If an accounting loss of £200,000 would not be intolerable, then it is best to ignore the accounting exposure.

Similar thought processes should be devoted to the question of conflicting maturities.

Example 16.3: maturity of hedge

Shipbuilders Inc. of USA has an instalment of Y200 million payable in month 26, and reporting dates at the end of months 6 and 18. It wishes to lock into the present exchange rate structure for this instalment. The exchange rates and deals shown in table 16.2 are open to it now.

Shipbuilders Inc. can

1 buy forward 26 months now and lock in a final loss of $182,000, compared with the current spot rate, or
2 buy forward 6 months now, locking in a loss for the first six months of

Table 16.2

	Rate $1 = (Yen)	Cost ($000)	Extra cost over spot ($000)
Spot	121	1653	—
6 months fwd	118	1695	42
26 months fwd	109	1835	182

$42,000, intending to buy forward again in month 6 either for month 18 or for month 26 at the forward rates available in month 6 for those forward dates.

Due to interest parity, the 'losses' of $42,000 and $182,000 represent the forfeiting of the Y/$ interest differential for either 6 or 26 months. The effect of the forward contract is equivalent to restoring interest costs to dollar interest rate levels.

What is the accounting effect at month 6 of a 26-months forward contract? If the forward contract was not *initially* entered into as a *specific* hedge against this yen payable amount, then under SFAS 52 the yen premium must be apportioned over the period of the forward contract, so that only $42,000 would be charged against the current year. The effect in this non-specific case would therefore under SFAS 52 be the same, irrespective of whether Shipbuilders buy forward for 6 or 26 months. Moreover, this would come to the same effect on current results as a spot hedge, where the premium would be replaced by the effect of the interest differential.

If on the other hand the hedge was *specific from the outset*, SFAS 52 does not appear to permit this apportioning treatment. The UK standard SSAP 20 on the other hand is silent on non-specific hedges. All it says is: 'where a *trading transaction* is *covered* by a *related or matching* forward contract, the rate of exchange in that contract *may* be used'. If the company had covered forward for 26 months, then it seems that at month 6 it 'may' under SSAP 20 use either Y109 or Y121, but not Y118. Moreover it has the choice between Y121 and Y109 only if this is a trading transaction (doubtful of a loan instalment). If not, then Y121 must be used.

If Shipbuilders is bound by SSAP 20, it must carefully consider the position. A true and fair view is a loss attributable to this year of $42,000. Many UK companies would adopt this treatment and ignore the standard. The same result can be achieved in compliance with SSAP 20 by buying forward only to month 6, the balance sheet date. This is course 2 above. This would incur some extra dealing costs and some uncertainties about the effect on the cash position between month 6 and 26. The ultimate outcome over the total period should be similar as long as the yen/dollar interest differential has not materially changed by month 6. (See also chapter 13, section 13.2.2 and appendix section A1, point 7). A company governed by SFAS 52 should perhaps consider whether it wishes to set up an unspecific hedge.

More questionably a company short of profit this year might adopt the apparent permission in SSAP 20's use of the word 'may', accrue none of the loss and hope for a subsequent rise by sterling against the yen.

To sum up, policy should normally be governed by the cash criterion. On the other hand the accounting consequences can be serious enough to require some consideration too, and in some cases they may affect the decisions taken.

16.5 Position risk management and general financial policies

Position risk management can come into conflict with other financial policies. The most likely ones are (1) its target gearing ratio and (2) policies to minimize interest expense or maximize interest income. Conflicts are often more apparent than real, if we remember (a) the possibility of set-off agreements to minimize gearing effects, and (b) interest parity and the international Fisher effect.

Any sound conceptual framework for managing these issues should start by recognizing that the hedging of currency positions always implies a forward date and a forward premium or discount against the current spot rate, and that this premium or discount is equal to the difference between the Eurocurrency interest rates of the two currencies concerned. In short, hedging *is* a change in the company's interest profile: it is a time-related transaction, just like borrowing or investing.

16.5.1 The interest rate trap

Currency risk managers owe to John Heywood (1984a) the phrase 'interest rate trap' which he first used in 1978. It describes the process which ruined at least one famous UK company. Like many others, it borrowed a large sum of medium-term fixed interest Swiss francs around 1970 to finance its sterling assets, at Swiss franc rates of interest well below sterling rates. As it happened, the Swiss franc rose against sterling by many times that interest differential. Due to its heavy currency loss the company could not meet its repayment obligations and lost its independence.

Any company caught in this trap has overlooked

1 that under the international Fisher effect it could expect to lose on the principal what it gained on the interest,
2 that any deviation from the IFE might be sharply adverse (as it turned out in 1970–6), and
3 that after tax (see chapter 15, section 15.8) under UK tax law the dice were in any case loaded against the company: the interest gain was taxable, but the loss on the principal amount of a liability was not tax-deductible.

16.5.2 Tax and accounting arbitrage and saving interest

The interest rate trap was a classic case where single-minded attention to the lowest rate of interest was wrong in principle. Those who fell into it probably failed to take account of the connection between interest rate differentials and market expectations. They expected the kind of free lunch which is unlikely in the financial markets.

However, the conflict between currency exposure and interest rate management can take more rational forms. The most obvious one is where the tax system is not neutral between currency movements on the amount owed and the interest differential, as in the UK or in Sweden.

In the US, however, the tax system is in most cases neutral. So if a US company needs to borrow $10 million for 12 months, with a forward premium on the D-Mark of 5 per cent, should it borrow D-Marks and save 5 per cent interest or dollars and lose the 5 per cent savings? Unless the company wishes to indulge in a sheer gamble, it should of course borrow dollars because the spot rate is more volatile than the interest differential. The D-Mark could rise or fall 40 per cent.

This rule of thumb would need to be reversed where the tax treatment rewards borrowing the stronger currency with the lower rate of interest, but the tax incentive would have to be steep to compensate for the unfavourable risk profile of that policy.

The tax incentive is unlikely to apply even where the foreign currency borrowing is covered forward, because the incentive is usually intended to prop up an overvalued currency. If it nevertheless did reward this 'covered arbitrage', then advantage should of course be taken of the tax saving. In that case the stronger foreign currency should be borrowed and covered forward. A more insidious temptation is accounting arbitrage. This arises where the gain or loss on the principal will appear in the accounts as a change in the reserves and the interest as extra profit. This temptation can be intense for a company desperate to improve its immediate earnings per share, perhaps because it is under threat of a hostile bid. It is not always easy to convince managers in that dilemma that any losses from recklessly incurred risks would attract attention in the searching analyses undertaken during a take-over battle. The best policy is still to pay the higher rate of interest and to avoid the risk on the principal amount.

16.5.3 Position risk hedging and gearing policy

Generally, a company should optimize its gearing ratio by financing profitable investment with debt up to the ideal ratio. The Modigliani and Miller argument has surely been laid to rest by now: it seems to be widely agreed that there are limits to how highly companies can safely gear their equities. Spot hedges, i.e. assets overlapped with debt just for the sake of balancing out positions in a currency, do not fall into the category of profitable investment. Commercial assets need to earn more than money market returns to earn their keep. Subject to the cost of extra bid–offer spreads, one way round this dilemma is to arrange the overlapping money market assets and debt to be covered by set-off rights with the same bank, as described in chapter 12, section 12.7, and illustrated in chapter 15, section 15.3.1.

16.6 Managing the effect of taxation

The chaotic state of tax law in this field was discussed in chapter 13, section 13.14. If there were a prevailing pattern, it would be that the dice are loaded against taxpayers who transact business across the exchanges. We there noted that tax-effective transactions must be distinguished from tax-ineffective ones in the process of computing the amount of position risk in any one currency. Moreover, the currency manager must carefully explore how each of the market hedging instruments will affect the tax liability in various countries. The uncertainty is greatest with the more recent innovations like currency swaps and currency options, but it also affects more traditional ones like spot and forward contracts, as we saw in example 16.3.

16.7 Managing exposure in hyperinflation currencies

We looked at hyperinflation currencies in chapter 4. The normal rules do not apply in these currencies because the volatilities are reversed, with inflation rates more volatile than interest differentials and controlled spot rates. There is no free market, there are no normal hedging instruments. Inflation is the key variable, but its actual size is not known with precision until some months after the event.

In these circumstances the only way to manage a subsidiary in such an environment without loss is to ensure that local managers are sharply aware that they are expected to achieve positive real returns equal to the parent's real cost of capital (PRCC). In local currency terms this means the highest of

1. PRCC plus the local inflation rate less parent currency inflation rate,
2. PRCC plus rate of depreciation of the local currency against the parent currency less the inflation rate of parent currency,
3. the local free market rate for short-term funds.

All three indicators have flaws; that is why performance must beat them all for safety. Information about the local inflation rate is neither prompt nor accurate, the rate of devaluation is heavily controlled by the central bank and is not in the short term dictated by market forces, the local free interest rate is influenced by many distortions in the market and is often negative in real terms.

If the subsidiary sees no prospect of achieving this criterion, then its viability must be questioned.

16.8 Managing the effect of exchange control

This book is not about controlled currencies and the risk of blocked funds. However, it is necessary to stress that where a currency is controlled, many of the normal rules of currency risk management are overridden by the need to remit funds from a controlled environment at almost any rate of exchange rather than none. The net present value of a blocked sum of money in a heavily controlled banking system is seldom much above zero, unless the removal of exchange controls appears imminent. So the currency manager's priorities can change quite dramatically between a controlled and an uncontrolled currency. The precise action which this requires varies enormously from country to country, as the regulations, and the various ways in which traders and others are permitted to operate, tend to be very detailed with infinite scope for variation.

16.9 Summary

Aggressive position risk management is not wrong in principle as long as it is properly disclosed, but the currency manager must justify why he should take a view against the consensus of the market. There is much evidence that the market is hard to beat systematically.

However, this leaves certain parts of the market as fair game for speculators, especially very short and possibly very long periods, and controlled markets in which money can be made out of central banks bound by artificial rules to deal at a loss in certain circumstances. The EMS exchange rates are a case in point. The currency manager can also expect to speculate profitably in conditions of tax arbitrage and where he is free from time constraints so that he can afford to wait whatever time it takes for the market to correct an over- or undervaluation of a currency.

The timing dilemma applies at major and minor levels, whenever a currency manager must deal, but has reasons to avoid dealing at what with hindsight may turn out to be an unfortunate time.

Accounting standards are not always realistic. Currency risk should on balance be managed against cash rather than accounting criteria; yet accounting effects cannot be ignored. Accounting conventions tend to affect legal and contractual gearing limits. They are in any case important where a company is under pressure to optimize short-term accounting results.

Managements should thoroughly understand the relationship between interest and exchange rates. The classic 'interest rate trap' should not confuse managers any more, but the desire to minimize interest expense or maximize interest income can give rise to rational conflicts with currency risk objectives where either the accounting conventions or the tax rules treat the two phenomena differently. Any trade-offs must be resolved with open eyes.

Currency risk management actions do not normally run the risk of stepping up balance sheet gearing, as long as set-off rights can be used without undue extra cost.

Taxation is a major complication for international transactions because it tends to be unpredictable, asymmetric and usually biased against the taxpayer, yet vital to currency management decisions. Exchange controls can dramatically change corporate priorities because blocked funds are of little value.

A hyperinflation environment can only be managed by requiring local operations to earn real returns equal to the real cost of capital.

Part IV

Organization and Control; Summary

17

Organizing, Controlling and Appraising Currency Risk Management

17.1 Poacher and gamekeeper

This chapter reviews the implications of what has been suggested in this study for the organization of the company or group, how currency risk management might fit into that organization, its relationship to the activities of other functions, and finally its control and performance measurement. Not all companies approach these issues realistically.

Currency risk management is a complex topic. It calls for some specialized attention, yet many of the tasks cannot be performed by specialists isolated in a back room. On the contrary, currency risk management must often serve non-specialist, even non-financial objectives. Many tasks need teamwork with commercial managers; typically with the commercial people in charge and the currency expert in an important, but advisory role. The problems are typically *business* problems, not just commercial or financial problems.

Few organization structures accommodate this relationship easily and without friction; yet even the best lubrication is not enough. Collaboration will not be effective with anything short of enthusiasm.

The central difficulty is that somewhere in the process there has to be a discipline which enforces exposure limits. This is the negative side of an otherwise dynamic and positive task. In most companies this is within the responsibilities of the finance director. The currency expert is likely to be a member of the finance function who therefore combines a control function along with his advisory task of supporting the commercial effort. He has to be poacher and gamekeeper at the same time. This calls for a high calibre of self-discipline and balanced judgement.

The difficulty is made worse by the fact that currency expertise of the required order is both scarce and costly. Few companies can afford a currency expert in every commercial team that needs currency advice.

17.2 Issues of organization and control

A checklist of topics to be determined and clearly communicated by top management should include these items:

1 How the company defines the various risks.
2 The company's priorities between the accounting and cash flow views of currency risk.
3 The benchmark currency in which the company measures its performance.
4 How defensive (risk-averse) or aggressive the company's policy is in currency risk management. Is active risk management restricted to making money out of 'natural' exposures?
5 To what extent exposures are to be managed for each overseas subsidiary, as well as globally for the group.
6 Precisely what is to be centralized or delegated, complete with a hierarchy of authority limits. It is helpful to highlight any places where this structure is an exception to general principles of decentralization in the group. The dimensions of this issue are listed in section 17.3.
7 The interrelation with commercial or trading decisions, such as the currency of sale or purchase, exchange rates to be used in pricing, or the costing of antenatal trading risks. The need of interdisciplinary teams, and allocation of responsibilities within those teams. Any variations in these rules for overseas subsidiaries.
8 How currency risk management should be related to other financial issues like funding, gearing and borrowing limits.
9 How currency issues are to be handled in corporate and strategic planning, and in capital investment decisions.

Most of these topics have been discussed in other chapters, but 6 and 7 are discussed in sections 17.3–6.

17.3 Centralization of currency risk management

17.3.1 The dimensions

The dimensions in which currency risk management can be either centralized or decentralized are

1 where and by whom currency dealing is done,
2 where and by whom exposures can be authorized and hedging decisions taken,
3 where and by whom it is decided in what currencies to quote prices,
4 in what currencies intragroup sales are invoiced.

Some interesting modern developments can be seen in multinationals like SKF which do their entire internal accounting in their own currency basket currency, and others who use the ECU for intragroup invoicing within Europe.

The extreme form of centralization is where the group centre does all dealing and takes all decisions. The opposite extreme is where each profit centre does its own dealing and takes its own risk management decisions. However, a complete absence of central guidelines and authority limits is rare (Davies and Collier, 1983).

17.3.2 The case for centralization

First, there is just one thing that a group of companies cannot decentralize: its credit rating and investment status in its financial markets. If the parent is listed, it will have its primary stock market quotation on one stock exchange like the New York Stock Exchange or the International Stock Exchange in London. The stock market treats such a group as a single financial entity with an integral investment and credit status. Similarly banks tend to regard subsidiaries as extensions of the parent, even if the parent will not formally guarantee them. The parent alone therefore has the critical interface with the financial markets. Partly owned subsidiaries may be an exception to this rule. It follows that only the corporate centre is sensitive to the effect of currency exposures on the group's financial standing and cost of capital. Managers outside the corporate centres may take decisions which are either imperfectly targeted or convey unhelpful signals to the financial markets.

Secondly, because only the centre has the key interface with the financial markets, wholly owned subsidiaries tend to need less experts for dealing with those markets than the parent. They may therefore lack some of the *technical* sophistication and experience needed to handle currency risk in volatile modern markets. Currency risk is not easy to handle; few groups can afford expertise in all their subsidiaries or other sub-units. Where the skills are concentrated at the centre, there is a strong case for letting the central experts take the critical decisions.

Thirdly, it is often contended that there are economies, particularly in dealing costs, if transactions are minimized, netted and then centrally handled. This case is examined in section 17.3.9.

17.3.3 The case against centralization

Many companies take the view that their group's commercial success requires strong 'local' control. Local here refers to any profit centre, whether it be geographically distant, or concerned with a different product or a different competitive market. It is hard for such a structure to be effective if there are any unnecessary restrictions on the local manager's power to take all decisions which influence that commercial success, and on his accountability for those decisions. Many currency risk decisions are highly germane to commercial success.

Secondly, the local currency manager is closer to the transactions of the local unit, and also to the local banking system and foreign exchange market. This is especially important if the local currency market is insulated by controls from the world banking market in which the parent deals.

17.3.4 What determines degrees of centralization?

There is much diversity in the extent to which companies centralize currency dealing, currency invoicing decisions, and risk management and hedging decisions. This has been studied by many, notably in the UK by Davies and Collier (1983), Glaum and Belk (1989) and Batchelor (1989). Its intragroup aspects are discussed in chapter 14. The diversity is indirectly confirmed by the companies referred to in the appendix to chapter 9.

Not surprisingly, this diversity of practice is to a considerable extent a consequence of the different commercial and organizational profiles of companies. In many multinationals the subsidiaries in different countries are in quite different businesses requiring quite different, relatively decentralized, management styles: other multinational companies are commercially homogeneous and some monolithic, with overseas subsidiaries integrated in the global business directed from the centre. SKF and IBM may be good examples of such integration.

Apart from these different commercial and operating profiles, companies also differ in their corporate cultures and management styles. These too have an influence on the trade-off in each case between pressures for and against centralization.

17.3.5 How are companies structured?

Practice in multinational groups can vary from total centralization, where all dealing is done by the parent, to a high degree of freedom for every world-wide profit centre to manage its own currency risks by its own criteria (Davies and Collier, 1983; Glaum and Belk, 1989; Batchelor, 1989). The variety of practice is likely to owe much to differences between the products, market positions and international spread of each group of companies.

Few companies stand at the extreme ends of the spectrum. Most international companies, as a minimum,

- issue guidelines stating the corporate objectives in managing currency risks,
- require prompt and accurate information about currency positions, so that the corporate centre can then at the centre adjust the consolidated position of the group to the desired level, and
- monitor and take central action to manage that group position.

This is of course just what Universal Saxophones plc did in example 14.3 in chapter 14, when it borrowed SFr16m in order to reduce the group exposure in Swiss francs to zero.

On the other hand very few groups centralize

- currency dealing for all their foreign subsidiaries, or
- decisions about the currencies in which units sell, or
- decisions about the exchange rates used to calculate export selling prices.

Many give guidance and advice, but few directly interfere in the affairs of overseas subsidiaries. Domestic subsidiaries are another matter, for the prevailing practice is to have only one currency dealing centre per country. The principles are discussed in sections 17.3.6–10.

17.3.6 Control of group exposure

The parent needs to control the group's currency gains and losses over the short and long periods for which it plans. This is important because group currency gains and losses have a direct impact on reported group results, net worth and gearing, which are the focus of attention in the financial markets. Even if the group does not wish to hedge its accounting exposure, it may still wish to watch it (chapter 9, section 9.12 and chapter 16, section 16.4).

For this task the parent needs to know all non-parent currency positions. The parent can then restore zero risk by taking a mirror-image position to the rest of the group's net total in each currency. It can do this, for example, by the use of spot or forward hedges or currency swaps. The biggest problem is often to get accurate up-to-date information on the net non-parent positions.

17.3.7 Communicating corporate objectives

The parent has to communicate its criteria and objectives, such as its yardstick currency. The topic was discussed in chapter 9. The group must have a common set of objectives. We saw in section 17.3.2 that it has a single critical financial market, for example the stock exchange on which the parent is quoted. If parts of the group disregard those objectives, the group's financial standing could suffer a setback. An example would be where the finance director has told the analysts that the group will not borrow Swiss francs or yen to save interest charges, and then has to disclose that the US subsidiary has incurred a major loss by doing just that.

Subsidiaries may of course have to watch other criteria as well: the Italian subsidiary must avoid insolvency in lire terms. Yet the subsidiaries need to know by what criteria the parent judges their performance.

17.3.8 Commercial interests

The parent needs to be sensitive to the commercial implications of currency gains and losses.

In chapter 14, section 14.8 we noted the risk of causing the insolvency of overseas subsidiaries. This can largely be controlled by delegating responsibility to local management who have a powerful incentive to watch this point.

Similarly, where a parent decides to centralize as much currency risk management as possible by selling to all its overseas subsidiaries in their own currencies, yet leaves those subsidiaries to make their own commercial pricing decisions, then those who make those decisions are in the dark about the effect of currency fluctuations on the group's competitiveness. They are imperfectly equipped to maximize group profits: the local incentive conflicts with the group's interests.

17.3.9 Saving dealing costs

Suppose the Austrian subsidiary sells a long dollar position forward, and the parent has a much larger short dollar position of its own. From the group's point of view the Austrian action aggravates the group's short position. If the parent wishes a zero group position in dollars, the Austrian forward sale forces the parent to buy all the more dollars forward, duplicating the cost of dealing spreads.

In a few groups this line of reasoning is taken to extremes, with all currency dealing for the whole or most of the world centralized at the corporate centre. In a very monolithic single-product group this may be justified. Yet do these groups give due weight to the diseconomies of dealing from a distance, the extra staff, telephone, telex and facsimile time, the delays this may cause to urgent local remittances, and finally the demotivation of local managers?

In present competitive wholesale markets currency dealing costs are modest. To have the Austrian subsidiary selling dollars while the parent has to buy all the more, may not be uneconomic. It matters more that objectives are harmonized.

17.3.10 Making the most of specialist skills

A decentralized group that wishes to manage currency risk for gain, may therefore ask its overseas subsidiaries to adopt a defensive hedge-everything policy, leaving only the corporate centre to deal aggressively for gain. It might see this division of functions as the way to get the best of both worlds. However, there are other ways.

17.3.11 The corporate centre as banker

The most extreme form of centralization is to make not only risk management, but also dealing the sole prerogative of the corporate centre: currency management in that case simply bypasses the subsidiaries and other profit centres.

Central dealing can, however, also be used for a much more devolved structure. This permits all profit centres to make their own currency risk management decisions, but requires them to deal exclusively with the group centre as their in-house banker. The group centre then at their request gives the profit centres spot or forward deals, swaps, or options, quoting the best market prices that they could have obtained by dealing direct. It then makes its own decisions about dealings with the outside world. The group centre is then in complete control of the group position, free to pursue its own policies; yet the operating units are equally free to run their affairs as they choose. Companies A and L in the appendix to chapter 9 adopt structures of this kind.

17.4 Integration with commercial management

Chapter 7 stressed the extent to which currency issues can be subordinate to commercial ones. This is because the success or failure of a business is widely believed to depend critically on how it selects its commercial markets and competes in them. We now examine the implications of this relationship for the way currency risk management is organized.

We have come across a number of problems which were important enough to warrant a high-powered decision process, but for which the best solution could not be found without the *combined* skills and experience of commercial and currency management. Example 12.3 of chapter 12 showed the case where the only way to manage antenatal trading risk was to cost the risk, and example 9.1 of chapter 9 examined the case of the customer who switched the currency in which he required quotations. Both called for commercial decisions which could not be rationally taken without currency judgements and skills. Advice from financial management will cover

- the possible range of currency outcomes over various future periods,
- the probabilities of various ranges of outcomes; and where needed,
- the maximum tolerable level of exposure in the light of the company's financial size (chapter 6).

In all such cases the commercial manager must be in ultimate command of the commercial decision, but he will be inadequately informed unless he and the currency manager have learned to act as a team and to respect, trust and value each other's judgements.

17.5 Motivating managers of subsidiaries

It has for some decades been understood that companies of medium and large size run more effectively if the head office confines itself to a bare minimum of tasks, leaving decentralized general managers to run divisions or subsidiaries or other sub-units of the parent group. Line management must not be distant from the commercial markets in which the group competes, because competitive markets are the critical battlefield.

17.6 Control of delegated powers

Where currency expertise is for one reason or another centralized as an exception to an otherwise decentralized management structure, there are two implications. First, the need for teamwork is paramount. Secondly, the central currency management function should as far as possible play a detached part, relying as much as possible on guidelines, routine advice on exchange rates and currencies, and as little as possible on an imposed right to be consulted on day-to-day decisions. This helps to reinforce the motivation of line managers to run their businesses successfully.

The corporate centre needs a clear view of what exposures are too small and fragmented to be worth managing, and to issue carefully defined authority limits. Units are free to manage exposures below those limits as they think fit. All currency positions must, however, be reported to the centre so that the group exposure can be monitored. The ultimate constraints on delegation are

- the integral nature of the group's standing in its financial markets, and
- the threshold of tolerable risk, described in chapter 6.

The process of delegation needs so much care because currency exposures have a way of being correlated and cumulative, both in time and across the spectrum of a group's sub-units. If the dollar is on a steep trend against sterling in either direction, then figure 4.1, for example, suggests that such a trend can go on for a long time (e.g. early 1980 to the end of 1984). However, few groups' dollar inflows and outflows are so naturally balanced that a policy of *laissez-faire* is safe. Small individual exposures, instead of cancelling out, have a way of accumulating to major gains or losses for the group.

The most effective place for the head office to manage this is in the parent company, leaving the profit centres to watch their own solvency criteria.

An effective decentralized structure should be impeded as little as possible. Currency risk management should achieve its central objectives as unobtrusively as possible.

17.7 Control of currency management staff

This is a difficult and important topic. In many companies currency dealers are relatively junior staff who handle often very large transactions, and implement them by telephone or other electronic communications. In a fast-moving market like the currency market there is no other way. The main risks are those of (a) improper cash payments out of the company, and (b) a build-up of excessive exposures.

The main safeguards are authority limits not only for the dealing department, but also for individual dealers, of constant reporting of positions to higher authority, and of a rigorous system of confirmation of deals. Company employees unconnected with the dealers should check all information slips from the banks against internal confirmation slips issued by the dealers. Helpful reviews of such control systems are found in Austen and Reyniers (1986, ch. 9) and Back (1988).

17.8 Performance measurement in currency risk management

Performance measurement in this field has attracted a great deal of attention, but few satisfactory solutions.

17.8.1 Treasury as profit centre

One typical case is where the parent company sets up a separate finance subsidiary, which acts among other things as a reinvoicing company. This type of vehicle was described in chapter 15, section 15.9.6. We are not here concerned with netting or transfer pricing, but with performance measurement.

When these vehicles were first set up, their financial results tended to be regarded as a measure of exposure management performance. If a vehicle company had made a profit, it had done well; if a loss, badly. The inadequacy of this was soon recognized. Company K in the appendix to chapter 9 is explicitly conscious of it.

Some of these vehicles deal with their internal counterparties at the bid–offer spreads which those subsidiaries could obtain for themselves in the market at their own level of size and dealing turnover, but deal with banks at lower spreads offered to large customers. The vehicle pockets the difference between the dealing margins offered to customers of different sizes. This built-in profit is a fair part of the answer to whether the vehicle is financially worth having or not, and should be set against the overhead costs of running the vehicle.

Yet that is not the question asked by *performance measurement*. Performance measurement is concerned with opportunity gains or losses achieved by the currency manager, against some other benchmark course of action open to him when he took his decisions (Cooper and Franks, 1987). The question is not whether the vehicle is worth having, but whether the currency manager could and should have managed the exposures more successfully.

In other words the vehicle or profit centre does not by itself greatly advance the task of performance measurement. At best it may purify the accounting records used as raw material for performance, by isolating treasury operations from other transactions. It does not, however, contribute to the analytical task of performance measurement: this always requires the *recording of hypothetical alternative courses of action, and their outcome*.

17.8.2 Opportunity criteria of performance

In their most helpful review Cooper and Franks (1987) set out the opportunity criteria framework. For the typical problem of measuring a hedging decision, i.e. to cover a position with a forward contract, what is required is a comparison of the outcome of that action with an alternative benchmark course of action like dealing at spot on maturity, but this comparison must be further adjusted for the increase or reduction in risk caused by the transaction under review. Risk is valued by market measures of variability and volatility of exchange rates and the yield of extra returns from risks. In the present case the decision to cover forward reduces risk and therefore requires an adverse adjustment to the outcome of the benchmark alternative: dealing spot on maturity.

In many companies with few and large exposures this is the appropriate standard of measurement. Where exposures and exposure management decisions are numerous and fragmented, the totality of opportunity comparisons might be a sufficient experience of dispersion and volatility, with less need for the risk adjustment. It might be neither economic nor necessary to evaluate individual decisions.

17.8.3 Selecting the benchmark

As Cooper and Franks (1987) stress, the benchmark course of action must be one which was open to the decision taker at the time he made his decision. Most other writers (e.g. Donaldson, 1980, 1987; Back, 1988; Kenyon, 1981) have stressed that there are three possible standards, the forward rate at the time of action, the spot rate at maturity, and the most favourable rate that was with hindsight available at any time between those two dates. This last standard does not pass Cooper and Franks' test of a decision open to the currency manager at the former date. In other words, any course of action that could be adopted only with hindsight is not a horse that should be entered in this race. The other writers had arrived at similar conclusions. Company K in the appendix to chapter 9 uses a compromise benchmark of 50 per cent. (This discussion deliberately ignores the distinction between forward rates on the one hand and spot rates plus interest effects on the other. The relationship was clarified in chapter 3 and applied in chapter 12.)

17.8.4 The timing problem revisited

Example 16.1 in chapter 16 concerned a timing dilemma. Universal Music had to decide whether to lock its major £40 million sterling asset in at a dollar value of $72.8 million at the current spot rate of $1.82 = £1, or whether to wait for sterling to rise to a higher dollar value. Alternatives considered in that example were

- cover now,
- leave uncovered but decide now to cover as soon as the rate reaches $2.00, i.e. has risen by 10 per cent.
- sell one-half = £20m for dollars now and leave the other half open subject to the trigger rate of $2.00.

In the last two cases the open position would in any case be kept under review (see below), and the decision should also include a stop-loss downside rate at which the open position would also be closed out. Clearly a stop-gain/stop-loss type of decision passes the Cooper and Franks test of being open to the currency manager at the time of decision. It could, however, only be used as a benchmark if it was recorded as a course considered but rejected in favour of either cover or complete inaction.

A feature of the timing dilemma is that between the time that the risk is first spotted and its maturity (even if that is only a few months away), there will be thousands of different rates at which the position could be closed out for that maturity date. This is because the market is moving all the time, so that there is a multiplicity of possible rates each day, even from a single bank. This, coupled with the fact that a hedge–no hedge decision does not have to be locked away until the exposure matures, explains why the open position needs to be kept under review.

17.8.5 Monitoring the use of more advanced instruments

The discussion has so far been simplified by assuming that decisions are to hedge or not to hedge, and that hedges are always spot or forward hedges. It is not difficult to refine the principles so as to bring in swaps and options and their derivatives, and above all to devise tests for whether the most economic among the various instruments was in fact used. It is, however, important to bear in mind that, except against antenatal trading risk, an *option* is something better and more costly than a mere hedge, and needs to be carefully evaluated in the light of its extra value.

17.8.6 Monitoring antenatal trading risk decisions

In trading risk there is the mechanical difficulty of capturing in the system the rate used in the pricing decision, and comparing the dealing rate with that pricing rate. Where companies sell from price lists, currency movements introduce an often mystifying volatility into gross margins on sales. Cooper and Franks (1987) here simply suggest that the currency manager should at the time of each decision select and record his own rejected benchmark course of action.

17.8.7 Measuring the dealer's performance

Risk management decisions are not the only decisions that need to be monitored. A dealer's job is to shop around for the best available rate, and in some companies the dealer is given some latitude in timing: he may, for example, be free to deal at any time on the day concerned up to 4 pm. The best way to monitor performance depends on how many deals a dealer makes in a week. If he makes hundreds, then perhaps a random sample only should be monitored. The best yardstick would be to ask a market-making bank (see chapter 4, section 4.11) to supply its rates for the times in question, and perhaps its high and low dealing rates for the days in question. These would serve to establish benchmarks.

17.8.8 Performance measurement and motivation

Performance measurement standards and benchmarks must be chosen with care and with a sharp eye on how they may motivate those appraised. A biased system can easily induce either apathy or risk aversion. So can unattainable goals. A performance measurement system should seek fairly to find performance worthy of praise as well as room for improvement. Demotivation is always easier than motivation!

17.9 Summary

Currency risk management is not by nature a friction-free activity. Currency expertise has to offer vital information to commercial decision takers, and has to act as a brake on excessive risk concentrations, whilst being generally the junior partner in the relationship with commercial management. To make this frictionless requires tact, teamwork and clearly communicated objectives, guidelines and authority limits for accepting and managing risks. The teamwork must be driven by enthusiasm and trust. Shotgun weddings are not enough. Problems should be seen as business problems, not just commercial or financial issues.

Decentralization has great management benefits. In currency risk its limits are set by the company's or group's single credit and investment rating in its financial markets and by the scarcity of currency expertise. This calls for great discrimination between powers and tasks to be delegated and to be kept at the centre. Dealing for overseas subsidiaries is seldom best done by the parent, but guidelines on exposure limits must be set by the centre. The device of using the centre as compulsory banker for all operating units, but leaving them free to manage their currency positions as they think fit, may often get the best of both worlds. The parent must at the very least enforce the prompt reporting of all exposures and then control the net group exposure by adjusting its own position in the markets. This type of structure has the virtue of retaining the maximum motivation of subsidiary managers to run their businesses profitably.

The control of powers delegated both to subsidiaries and to central and local currency management staff requires clear objectives, clearly communicated authority limits and an adequate internal check on deal confirmations and exposed positions.

Performance measurement is not achieved by merely turning the treasury into a profit centre and watching its profit or loss. The test of success is the risk-adjusted opportunity cost of actions taken, which has to be measured against benchmarks of alternatives rejected and risk effects. Yardsticks applied must be unbiased and result in praise as well as criticism if currency managers are not to be demotivated.

18

Executive Summary

18.1 Floating exchange rates (chapters 3–5)

1 Freely floating currencies have very volatile exchange rates. Swings of between 5 per cent and 40 per cent in a year and 5 per cent in a single day are possible. These swings are not predictable. Professional forecasters have not systematically beaten the market forward rate by sufficient margins to justify their fees. It is not that the forward rate is a useful forecast, just that others are little better, mostly worse.

2 Freely floating currency markets are closely linked to international market interest rates. In the long run they are also, less closely, linked to relative inflation rates. Currencies with higher interest or inflation rates tend to fall against those with lower interest or inflation rates. The link with interest rates is shorter term, and the looser link with inflation operates in the much longer term.

3 Between *freely floating* exchange rates money is only likely to be made over very short periods, say a few dealing hours. Apart from that anyone who claims he can systematically make gains from exchange rates might find it hard to prove his claim.

4 Generally, the time-horizon over which we look at the exchange markets makes a lot of difference. For periods of more than a few months, a business should watch the *combined* effects of its exchange gains and losses and interest rates, especially after tax: not just at exchange gains and losses on their own.

18.2 Controlled currencies

5 Most of the world's currencies do not float freely, but are managed by their central banks against a major currency or group of currencies. In

Europe the EMS currencies and the Scandinavian currencies are a case in point. Here the artificial rules can sometimes make profitable speculation possible – at the expense of the central banks.

6 None of the recommendations in this executive summary apply to heavily controlled currencies. Their exchange rates are a long way from their free market rates, and normal market instruments are not available or traded in these currencies. Dealings with each such currency must be governed by the circumstances of that currency and its particular regulations.

18.3 Risk management (chapter 6)

7 Risks can be one-way or two-way. Currency and commodity price risks, for example, can end in gains just as much as losses. Earthquake risks, on the other hand, are one-way risks: only insurers have a chance to gain from them.

8 Every risk is a cost. That cost may be hard to quantify, but that does not stop it being a cost.

9 A risk can be intolerable when its worst outcome could end the independent survival of the business. Currency risks can be intolerable. A currency exposure of $3 billion could easily lead to a $1 billion loss. A loss of that size may be within the tolerable limit for some global giants, but not to a company which is merely large. Intolerable risks cannot be accepted uninsured or unhedged. A single risk is vulnerability to a sinlge event outside the control of the business, such as a fall of the dollar by one-third. The fall in the dollar may cause loss to the same company in more than one profit centre, place or activity. It is risk *concentrations* that can make exposures intolerable.

18.4 The place of currency risk in business management (chapter 7)

10 Currency risk is not often a free-standing management task, unrelated to commercial and other business objectives. Where a customer wants a price to be quoted in his rather than our currency, commercial rather than financial objectives may have to prevail, but both are relevant, and risk management needs to heed and understand both.

11 Like most business problems, currency risk must often be managed with at least one eye on short-term business results.

12 Currency risk can seldom be managed passively, i.e. with the risk profile accepted as given. Where it can be managed passively, the

only decision is whether to use a financial hedge or not. In most situations, however, managers have the opportunity and therefore the duty to manage the risk profile itself.

18.5 Classification of currency risks (chapter 8)

13 Currency risks come from two kinds of external threats:

(a) A rise in the *real* exchange rate of the currency in which we incur our costs against our competitors' currencies. This means a rise in its nominal exchange rate by more than is warranted by the difference between their and our inflation rates. This makes our costs less competitive. We call this competitiveness risk.

(b) Movements in *nominal* exchange rates. These cause risk first where we have a mismatch between our currency of cost and the currency in which we quote prices to customers. We call this trading risk.
Nominal exchange rate movements cause risk secondly where we have a mismatch between assets and liabilities, or future cash inflows and outflows in a currency other than our yardstick currency (in which we measure our performance). We call this position risk.

14 Table 18.1 compares trading, position and competitiveness risk.

Table 18.1 Classification of currency risk

	Financial		Economic
	Trading	Position	Competitiveness
Threat from FX rate	Nominal	Nominal	Real
Mismatch	Cost v. price	Net position	Irrelevant
Exposure			
Transactions	Contingent	Certain[1]	Certain or uncertain
Prices	Committed[2]	Committed[2]	Uncommitted[2]
Exposed items already on balance sheet?	None	Most	None
One risk per	Pricing decision	Currency	Commercial offering with separate costs
Can be viewed in cash or accounting terms	Yes	Yes	Irrelevant

[1] Exposures are treated as 'certain' if business managers regard them as certain.
[2] They are *position* exposures only if their prices are also 'committed' and do not depend on pricing decisions yet to be made by the business – otherwise they are part of competitiveness exposure.

18.6 Corporate objectives in currency risk management (chapter 9)

15 Corporate objectives in this field.

(a) are integrated with other objectives,
(b) are appropriate to each company's operational profile,
(c) vary in their approach to risk.

They vary between the extremes of

- locking into the current market structure (hedging everything) whenever possible, and
- wishing to make money out of taking open positions.

Some companies, however, are more concerned with the objective of 'smoothing' the effect of currency movements; with consistency in the effect of exchange rate movements between one year and another.

18.7 Competitiveness risk (chapter 10)

16 Competitiveness risk is a long-term problem. Trends in real exchange rates can sometimes be assessed for a few years ahead. Companies can profit from this either by switching costs to currencies likely to become more competitive or by competitive strategies which modify sensitivity to cost differentials. The essence of this risk is its effect on the competitive position, and responses should concentrate on commercial rather than financial action.

18.8 Trading risk (chapters 11–12)

17 The threat in trading risk is to margins intended in commercial pricing decisions. Trading risk does not arise in a business which never makes a pricing decision; nor is it a material problem for one that has little need to control its margins. It arises in tendering for contracts and in issuing price lists in currencies other than those in which costs are incurred.

18 Trading risk is a problem only in its antenatal phase, from the time when we have quoted a currency price until our customer is certain to buy from us. It cannot during that phase be hedged by a spot or forward exchange deal.

19 The primary aim in managing antenatal trading risk is to achieve an exchange rate no worse than was used in the pricing decision.

20 Until the seller becomes commercially sure of his sale, the risk can be managed by

(a) avoidance: quoting in the currency of cost,
(b) currency options or some of their derivatives,
(c) for large UK export contracts, by the Export Credits Guarantee Department's tender to contract cover,
(d) building the cost of the risk into the cost estimate, so as to make a better informed decision about whether and at what price to quote for the business concerned.

21 All these tools bridge the antenatal period only. When the contract or business is certain, a deliberate choice should be made: either to close the exposure out, e.g. by a spot or forward currency deal, or to leave it open as part of the position risk.

22 All antenatal trading risk management needs a high order of teamwork between commercial and currency risk managers.

18.9 Position risk (chapters 13–16)

23 There is one position exposure per currency, subdivided by the dates when the various items are expected to become cash receipts or payments. For some fixed assets that may be a time-horizon of 20 or more years. Position exposure needs to be carefully defined. The yardstick currency must be identified, and a choice made between the accounting and cash definitions of exposure. In quantifying the position in a given currency, thought must be given to the items to be included and excluded, to the treatment of previously hedged transactions, and to the effect of tax.

24 A position exposure can be managed by adjusting it to a desired net level. The tools for this are spot, forward and interbank swap deals, futures, options and currency swaps. There are also internal measures: matching, netting, and leading and lagging.

25 The *currency option* is always something both dearer and better than a mere hedging instrument, because it limits the downside without restricting the upside.

26 Netting is not a hedging instrument, but a way to simplify the use of hedging instruments. Netting or reinvoicing vehicle companies can do this very effectively. Vehicle companies can, however, in some cases obstruct commercial management by insulating it from the currency environment of its markets.

27 In international groups of companies, indirect internal sales are best invoiced in the currency of whichever of the two internal parties does *not* decide prices to ultimate external customers: the party with the pricing decision should have the currency exposure.

28 *Group* position exposures are created or modified only by those intragroup transactions which shift the group's liquidity between countries. Examples are intragroup dividends, royalties, interest payments and leading and lagging, i.e. lengthening and shortening intragroup credit periods.

29 It is usually unsafe to manage just the group's exposures and to ignore exposure in each overseas subsidiary. The exception is where the potential currency losses in those subsidiaries would be too small to jeopardize their net worth criterion of solvency.

30 In hyperinflation currencies, both the problem and the available means of managing it are different. The only way to avoid losses is to require local subsidiaries or branches to earn positive real returns on the capital invested. Measured in local currency this must beat the local free money market cost of funds, and also the group's real cost of capital plus the higher of local inflation and devaluation against the parent currency. All three measures have to be used because none of them give a reliable and up-to-date signal of the current inflation rate.

18.10 Aggressive, defensive or smoothing?

31 Position risk can be managed either aggressively for gain or defensively to avoid loss. Some companies prefer the objective of leaving the impact of currency movements unchanged between successive reporting periods: they prefer to smooth rather than optimize or minimize the effect of currency movements. Defensive management adjusts each position to zero. Aggressive management of freely floating currencies is for those who either have reason to know they can beat market expectations of future exchange rates, or have special tax positions which load the dice in their favour after tax. Aggressive management is more likely to be successful with controlled or managed currencies or over very short periods.

32 Aggressive position risk management is difficult, but not wrong in principle, as long as it is a calculated and adequately controlled and disclosed policy, understood by investors. Nor should a policy of aggressive risk management restrict itself to the company's 'natural' exposures. Successful currency experts are so scarce that they should be allowed to choose their home ground for producing gains.

18.11 Timing dilemma

33 Position risk easily creates timing dilemmas, which give rise to very hard decisions. They arise where a deal should be done to reduce an open position to zero, but where investors might have reason to be critical if the deal was made with what turns out to be unfortunate timing.

18.12 Cash or accounting view?

34 Currency risk should on balance be managed with an eye on cash rather than accounting effects. The conflict is largely a question of how fixed assets are valued as part of the position exposure. Historical cost valuations of fixed assets can be wildly unrealistic. Nevertheless accounting effects cannot be wholly ignored. Vital matters like solvency tests, borrowing powers and gearing ratios in loan agreements and other debt instruments are usually governed by accounting definitions. A company may also be under short-term pressure to produce certain accounting results.

18.13 Organizing currency risk management (chapter 17)

35 Many currency risk managers have an awkward combination of poacher and gamekeeper roles: to assist commercial managers and at the same time to prevent excessive risk concentrations. The organization must include very clearly communicated objectives, guidelines and authority limits for accepting and managing risks. A great deal of tact and enthusiastic teamwork is needed. The problems must be seen as *business* problems, not as either commercial or financial issues.

36 Decentralization is often a precondition of efficiency. In currency risk its limits are set by the company's or group's single credit and investment rating in its financial markets and by the scarcity of currency expertise. Delegation of powers must be selective and skilful. The objective should be to achieve control of exposures as unobtrusively as possible, so as to maintain the motivation of profit centre managers. There are two useful methods. First, much delegation is possible subject to guidelines issued by the corporate centre. As long as currency positions are accurately and promptly reported to the parent, the parent can control the net group position

by adjusting its own currency position. Secondly, operating units can be left free to manage their currency risks as they choose, as long as they deal exclusively through the central treasury as in-house banker. The centre under this scheme is obliged to accept all their instructions, but can then once again manage the group's net position by controlling all deals in the currency markets.

18.14 Control and performance measurement

37 Currency management and dealing needs to be controlled, because the risk of improper or unintended large losses is high in this field. The preconditions of control are clear objectives, clearly communicated authority limits and an adequate internal check on deal confirmations and exposed positions.

38 Performance measurement is not achieved by merely turning the treasury into a profit centre and watching its profit or loss. The test of success is the opportunity cost of actions taken, which has to be measured against benchmarks of alternatives rejected and risk effects. Yardsticks applied must result in praise as well as criticism if currency managers are not to be demotivated.

References

Adler, M. and Dumas, B. (1984) Exposure to currency risk: definition and measurement. *Financial Management*, summer, 41–50.

Ankrom, R. K. (1974) Top-level approach to the foreign exchange problem. *Harvard Business Review*, July–August, 41–50.

Austen, M. and Reyniers, P. (1986) *International Treasury Management Handbook*, Price Waterhouse and Euromoney.

Back, P. L. (1988) *Corporate Cash Management*, Woodhead-Faulkner.

Batchelor, G. (1989) The application of currency management policies within major UK companies. *The Treasurer*, May, 25–7.

Bell, S. and Kettell, B. (1983) *The Foreign Exchange Handbook*, Graham & Trotman.

BIS (1986) *Recent Innovations in International Banking*, Group of Ten study group, Bank for International Settlements.

Blake, D., Beenstock, M. and Brasse, V. (1986) The performance of UK exchange rate forecasters. *Economic Journal*, 96, December, 986–99.

Boyadjian, H. J. and Warren, J. F. (1987) *Risks, Reading Corporate Signals*, Wiley.

Brasse, V. (1983) The inaccuracy of exchange rate forecasting services in the UK. *City University Business School Economic Review*, 1, no. 1, spring, 35–44.

Brown, B. (1983) *The Forward Market in Foreign Exchange*, Croom Helm.

Buckley, A. (1986) *Multinational Finance*, Philip Allan.

Chown, J. (1986a) Futures and options – when to hedge? *International Correspondent Banker*, May, 44–5.

Chown, J. (1986b) Tax traps for the banker. *The Banker*, November, 28–30.

Chown, J. (1988a) Taxation of foreign exchange gains and losses. *The Treasurer*, 10, no. 10, January, 17–19.

Chown, J. (1988b) Association of Corporate Treasurers. Submission on the taxation of financial instruments, with introduction. *The Treasurer*, 10, no. 10, November, 57.

Chown, J. (1990) Tax Efficient Foreign Exchange Management, Woodhead-Faulkner.

Chown, J. and Evans, K. (1987) Taxation of foreign currency gains and losses; the UK Revenue Statement of Practice. *Journal of Strategy in International Taxation*, 3, no. 2, 139–64.

Chu, K. Y. and Morrison, T. K. (1984) The 1981–1982 recession and non-oil primary commodity prices. *IMF Staff Papers*, 31, no. 1, March, 93–140.

Cooper, I. (1985) Currency option prices. *The Treasurer*, 7, no. 5, May, 9–15.

Cooper, I. (1987) New instruments, an overview. In *New Financial Instruments*, Chartered Institute of Bankers.

Cooper, I. and Franks, J. (1987) Treasury performance measurement. *Midland Corporate Finance Journal*, 4, no. 4, 29–43.

Davies, E. and Collier, P. (1983) *Treasury Management in the UK*, Association of Corporate Treasurers.

Donaldson, J. A. (1980) *Corporate Currency Risk*, Financial Times Business Information.

Donaldson, J. A. (1987) *Corporate Currency Risk, A Reappraisal*, Financial Times Business Information. (Revised 2nd edn, 1st published 1980.)

Ducros, G. (1989) New strategies for a corporate treasurer. *The Treasurer*, 11, no. 10, November, 23–5.

Duker, K. (1989) Derivative products, *The Treasurer*, 11, no. 10, November, 6–13.

Dumas, B. (1978) The theory of the trading firm revisited. *Journal of Finance*, June, 1019–29.

Edwards, R. (1988) Exchange rate misalignment in developing countries. In *World Bank Occasional Paper No 2*, new series. The Johns Hopkins University Press.

Fama, E. F. (1970) Efficient capital markets: a review of theory and empirical work. *Journal of Finance*, 25, 383–417.

Frankel, J. A. and Froot, K. A. (1987) Using survey data to test standard propositions regarding exchange rate expectations. *American Economic Review*. 77, no. 1, March, 133–53.

Garner, K. G. and Shapiro, A. C. (1984) A practical method of assessing foreign exchange risk. *Midland Corporate Finance Journal*, 2, no. 3, fall, 6–17.

Gilbert, C. L. (1989) The impact of exchange rates and developing country debt on commodity prices. *Economic Journal,* 99, no. 397, September, 773–84.

Glaum, M. and Belk, P. A. (1989) The management of foreign exchange risk in UK MNCs: an empirical investigation. 12th Annual Congress of the European Accounting Association, 5–7 April 1989, University of Stuttgart.

Grauwe, P. de (1988) The long swings in real exchange rates – do they fit into our theories? *Bank of Japan Monetary and Economic Studies*, 6, no. 1, May, 37–60.

Grilli, E. R. and Yang, M. C. (1981) Real and monetary determinants of non-oil primary commodity price movements. IBRD working paper no. 6, December.

Hacche, G. and Townend, J. C. (1981) A broad look at exchange rate movements for eight currencies, 1972–80. *Bank of England Quarterly Bulletin*, December, 489–509.

Heffernan, S. A. and Sinclair, P. (1990) *Modern International Economics*, Blackwell.

Hertz, D. B. and Thomas, H. (1983) *Risk Analysis and its Applications*, Wiley.

Hertzell, S. and Caspar, C. (1988) Coping with unpredictable currencies. *The MacKinsey Quarterly*, summer, 12–24.

Heywood, J. (1984a) *Foreign Exchange and the Corporate Treasurer*, 4th edn, A. & C. Black.

Heywood, J. (1984b) *Using the Futures, Forwards and Options Markets*, A. & C. Black.

IMF (1981) *Annual Report 1981*, International Monetary Fund.

IMF (1985) *Annual Report 1985*, International Monetary Fund.

Jensen, M. and Meckling, W. (1976) Theory of the firm. Managerial behavior. Agency costs and ownership structure. *Journal of Financial Economics*, October , 305–60.

Kenyon, A. (1981) *Currency Risk Management*, Wiley.

Kenyon, A. (1985) Are British companies more timid? *The Treasurer*, 7, no. 10, November, 7–10.

Kenyon, A. (1988) Conflicts in risk management. *The Treasurer*, 10, no. 9, October, 15–16.

Levich, R. M. (1982) How the rise of the dollar took forecasters by surprise. *Euromoney*, August, 98–111.

Lighterness, T. J. (1987) Managing economic exposure. The Rio Tinto-Zinc Corporation plc. *The Treasurer*, 9, no. 2, February, 13–18.

Macdonald, R. and Taylor, M. P. (1989) Economic analysis of foreign exchange markets: an expository survey. In R. Macdonald and M. P. Taylor, *Exchange Rates and Open Economy Macroeconomics*, Blackwell.

Mathur, S. S. (1988) How firms compete: a new classification of generic strategies. *Journal of General Management*, 14, no. 1, autumn, 30–57.

Oxelheim, L. and Wihlborg, C. G. (1987) *Macroeconomic Uncertainty*, Wiley.

Porter, M. E. (1980) *Competitive Strategy*, The Free Press.

Rothkopf, M. H. (1975) On measuring risk. Working paper, Xerox Palo Alto Research Center, quoted by Hertz and Thomas (1983).

Sarwal, A. (1989) *KPMG International Handbook of Financial Instruments and Transactions*, Butterworth.

Shapiro, A. C. (1989) *Multinational Financial Management*, 3rd edn, Allyn and Bacon.

Slovic, P., Fischoff, B., and Lichtenstein, S. (1980) Facts versus fears: understanding perceived risk. In R. Schwing and W. A. Albers (eds), *Societal Risk Assessment: How Safe is Safe Enough?* Plenum Press.

Sweeney, R. J. (1986) Beating the foreign exchange market. *Journal of Finance*, XLI, no. 1, March, 163–81.

Taylor, M. P. (1989) Covered interest arbitrage and market turbulence. *Economic Journal,* 99, no. 1, June, 376–91.

Walker, D. P. (1978) An economic analysis of foreign exchange risk. Research Committee Occasional Paper 14, Institute of Chartered Accountants in England and Wales.

Walmsley, J. (1988) *Foreign Exchange Handbook*, Wiley.

Wihlborg, C. G. (1980) Currency exposure: taxonomy and theory. In R. M. Levich and C. G. Wihlborg (eds), *Exchange risk and exposure*, D. C. Heath.

Wilson, S. J. (1988) Economic risk. MBA dissertation, City University Business School.

Wolff, C. P. and Reyes, C. G. (1989) Exchange rate volatility. In R. Z. Aliber (ed.), *Handbook of International Financial Management*, Dow Jones-Irwin Publishers.

Index